The Seven States of Minnesota

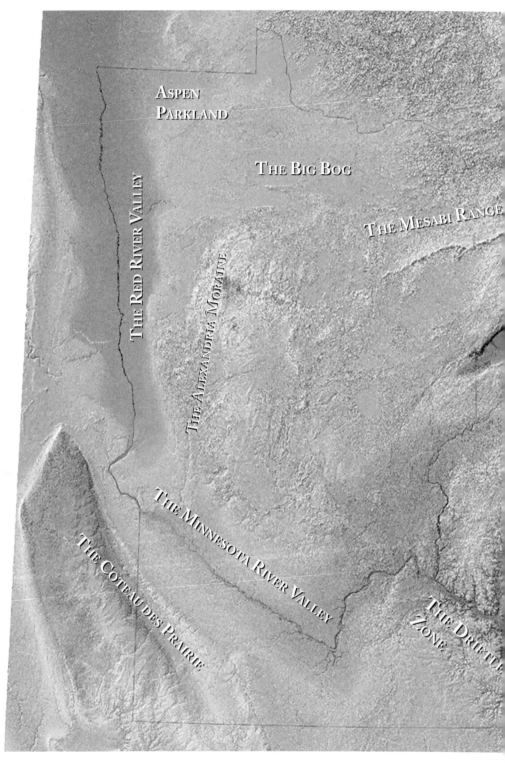

ASPEN PARKLAND

THE BIG BOG

THE RED RIVER VALLEY

THE MESABI RANGE

THE ALEXANDRIA MORAINE

THE MINNESOTA RIVER VALLEY

THE COTEAU DES PRAIRIE

THE DRIFTLESS ZONE

A few of the prominent features that contribute to
Minnesota's varied landscape

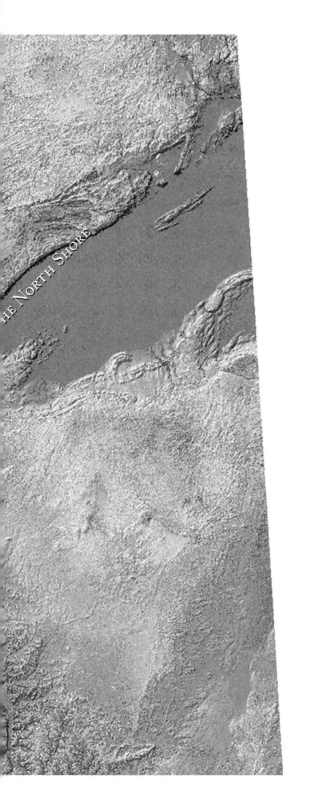

The Seven States of Minnesota

John
Toren

NODIN PRESS

All photographs are by the author with the exception of historic images on pages 108, 172, and 182.

Audio versions of some portions of the text appear in edited and modified form on travel CDs produced by Open Road Adventures.

Library of Congress Cataloging-in-Publication Data

Toren, John.
  The seven states of Minnesota / John Toren.
     p. cm.
  ISBN-13: 978-1-932472-51-6
  ISBN-10: 1-932472-51-7
  1. Minnesota--Guidebooks.   2. Minnesota--Tours--Guidebooks.   I.
Title.
F604.3.T67 2007
917.7604'54--dc22

                                   2007041503

Nodin Press is a division of Micawber's, Inc.
530 N. Third Street, Suite 120
Minneapolis, MN 55401

to my parents, Paul and Ellie Toren,

who introduced me to the outdoors

Acknowledgements

My thanks go first of all to publisher Norton Stillman for agreeing to take on this project. I'd also like to thank Sarah Moffett, the producer of the Open Road Adventure series of travel CDs, for whom some of the research upon which I have drawn in these pages was originally conducted. Special thanks to Tim Wahl, who created the files from which the maps were constructed. (Any errors or crudeness in the final renderings are my responsibility alone.) Thanks to Jim Klobuchar for permission to reproduce a few paragraphs from his recent book *Walking Briskly Toward the Sunset*. Also a word of thanks to Philip Fradkin, the author of *The Seven States of California (1997)*. That book is far longer and less travel-oriented than mine, but the titles do bear a striking similarity.

A word of thanks is due to the Minnesota Historical Society, which has sponsored and conducted so much valuable research about the state, and continues to maintain an impressive network of historic sites; and to the Minnesota Department of Natural Resources, which maintains the state's park system and also a remarkable array of technical information resources.

Most important of all, I'd like to thank my wife Hilary, who has accompanied me on travels almost too numerous to count, both across the state and also to places further afield. I drive, she reads from the travel books. We plot our next move, we explore, we linger.

CONTENTS

A gravel road leading out toward the Weaver Dunes, with the bluffs on the far side of the Mississippi visible in the distance.

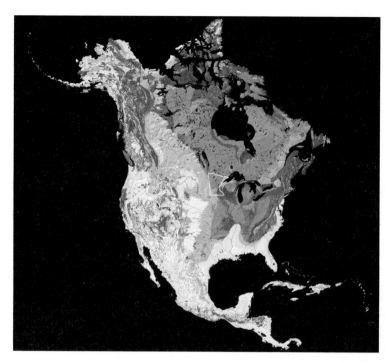

Minnesota: right in the center of things

INTRODUCTION:

BEING AT THE CENTER OF THINGS

It's a nice feeling, being at the center of things. And that's the way it feels when you're living in, or traveling through, the state of Minnesota. Politically the state will never be central, no matter how many unsuccessful presidential candidates it produces. And although it does have a lot to offer culturally, it will never have the population base to ramp itself up to the very top tier in that category. No, the centrality I'm referring to is a geographical one.

This geographic centrality is a subtle thing. It has far less visceral impact than you get when standing at the end of Oregon's Cape Lookout, for example, which gives you the sense that you're on the *edge* of things. And there are any number of places in Montana and Wyoming that give you the feeling you're at the very *top* of things. And at the bottom of the Grand Canyon...well, I think you get the point.

There is no place where you can stand and take in Minnesota's geographic centrality. It only becomes apparent as you move about from place to place. But it's interesting to note that the Great Plains lie right at Minnesota's western doorstep, spreading their way across the southern and western margins of the state like a trail of grass and mud that somebody tracked in. Meanwhile, the majestic and forbidding expanses of the Boreal Forest make their way into the northeast, creeping down from the tundras of Canada along the North Shore of Lake Superior. The pines and hardwood forests of the Great Lakes region cut an impressive swath across the state's midsection, making it a vacation destination for many visitors looking for lakes and fish and a week or two of relaxation. And the southeast corner of the state can lay claim to rattlesnakes, remarkable river bluffs, oak savanna remnants, and a slightly different mix of flora and fauna making its way north into Minnesota along the Mississippi Valley.

Geographers have identified a spot a few miles outside the town of Rugby, North Dakota, as the *absolute* center of North America. But the centrality I'm referring to is less mathematical than ecological, and it belongs entirely to Minnesota. Nor is it entirely a matter of vast biospheres meeting and commingling within our borders. Things are also flowing in the other direction. Minnesota can lay claim to three great watersheds, with the Mississippi carrying water south to the Gulf of Mexico, the Great Lakes draining east to the Atlantic Ocean, and the Red River meandering sluggishly north to Hudson's Bay and the frigid waters of the Arctic.

The residents of Denver, Reno, or Seattle may well chuckle at these refinements in analysis. And it's true that it isn't much of a stretch from the shores of Lake Superior, the lowest point in the state, to the towering heights of Eagle Mountain a few miles to the west. Most of the state undulates within an even narrower range in elevation. Yet to those who travel across Minnesota from, say, southern Saskatchewan, or any other truly expansive place on the plains, the state is anything but flat. Other parts of the country may be more dramatic, but the landscapes of Minnesota are no less interesting.

That is what this book is all about.

WHY SEVEN?

The decision to carve up the state into seven regions was neither arbitrary nor entirely precise. Tourist agencies often make use of four zones (one of which is the metro area), but that hardly seems adequate to convey the richness of the varied culture and terrain we'll be passing through. The Minnesota Department of Natural Resources divides the states into ten regions and twenty-two subregions, which is illuminating but far too complex for our purposes. In any case, these itineraries are designed to highlight historical and cultural as well as ecological and geological points of interests. We will leave it to the experts to determine whether the town of Brimson lies in the Toimi Uplands Region or the North Shore Highlands (though that might be an interesting thing to think about). Our goal is to provide a framework for exploring the fascinating and sometimes undiscovered areas of Minnesota by providing a few insights and observations, a few dining and lodging tips, some directions, and more than a bit of background—historical, geological, ecological, cultural, and aesthetic.

I used the word *aesthetic* a moment ago. You're never too old to take a road trip, but you may have forgotten just how beautiful a field of corn can look in mid-July or how enchanting a forested understory becomes in early May when it's festooned with Virginia Bluebells. It might be more interesting than you think to visit a county historical society, tour a snowmobile factory, or learn a little more about the exploits and lifeways of the Dakota and Ojibwe women and men who were here long before explorers and traders first arrived from Europe.

Maps

In order to make full use of this guide, however, you're going to need a map. A highway map will do, though a more detailed atlas of the state would help in some cases. The atlas in the Delorme series is good, though the Vincent Atlas of Minnesota is easier to read and contains quite a few obscure sites that aren't included on other maps of the region. The maps that accompany the text here are designed merely to give you an overview of the locations being described and to convey something of the topography you'll be passing through.

The seven regions, in brief, are as follows:

1) The Bluff Country of the southeast corner of the state, formed by the Mississippi Valley and neglected by recent glaciers.

2) The Southern Plains, which were once covered with tall-grass prairies, though they're now largely agricultural.

3) The Heartland of lakes and forests that reaches northward from the Twin Cities across the central part of the state.

4) The Arrowhead of pine forests and exposed pre-Cambrian bedrock that extends down from Canada to give us the Boundary Waters Canoe Area Wilderness and Lake Superior's North Shore.

5) The Boglands left by Lake Agassiz, which make the central north a haven for orchids, owls, and Labrador tea but an impenetrable wasteland for most of us.

6) The Iron Range, which brought immigrants in droves from Europe to create one of the most distinctive cultures in the state, and also a distinctive landscape of gaping pits and heaping piles of slag.

7) The Red River Valley, Minnesota's "back door" to Winnipeg and the flattest part of the state, though it's rimmed with glacial dunes and aspen parklands.

Some of these regions make a tidy unit. Others are unwieldy enough to require subdivisions, so that there are actually twelve regions described within the pages of this book. (Well, I didn't want to scare anyone off right away.)

And then we have the problem of transitions. Lanesboro lies in the valley of the Root River, one of the Mississippi's main tributaries. I've included it in the section on the Rochester plateau, because it's quite a ways inland from the Mississippi, and makes an enticing destination for travelers passing through the farm country south of the Twin Cities. The town of Ely appears in the Range section, because iron ore was first commercially mined in Ely, and it would be impossible to tell the story of the Range without including it. But Ely is also a gateway to the Boundary Waters wilderness, and thus requires an entry in the Arrowhead section as well.

Milan sports a fine group of grain elevators.

How to Travel

There are many ways to take a trip. This book should provide a framework of highlights for anyone interested in exploring the state of Minnesota. There is less information about coffee shops than fur traders, I'm afraid, but coffee-shops do come and go, while the lore of the countryside remains largely the same. Much of the delight in exploring new territory lies in discovering what's out there *now*. It's worthwhile buying a weekly newspaper in any small town just to find out what the locals are currently thinking about. The want-ads can also be interesting. Public libraries and grocery stores are fine places to get the feel of a community, and eavesdropping on café conversation can also be rewarding.

In those parts of the state that are heavily touristed, there's a lot to be said for traveling during the spring or fall months. Itasca State Park will seem different if you arrive in early May, when you've got the place largely to yourself. And when accommodations and campsites are freely available, it becomes easier to relax and linger, to rent a canoe for an afternoon paddle or follow that inviting, but perhaps not quite so direct, country road. To my mind much of the pleasure in exploring the state lies in watching the landscape rise and fall or visiting a town that you've seen on the map for decades and have always wondered about…

THE BLUFF COUNTRY

We sometimes attach an element of romance to those drifters, hitchhikers, and tramps who wander from job to job and place to place, unencumbered by long-term commitments—individuals such as the ones portrayed by William Holden in *Picnic* or Jack Nicholson in *Five Easy Pieces*. But what are we to make of the quality of "driftlessness"? It's like a Zen koan.

The Mississippi River Valley downstream from the Twin Cities is known as the Driftless area. During the most recent Ice Ages, which ended perhaps twelve thousand years ago, this part of the continent escaped the scouring impact of the sheets of ice, and also the deposits of glacial "drift" that spread out across the countryside as the glaciers melted. Unlike other parts of Minnesota, which are typically covered with fifty feet of drift at least, the rugged terrain of the Driftless Zone reflects more than half a million years of continuous erosion through ancient layers of sedimentary rock.

Geologists don't much like the term "driftless," however. They point out that the area was scoured by previous Ice Ages, and is therefore hardly driftless. They prefer to call it the Karst country.

The word "karst" derives from a Paleo-European word "karra" which means simply "stone," though geologists use the term more specifically to describe limestone regions that have developed sinkholes, underground streams, and caverns. A sinkhole is formed when the roof of a cave collapses. Surface water sometimes sinks down into the earth through fractured bedrock (hence a "disappearing" stream) either joining an aquifer or continuing as a stream underground. These streams can re-emerge as powerful springs, often having been cooled during their underground journey. Such streams are often superb trout habitat.

But for the casual visitor, the region's two most distinctive features are its handsome rivers—the Cannon, the Zumbro, the Whitewater, and the Root—that roll down to the Mississippi, creating attractive valleys as they descend through the layers of limestone; and the bluffs that rise as much as 600 feet above the level of the river. These are the features that make the stretch of Highway 61 between Hastings and the Iowa border one of the most scenic drives in the United States.

Mounds Park

Mounds Park is located on the bluffs just downstream from downtown Saint Paul, (take Burns Avenue west off of Highway 61, just south of I-94). The city of Saint Paul established the park in 1893, which may seem like a long time ago, but that's almost yesterday when placed in the context of the mounds themselves, which may be as much as two thousand years old. The river valley that lies below you was carved more than ten thousand years ago as meltwater from Glacial Lake Duluth (the gigantic precursor of our own Lake Superior) made its way south through the valley. At that time there was a waterfall a few miles upstream, near the present site of Fort Snelling, that was ten times longer than Niagara Falls is today.

The park has pedestrian paths, gardens, and a magnificent view of the river. You can look out at the railyard, the wooded bluffs on the opposite bank, and the river flats that contributed so much to the development of the city a hundred and fifty years ago. Barges and trains pass by below, loaded with grain or coal, and airplanes arrive and depart from Holman Field. Looking west, you can see the quaint cluster of buildings that make up downtown Saint Paul and the buttery marble of the state capital, but it's the vista downstream and the mounds near at hand that command our attention.

Six burial mounds, covered in summer with grasses, milkweed, and wild grapes, sit in majestic simplicity here on the crown of the bluff. They were built by Hopewell peoples who lived in the area between 1500 and 2000 years ago. The Hopewell traveled and hunted throughout a region stretching from Ohio to Minnesota, though they also depended heavily on agriculture, and had a trade network extending for hundreds of miles across the interior of the continent. They had a rich ceremonial and spiritual life, to judge from the few tantalizing traces that remain—including the great mounds themselves. Excavations of mounds similar to the ones here in Saint Paul have unearthed magnificent clay and ivory objects and ornaments, many of them in the shape of owls, wildcats, bears, turtles, and other animals; and also pearl necklaces, ear ornaments, bracelets, and copper headdresses. Silver from Ontario, obsidian and grizzly teeth from the Rockies, mica from North Carolina, and marine shells from the Gulf of Mexico have been found among their artifacts.

The Hopewell were the first residents of the area to cultivate a crop for which the State of Minnesota is now famous—corn. Although most of the mounds they built seem to have been used for burials, some of the massive ones served no other purpose than to trace large animal shapes onto the landscape. (A good place to see these earthworks is at Effigy Mounds National Monument, on the bluffs above the Mississippi just across the border in Iowa.) Although the mounds here in Saint Paul lie on the fringe of the Hopewell world, some Hopewell constructions further to the south have walls twelve feet high and more than a thousand feet long, which suggests that they may have served as platforms for elaborate temple structures.

The Hopewell peoples vanished around 500 AD. No one knows why. In more recent times, Dakota Indians used the same bluff site for burials, often wrapping the bones of their deceased in buffalo skins and interring them along with household items, foods, and occasionally a favorite horse. In fact there was a village named Kaposia at the base of the bluff we're standing on as early as the mid-eighteenth century. It was occupied during the summer months by as many as 400 Mdewakanton Dakota, among them a succession of chiefs carrying the honorific title Little Crow. As various treaties were signed between the Dakota and the American government, this summer village was removed first to the far side of the river and then to a location on the narrow strip of reservation land in the Minnesota River Valley to the west.

At one time there were thirty-seven mounds on the bluffs in the Mounds Park area, though today only six remain. Excavation of such sites, which are sacred to the Native peoples, is now prohibited.

Hastings

Hastings is one of the oldest towns in Minnesota. It was established in 1850, and many buildings from its early years still line its attractive Main Street. Nowadays the three-block section of town facing the river offers an interesting selection of cafés, restaurants, bars, and shops. (A good bet for casual dining is The Levee, 100 Sibley Street, which has outdoor seating in season. 651-437-7577)

All told, Hastings has more than sixty structures on the National Register of Historic Places. But the town's history extends even further back than its buildings. In 1820 a keelboat moving upstream from Prairie du Chien, Wisconsin, to re-supply a military encampment at what would later become Fort Snelling, was forced by encroaching ice to encamp at the site. The men spent the entire winter there, bringing the supplies they were transporting further upstream in smaller, more manageable loads as they were needed by the troops.

In 1853, two years after the Dakota had ceded their land west of the Mississippi to the government, Hastings was officially platted, and it grew rapidly. Four years later it was incorporated as a city. Its location on the river made it a convenient place to live, and the location was further enhanced by the fact that in many years, due to the vagaries of rainfall and shifting channel currents, it was the last town on the Mississippi to which river boats could navigate. A tiny but ferocious river, the Vermillion, (popular today with whitewater kayakers) runs through the heart of town just south of the prominent grain elevator on the left side of Highway 61. It drops more than 100 feet on its way through Hastings toward the Mississippi. Though the casual visitor will probably never see this river, during the city's early years it provided more than enough hydro power to run the many flour mills that sprang up to supply the needs of local farmers, and also to power the lumber mills that cut the massive rafts of timber being floated downstream from the pine forests on either side of the St. Croix River.

Blessed with so many natural advantages, and with ample supplies of local commodities moving through town to be processed and shipped to far-flung places along the river, it is no wonder that Hasting grew swiftly. At one time it could boast of ten hotels, four breweries, and saloons almost beyond number. As you drive through town, it might be worth taking a spin down a few of the side streets to see some of the elegant Victorian mansions that remain from that era. The city hall, with its classic dome, which you may notice looming above the trees as you come into town from the north, is also worth a look. The building served as the Dakota County Courthouse for more than a hundred years. It was purchased by the city and renovated in 1993. You can visit during normal business hours and examine works of art celebrating the city's culture and traditions.

Perhaps the most impressive of the city's domestic structures is the LeDuc-Simmons mansion (1629 Vermillion St.), set well back from the street on the east side of Highway 61. It was built in 1865, and recently re-opened for tours following a lengthy period of renovation. The house has fifteen rooms, nine fireplaces, servants quarters, and a third-story chapel. General William LeDuc was a local luminary

and Civil War hero who eventually became secretary of agriculture to President Rutherford B. Hayes.

The LeDuc-Simmons Mansion has been referred to as the most romantic example of Gothic Revival architecture in the nation. Well, who can say? There is little doubt that the designs LeDuc used in building his estate were heavily influenced by the writings and philosophy of architect Andrew Jackson Dowling. Dowling's books on country architecture were widely read and consulted in those days, and did much to spread the "Carpenter" Gothic and Hudson River Bracketed architectural styles among Victorian builders. We might consider him the Martha Stewart of the 1840s.

What makes the LeDuc mansion especially pleasing to the visitor is that not only the house, but also the grounds—including barn, ice house, and outbuildings—are still standing. In fact, it may be one of the few remaining Dowling-inspired estates left intact in the nation.

Just down the way from the LeDuc Mansion, on the same side of the street, you may happen to spot the ConAgra mill. That mill (though not that building) was established in 1853 by Harrison Graham, whose family invented Graham Crackers. The mill was later owned by Stephen Gardner, famous as the inventor of the milling process that produces "patent flour." LeDuc himself once owned the mill too. It is still in operation, and is widely thought to be the oldest continuously operating mill in the state.

If you pull into the little park just past the mill, you'll be able to walk over to the path that will lead you downstream to the cataracts of the Vermillion River I mentioned a moment ago. It's a pleasant place to have a picnic, and as you listen to the faint roar emanating from the nearby mill—much louder than the roar of the waterfall—you can think of the millions of pounds of flour that have issued from those grinding rollers to feed a hungry world since settlers first arrived in the area 150 years ago.

There are at least three ways to get from Hastings to Red Wing. You can follow Highway 61, or take the short cut by turning left on Highway 316, which re-connects with Highway 61 down the way. This short cut will also take you past the turn-off to Treasure Island Casino. The casino turnoff is worthwhile, if not for the gambling, then simply to leave the bustle of traffic behind for a while and explore the winding back-ways through the sloughs of the Mississippi, where black-billed cuckoos, bitterns, grebes, rails, and herons nest.

Highway 68 becomes Highway 18, which eventually reconnects with Highway 61. If you happen to go this way, it might be worthwhile taking yet another short detour, following a well-marked route, to nearby U.S. Lock and Dam #3. The viewing platform here allows you to get a good look at the river as well as the lock, and the visitor's center outlines the history of the Army Corp of Engineer's efforts to keep the Mississippi navigable.

The Cannon River

The Cannon is a fine little river. The French called it Riviere aux Canots—that is to say, the "river of canoes." It remains unclear whether they found it a convenient water route to the prairies to the west or merely a good place to cache their canoes before proceeding on foot upstream. In our times the Cannon has become a popular river for tubing and canoeing. A scenic bike path also runs along the river from

Cannon Falls to Red Wing along cliff-sides that occasionally tower as much as 360 feet above the river.

The village of Welch makes a good starting point for biking, canoeing, or tubing on the Cannon. The well-marked exit lies on Highway 61 a few miles east of Highway 316. (If you've taken the Treasure Island route, you'll have to backtrack west when you return to Highway 61.) Just turn south at the sign for Welch and follow the winding road that descends to the village. The village itself consists of little more than a café and a shop that rents tubes and canoes and also shuttles canoeists up to Cannon Falls to begin their descent. Bicyclists can proceed on through town and across a bridge to the easily-spotted barn and parking lot on the other side. The route west to Cannon Falls is more scenic than the trip east to Red Wing, but both make for a pleasant twenty-mile ride through the woods. And the rest of us can simply enjoy the picturesque beauty of the valley before returning the way we came to Highway 61.

Red Wing

The approach to Red Wing from the north, down a gentle slope from the plateau above, is so attractive that even the fast food restaurants look inviting. And the town itself gives every appearance of being a community that has neither died nor been artificially gentrified beyond recognition. Red Wing's downtown streets have the usual mix of restored buildings, thrift shops, and clothing and furniture emporiums, but it also has attractive churches and parks, and several swanky bars and restaurants. The T. B Sheldon Memorial Auditorium (443 W. 3rd St.), built in 1904, was the nation's first municipally-owned and operated theater. Recently restored, it's impressive both inside and out, and recalls to mind the days when Lillie Langtry, Mark Twain, Buffalo Bill, and other celebrities toured the region by riverboat, wowing the locals.

At the far end of Main Street stands the venerable St. James Hotel, which opened in 1875 to accommodate visitors during a period when Red Wing was briefly the world's largest wheat market. The hotel was restored in 1979, and now caters to weekend holiday-makers from the Twin Cities. (651-388-2846)

Barn Bluff towers over downtown Red Wing. The local Dakota
called the place "mountain in the water."

From the top of Barn Bluff there are beautiful views in several directions. Looking down at the narrow river and the large island just below
you, it's easy to see why riverboat captains considered the sharp bend
at Red Wing to be one of the most difficult sections on the entire river.
There are several paths leading up to the top of Barn Bluff, but chose
wisely, because some are steeper than others. More difficult than climbing
the bluff, perhaps, is finding a route to the base of it along city streets that
are abruptly terminated by the passing highway. Inquire at the Chamber
of Commerce, which is located down by the river on Levee Street, and
while you're down there, you might as well explore the riverside parks.
You can still watch river barges being loaded with grain here.

Red Wing's first recorded white visitor was Father Louis Hennepin, a Franciscan priest who arrived in April of 1680. More than a
hundred years later Zebulon M. Pike landed and held a conference
here with an old Dakota Chief named Hupahuduta (meaning "a
swan's wing dyed in red.") In those days Red Wing was the name given
to whoever happened to be local chief. The band of Mdewakanton
Dakota that lived in the vicinity referred to the locale either as *Proy-
mueche* (meaning "mountain in the water") or *Hemminnicha*, (which
means "wood, water and hill."). It is now known rather prosaically as

Barn Bluff. That name was originally conferred on the beautiful knob by the French, who called it La Grange.

The image of Red Wing, which once served as a talisman for a long line of Dakota chiefs, is now familiar to us mainly as the logo for Red Wing Shoes, which employs 1400 people at its Red Wing plant and quite a few more at plants in China and at other places around the world. The company was established in 1905, and by 1915, with the help of contracts from the U.S. Army, was making 200,000 pairs of shoes a day. By 1985 the company was making 2 *million* pairs of shoes a day, and it continues to be a respected maker of shoes and boots throughout the world.

Red Wing was also once famous for its pottery, though now only antique collectors take an interest—the Red Wing Pottery closed its doors in 1967. You can still stop by the old pottery factory, easily spotted down on the flats as you come into town from the north, to purchase antiques, seconds, and pots newly made in the old crock traditions.

Frontenac

The highway leaves the river south of Red Wing, passing between towering bluffs before returning to the river at Frontenac. When we meet the river again we find that it has transformed itself from a narrow and powerful channel to a broad expanse of water—Lake Pepin.

To get a good view of the lake, take the left turn at Frontenac up the hill to Frontenac State Park (651-345-3401). It's a lovely hilly place with magnificent overlooks at the top. As you wind your way up the hill toward the bluff, take a look at the fields on the left hand side of the road. You may see a herd of buffalo grazing on the hillside. Buffalo once roamed freely throughout these grasslands, and west all the way to the Rocky Mountains, though these animals are probably corn-fed. Yet the sight of them may evoke the times when most of the inhabitants of the region moved their camps season by season and lived off the land.

On your way up the hill you might also see towees and field sparrows here and there amid the tall grass, and perhaps a red-tailed hawk soaring on the updrafts as it examines the grassy fields below for scurrying rodents. (A red tailed hawk can spot a mouse from a mile away and identify scrumptious spiders and beetles from far above the earth.)

If you happen to see a smaller hawk with pointed wings hovering furiously twenty feet above the ground, you're probably looking at a kestrel, the smallest local member of the falcon family. It subsists largely on grasshoppers and other insects.

And if you open the window and listen carefully, you may hear the melodious gurgle of a nearby meadowlark hiding in the grass, or perhaps even sitting on a fence post with his golden breast exposed to the sunlight. That is the sound of the prairie.

Once you've reached the parking lot, you can stretch your legs by walking out to the point. Jeptha Garrard, a brother of the two men who founded the village of Frontenac just below the bluff, used to jump from this point to test the flying machines he'd devised. His contraptions didn't work, but Jeptha survived the experiments and moved back to Cincinnati where he lived to the ripe old age of seventy-nine.

This bluff-top location might be a good place to reflect for a moment on the early history of the Mississippi itself. The bluffs we see lining the banks of Lake Pepin are made of sand that was deposited on the bottom of a shallow sea hundreds of millions of years ago. In relatively recent times—perhaps 15 thousand years ago—the rushing waters of melting glaciers cut a path through the long-hardened sandstone, forming the body of water we now know as the Mississippi River. In those days the river was immense and the countryside lying below us was under water. The glaciers have long since spent their wad, of course, leaving a very large puddle—Lake Superior—and some handsome river bluffs. As the glacial melt-water receded the drainage of the upper Mississippi shifted away from Lake Superior into its current more-westerly path across the state. Meanwhile, the Chippewa River, which flows south through northern and central Wisconsin to enter the Mississippi at the lower end of the lake, continued to deposit silt as it reached the larger but slower-moving river. Eventually these deposits formed a dam that partially blocked the Mississippi's flow. The result was Lake Pepin.

If you take a stroll along the bluff tops you might come upon a giant boulder that once carried religious significance for the local Dakota Indians. No one seems to know what that significance was, but the rock's name is suggestive. It's called In-Yan-Teopa, which means "stone door/ place of entrance."

There are several paths leading down from the bluff into the forests that cover its flanks. On a hot summer day the forests can be cool, and in late spring it's a good place to observe the colorful warblers that migrate through the area. One of the paths will take you past an old quarry cut into the bluff-side. In 1883 limestone from this quarry was used to construct part of the Cathedral of St. John the Divine in New York City.

Whether you come to camp, hike, picnic, birdwatch, or simply take in the bluff-top scenery, Frontenac State Park is one of Minnesota's jewels. (For more information about the park call 651-345-3401.)

U pon leaving the park turn left toward the river, (rather than right toward the highway). You will soon be entering Old Frontenac. This quaint village was the handiwork of Israel and Lewis Garrard, who first visited the area on a hunting trip in 1854.

Israel and Lewis came from a distinguished family. Their maternal grandfather was one of the founders of Cincinnati, their father had been the governor of Kentucky, and their stepfather, John McLean, was U.S. Postmaster General under presidents Monroe and John Quincy Adams. McLean later served on the U.S. Supreme Court for more than thirty years, and is best known, perhaps, for writing the dissenting opinion in the Dred Scott case. (In fact, some scholars feel that the vehemence of McLean's dissenting views may have driven Chief Justice Roger Brooke Taney into a harsher and more polarizing opinion than he had originally planned.)

We have already been introduced to Jephta Garrard, who built flying machines in a barn behind his brother's house. Though the contraptions never took off, Jeptha did later receive a patent for a device to make oil heaters burn oil more efficiently. Another brother, Kenner, was a West Point graduate who fought for the North in the battles of Fredericksburg, Chancellorsville, and Gettysburg, attaining the rank of brigadier general.

But for Israel Garrard, hunting was clearly the thing. After spending a few weeks in the pristine area, which was then largely uninhabited and

One of the finer houses in Old Frontenac

teeming with wildlife, he purchased a parcel of land beneath the bluff from a Dutch immigrant named Westervelt. Westervelt had bought the land a few years earlier from James "Bully" Wells, who had opened a trading post there in 1839 on land owned by his Dakota wife.

By the following year Israel had completed a hunting retreat in the French Colonial style, which he named St. Hubert's Lodge in honor of the patron saint of hunters. Westervelt's own lodge, completed a year earlier in the Greek revival style, stands on a neighboring lot. Brother Lewis returned a few years later, and Kenner was also later convinced to join the group.

The onset of the Civil War put an abrupt halt to Israel's plans for developing the area, but other settlers began to arrive, and soon the neighborhood could boast of a sawmill, a brewery, a general store, and a saloon. Upon their return from the war, Isreal, Lewis, and Kenner set to work developing the area as a genteel tourist destination, and wealthy folk were soon travelling up the river on paddle-wheelers to spend a few weeks hunting, fishing, sailing, or just relaxing in the newly renamed "Frontenac." For a brief interval Frontenac came to be known as the "Newport of the Northwest."

The Lakeside Hotel can still be seen down on the waterfront, though parts of it have been demolished. President Grant once stayed there, as did members of the Randolph Hearst family, among many others. But as you can see, all of the commercial establishments have long-since vanished from Old Frontenac, which gives it a pleasantly sleepy, time-forgotten feel. This may also explain why the entire community of Old Frontenac is on the National Register of Historic Places. It was the first Minnesota community to be given that designation. Israel Garrard would probably be happy to hear it. When the Chicago, Milwaukee, and St. Paul Railway proposed building a rail line through town in 1871, Isreal controlled enough of the property to refuse the request. As a result, the rails were built along a path that now follows the highway, bypassing the town, and both businesses and residents gravitated away from Old Frontenac to nearby Lake City, which continued to grow as a result of its proximity to both river and rails.

After exploring the village, proceed south (downriver) on the gravel road which will take you back to Highway 61. Along the way you'll pass Villa Maria, a large brick building on your right. Isreal Garrard sold the land to the Catholic Church and a large Ursiline convent stood here until 1963, when it was struck by lightning and suffered severe damage. The remaining buildings, along with a few recent additions, now serve as an inter-denominational retreat center. A scale-model in the parking lot will give you an idea of what the convent originally looked like.

Fort Beauharnois

The first European post erected in what is now Minnesota, Fort Beauharnois, stood somewhere in the vicinity of Villa Maria. It was built by the French in 1727, when Cardinal Fluery was directing the French crown for the young Louis XV, and the operas of Rameau were all the rage at the French court. In those days the Mississippi had only been recently discovered, and it was still widely thought that it might serve as an inland route to the riches of the East Indies. Until such time as that passage through the continent was discovered, there were plenty of valuable furs to be collected in the remote reaches of the interior.

Not long after the fort had been hastily constructed, the Jesuits who accompanied the party celebrated the feast of St. Charles in the rough-hewn chapel. Father Guignas later described the event in his journal:

We did not forget that the fourth day of [November] was the saint's day of the general. Holy Mass was said for him in the morning, and we were well prepared to celebrate the event in the evening, but the slowness of the pyrotechnists and the variableness of the weather led to the postponement of the celebration to the four-teenth of the same month, when some very beautiful rockets were shot off, and the air was made to resound with a hundred shouts of 'Vive le Roy' and 'Vive Charles de Beauharnois' . . . . What contributed very much to the merry-making was the fright of some Indians. When these poor people saw fireworks in the air and the stars falling from the sky, the women and children fled, and the more courageous men cried out for mercy, and earnestly begged that we should stop the astonishing play of the terrible medicine.

The site chosen for the fort proved to be too wet during the spring run-off, however, and a second fort was built the following year on higher ground—perhaps on the very site where Villa Maria now stands.

Fort Beauharnois didn't last long. Trade was not as profitable as had been expected, and the natives were not as docile as they had first appeared. There were sporadic conflicts with both the Dakota and the Fox Indians, who controlled large sections of the inland passage from Lake Michigan to the Upper Mississippi. Finally, on 17 May, 1737, the post was burned to the ground and the French departed.

Several times in subsequent years representatives of the Dakota nation made the long journey to Quebec in hopes of convincing the Government of New France to re-establish the fort and revive trade relations. In 1750, a second fort was built in the vicinity and it remained in operation until the French abandoned the entire territory ten years later following the defeat of General Montcalm in the Battle of Quebec.

Lake City

Farmers have been suspicious of millers since the days of Aesop, for the simple reason that it's difficult to tell whether all of the grain you brought to the mill is actually coming out the other side as processed flour! During settlement days Lake City millers developed a reputation for honest dealing, which was good for trade.

At the turn of the twentieth century Lake City was also the regional center for the clamming industry. At first the clammers directed their efforts toward finding pearls and discarded the shells, but it was not long before enterprising locals were turning the shells into buttons, barrettes, cuff links, and other personal items. At its peak more than 500 workers scavenged the riverbeds looking for shells to supply the button factories in town. The residue from the button-manufacturing process, in turn, was added to hog and chicken feed. Finding a pearl, which might be sold in New York for $3,000, remained a powerful incentive for the clammers, but even the sale of chicken feed was likely to turn a profit.

Lake City has been the victim of several devastating fires, and relatively few buildings remain along its main streets from early times, but the city has been singled out by the Minnesota Historical Society as having the largest variety of nineteenth-century residential architecture of any town of its size. Why not take a spin around the back-streets and see for yourself?

❊ HOK-SI-LA CAMPGROUND ❊

LAKE CITY'S MUNICIPAL campground may look like a bug-infested slough from the highway, but beyond the dark and towering forest you see from the road lies a gem of a campground where trailers are prohibited and even automobiles are allowed into the camping area only briefly to drop off equipment and supplies. As a result the campground is relatively quiet, which makes it all the easier to hear and spot the migrating warblers that pass through the treetops in droves each May. Fishermen can pull their boats right up to the campsites here, making it easy to get out for some early morning fishing on the sparkling lake. And the trains that pass on both sides of the river throughout the night invariably blow their whistles—a haunting sound that will infiltrate your dreams and summon the romance of earlier times on the river. (651) 345-3855

During the summer months Lake City benefits from the presence of the largest recreational marina on the entire Mississippi. A walkway extends for several miles along the waterfront, and it's a pleasant place to get out and stretch your legs. As you stroll along the waterfront, it might be fun to reflect on what may well have been the most famous event associated with Lake City. On July 2, 1922, Ralph W. Samuelson, a resident of the city, invented the sport of waterskiing.

Ralph was only eighteen at the time, but he had already been dreaming of waterskiing for quite a while, inspired by the way barrel-staves glide down snowy hillsides during the winter months. After a number of unsuccessful attempts to ski behind an aquaplane, the enterprising youngster convinced his brother Ben to pull him on a rope behind his boat. He also made the decision—which was crucial to the success of the experiment—to boil the tips of the planks he was using and then clamp them into an upward curve. He bought some rope, hired a blacksmith to fashion an iron ring to use as a handle—and the rest is history.

For the next few years Samuelson was the star attraction at water carnivals throughout Minnesota. Three years after his initial triumph, he scored another "first" by flying off a ramp that had been greased with lard—thus inventing ski jumping! That same summer he also succeeded in skiing behind an airplane traveling at 80 miles an hour.

Samuelson's later life was more mundane, but his role in developing the sport of water-skiing resurfaced when a reporter vacationing in Lake City saw his antique skis hanging on the wall of a local boathouse, inquired about them, and later wrote a story about Samuelson's now long-forgotten exploits. Approaching seventy years of age, Samuelson returned to celebrity once again as The Father of Water Skiing. Lake City erected a monument in his honor, and he was also guest of honor at the 1972 National Water Ski Championships in Seattle, Washington, during which the sport's fiftieth anniversary was celebrated.

Samuelson's second pair of skis—the first set cracked—are now on display at the Water Skiing Hall of Fame in Winter Haven, Florida.

Lake Pepin

The name Lake Pepin first appears on a map of New France published in 1703. Presumably the name refers to the Frankish king Pepin, who was born in 714. Pepin's greatest claim to fame is as the father of Charlemagne, the ruler who united Northern Europe for the first (and only) time and attempted, with the help of the pope, to revive the Roman Empire. Today the name may only remind us that all of the countryside roundabout was once claimed by, though it has never really been possessed by, the French crown.

As we proceed down the shores of the lake perhaps we ought to spend a few minutes reviewing that period in history when the Upper Mississippi was an enticing destination for those seeking scenery and wildness—preferably from the comfortable chair on a passing steamboat. Such journeys find their modern equivalent in well-accouters treks to the remote reaches of Mongolia, New Guinea, or the Amazon, where the quest for contact with a more primitive way of life has been made easier by airplanes, jeeps, and helicopters. Few travelers who came upstream by steamboat from Rock Island or St. Louis in the 1830s were looking to settle and farm—the land was still unavailable. Most were hungry for first-hand experience of the pristine beauty of the river bluffs and the unusual lifeways of the Dakota tribes. As the poet William Cullen Bryant once put it: "This area ought to be visited by every poet and painter in the land."

Among the first of such "tourists" was Giacomo Beltrami, an Italian merchant and adventurer who made his way upstream on board the steamship *Virginia* in 1823. Comparing his experiences with those of yet an earlier time, he wrote, "I know not what impression the first sight of the Phoenician vessels might make on the inhabitants of the coast of Greece, or the Triremi of the Romans on the wild natives of Iberia... but I am sure it could not have been stronger than that which I saw on the countenances of these savages at the arrival of our steamboat." A few years later the famous artist George Catlin made the trip, and recommended that a fashionable tour be developed along the Upper Mississippi. The idea took hold, and before long men and women of means in increasing numbers were enjoying the salubrious weather and perhaps a glimpse or two of the fascinating native inhabitants. Literary transcendentalists, who often expressed the virtues of wildness and the corrupting influence of society, also made the trek, including Henry David Thoreau, the author of *Walden*, who came to Minnesota twice and spoke on his return of a new heroic age during which simple and obscure men would build a new and different type of castle in the West, and throw bridges across "a Rhine stream of a different kind."

In 1854 a Grand Excursion of steamboats was organized to visit the Upper Mississippi en masse. Twelve hundred people ventured north in that flotilla—more than the population of most of the towns the visitors passed along the way. And with the opening of the lands west of the Mississippi to settlement in 1853, such tourists were joined by immigrants arriving in ever increasing numbers. In 1854, 256 steamboats arrived in St. Paul. Four years later the number had quadrupled to 1,068.

The expansion of rail lines put an end to most steamboat traffic by 1870, but there has been a revival of interest in recent years, and you might just catch sight of a paddle-wheeler as you make your way along the river, though you're far more likely to see a caravan of barges carrying coal to one of the power plants upstream.

Reed's Landing

The Mississippi Valley is a haven for bald eagles throughout much of the year. During the spring break-up you can often see them soaring overhead or floating aimlessly downstream on big chunks of ice. Reed's Landing is one of the better places to spot them. Pull off the road into town and scan the treetops in the distance, where fifteen or twenty eagles may be perched.

Reed's Landing developed across from the mouth of the Chippewa River, and for several decades it was a center of the western Wisconsin lumber trade. Lumbermen would hang around the landing—sometimes more than 300 at a time—waiting for the logs to emerge from the mouth of the Chippewa, at which time they would proceed to bind them into huge rafts and escort them downstream to mills in Winona and points further south. The workers at Reeds Landing fashioned two thousand of these rafts a year, on average, until the railroads began offering a cheaper means of transporting the timber in the 1880s. Eventually the supply of trees petered out altogether and the town sank into insignificance. It's hard to believe that Reed's Landing once had seventeen saloons, twenty hotels and boarding houses, and 1800 residents!

The most distinguished edifice in Reed's Landing today is the brick schoolhouse. It was built in 1870 and is thought to be only the second brick schoolhouse built in Minnesota. These days it serves as the Wabasha County Historical Society Museum, and if it happens to be open, you can visit an old-fashioned school-room, a country store, an exhibit on the life of Laura Ingalls Wilder, who once lived nearby, and various artifacts related to the early history of the area.

Wabasha

Wabasha is the oldest community in Minnesota, having been continuously inhabited since the mid-1830s. Settlement was scanty in the early days, of course, and when Wabasha County was established as part of the Minnesota Territory in 1849, it ran all the way to the Missouri River, in the middle of what is now South Dakota!

The town is named after three generations of war chiefs who lived south of the area seasonally. The third of the Wabashas participated in negotiations leading up to the Treaty of Traverse des Sioux in 1851, whereby his people gave up most of what is now southern Minnesota in exchange for annuities and education in the white man's ways. Chief Wabasha was later instrumental in arranging for the release of a number of white prisoners from Camp Release during the Dakota Wars of 1862. The name Wabasha itself refers to a red military cap that was given to the first Wabasha by the British in Quebec in 1763. Thus do the cultures and histories of great nations become intertwined.

The town of Wabasha is known today for its newly-opened Bald Eagle Center, which overlooks the river. The center houses a gift shop and a number of informative displays, as well as a care center for injured eagles and other raptors. Wabasha also carries the distinction of being a port of call for several steamboats that currently ply the Mississippi River, including the Delta Queen.

It is not merely a coincidence that the film *Grumpy Old Men*, starring Walter Matteau and Jack Lemon, was set in Wabasha. The man who wrote the screenplay, Mark Steven Johnson, is from Hastings, and he often visits his grandfather in Wabasha. The citizens of Wabasha are proud of their associations with this comic film, though in fact, most of it was shot in Saint Paul, Faribault, Red Wing, and Center City.

Minnesota's oldest hotel, the Anderson House, is located downtown. It opened for business in 1856, and has recently been restored to its early small-town elegance.

Kellogg and the Weaver Dunes

Just south of Wabasha, Highway 61 leaves the river for a few miles and we come to an area of fascinating ecological diversity. Parts of it aren't so easy to get to, however—which may explain why they remain so interesting. The Weaver Dunes complex is composed of the Weaver Bottoms—a broad shallow lake formed by the old Zumbro River Channel wetland habitats; and the Weaver Dunes—an area of odd dunes covered with grassy vegetation, some of which rise up to thirty feet above the surrounding countryside.

You cannot see this intriguing area well from the highway. What you do see, looking off to the east, are farms and wetlands, with the familiar line of bluffs off in the distance on the far side of the Mississippi. Adventurous travelers might try to find their way into it by following any of the minor highways leading east and south from Kellogg between Highway 61 and the river, though the best way to penetrate the Dunes is by taking County 14 east from Highway 61 about five miles south of Kellogg. Continue north on County 84 and you'll pass some subtle and interesting landscapes. The area is beautiful in itself—a sort of land that time forgot—and it's also the home of what may possibly be the world's largest population of Blanding's turtles.

The Blanding's turtle is a semi-rare species that looks a lot like a WW II American Army helmet—with legs. Scientists estimate the population of Blanding's turtles on the west side of Weaver Dunes alone at between 2500 and 4600 individuals. That's a lot of turtles. The area possesses the perfect combination of calm, shallow waters that are rich

The Weaver Dunes, a turtle paradise

in aquatic vegetation for feeding, and sandy uplands for nesting. Unfortunately for the turtles, local roads bisect these two zones, both of which are essential to the turtle's health and reproductive vigor.

If you visit this area in midsummer, you might catch a spectacular display of the rough-seeded fameflower, which blooms daily for three hours every afternoon before sunset. The sandy soils of the dunes area also happen to be perfect for growing watermelons, and a watermelon festival has taken place every year in Kellogg since 1946 on the weekend after Labor Day. This four-day celebration includes something for everyone: a softball tournament, tractor pull, Watermelon Queen coronation, flea market, carnival rides, a dance, and two parades—one for the kids on Saturday and a grand parade on Sunday.

Beaver

As we continue downstream along the river toward the town of Weaver, it might be worth reflecting on the early history of settlement in the river valleys that cut up through the bluffs to the plateau above. In those days many of the valley hillsides were shorn of their timber and planted with crops. With each passing year more trees would be felled, and cattle and later goats would be grazed on the hillsides. The wood was used both for building and for fueling the passing steamboats; and it was convenient to be farming so close to the river, where the transportation, mills, feed, and farm supplies were located. Few early settlers stopped to consider the role played by the trees in holding the soil onto those slopes.

The citizens of Beaver, Minnesota, found out the hard way. The town was first settled by New Englanders in 1854, and is the oldest village in the Whitewater River Valley. It proved to be a pleasant place to live and farm, but as deforestation continued up and down the valley, flooding became more common. The source of the problem was recognized early on, though nothing much could be done about it until local farmers could be persuaded to stop cutting and burning the hillsides, or government funds could be found to purchase key parcels of land. In 1919 Whitewater State Park was created but land use practices nearby remained primitive and flooding increased, reaching a peak in 1938 when the town of Beaver flooded 28 times.

If you turn right on Highway 74 in Weaver, you can drive up into the valley and give the town of Beaver a look. There isn't much to see there now except a graveyard.

If you do find the graveyard, stop to take a look at a few of the graves. Maybe you'll spot the grave of Richard J. Dorer. Does the name sound familiar? You've probably seen it on your road map. The Richard J. Dorer State Forest is made up of a patchwork of forest lands purchased by the state in an effort to rehabilitate the area. Dorer himself was employed by the Minnesota Department of Conservation, and he was a driving force behind the movement to replant the hillsides with grasses, shrubs, and trees, terrace the upland fields, and bring more sensible conservation practices to the area. The beauty we see as we pass along the highway and the rich plant and animal life that has returned not only to the hillsides, but also to the marshes and river bottoms, is the result of decades of environmental concern, scientific study, and shrewd governmental action by Dorer and others like him—state employees, local residents, outdoorsmen, and nature-loving volunteers.

You might want to continue up Highway 74 past Beaver to Whitewater State Park, which is nestled in the hills halfway between the river bottom and the gently rolling farmland to the west. The park has excellent trout fishing, camping, and ten miles of hiking trails. Several of the trails will take you to magnificent overlooks, and in mid-summer the bird feeders at the visitors' center offer a living textbook of common Minnesota species.

The countryside surrounding the park is also rather unusual, with white pines and other species that are commonly found growing naturally only much farther north. During the last glacial period, this area marked the edge of the glacier's advance. These species are remnants of that much colder period in the area's history.

Upper Mississippi River National Wildlife and Fish Refuge

On the other side of the Highway 61 we catch sight once again of the Weaver Bottoms. Pull off at the wayside rest at mile marker 45 and take a look around. From mid-October through November this is one of the premier spots in the Midwest to see tundra swans, and a variety of other species—ducks, pelicans, shorebirds—might be present at any time of the year. This entire area is managed by the Upper Mississippi River National Wildlife and Fish Refuge.

This refuge is the longest in the contiguous United States, extending 261 miles along the river valley from the mouth of the Chippewa River all the way to Rock Island, Illinois. It owes its existence in large part to a Chicago advertising man, Will Dilg, who often spent his summers fishing in the area. When Dilg heard of a plan to straighten the river and drain much of the backwater, he went to work on an alternative plan: to turn the entire area into a wildlife refuge. Almost miraculously, only one year later, with the help of the Isaac Walton League (which Dilg had formed a few years earlier), Congress in 1924 passed the Upper Mississippi River Wild Life and Fish Refuge Act, which authorized the government to purchase and set aside land in the area as wildlife habitat. Today the Refuge encompasses almost a quarter of a million acres, ensuring that many of the ducks, swans, geese, pelicans and other birds that migrate through the area annually will be able to complete their journey.

The Isaac Walton League is not a high-profile organization today, though it still works effectively on environmental issues that may seem unglamorous to others. Under Dilg's early leadership, the organization quickly became by far the largest in the country, and by 1925 it had more than 100,000 members, many of them businessmen who were dis-inclined to see their favorite fishing holes disappear forever, and were concerned, more generally, that the United States was attempting to take the ruggedness, not only out of the rivers, but also out of the nation's character. As Dilg explained in the league's journal: "we are composed of thousands upon thousands of HE MEN."

The Mississippi habitats have proven to be as difficult to manage effectively, however, as they once were to navigate.

An ambitious program was started during the 1930s to build a series of locks and dams along almost the entire length of the Upper Mississippi River. The idea was to make the river deeper behind the dams, so that the Army Corp of Engineers could maintain the 9-foot channel depth required for commercial barge traffic. Slowing down the river led, however, to increasing deposits of sediments in the backwaters, which, in turn, threatened to ruin the precious waterfowl and fish habitat. Balancing such commercial and environmental interests along the course of a mighty and unpredictable river has been an ongoing challenge for the U.S. Fish and Wildlife Service, the Army Corp of Engineers, and various state and local agencies up and down the river.

Perhaps the success of their efforts may be measured by the spectacular spring and fall migrations, during which millions of birds ranging from tiny warblers to enormous eagles, herons, and pelicans pass through the valley, while the waters below continue to support walleye, crappies, catfish, bass, and even such unusual species as the lake sturgeon, paddlefish, and American eel.

You have probably seen a barge or two making its way slowly upstream during your journey. These vessels remain an efficient way to transport coal, grain, and other bulk commodities. Today more than twenty thousand barges ply the river annually.

The barge traffic on the river is not what it once was, however. The number of barges moving through the locks has fallen by 40 percent in the last fifteen years, and barge fleets are being reduced. The Army Corp of Engineers has come in for mounting criticism, therefore, even from within its own organization, for continuing to forecast, against the grain of scientific and economic analysis, that barge traffic will *increase* significantly in the coming years, in order to justify proceeding with its long-delayed plan to lengthen the river locks. "With each passing month," one observer recently reflected, "the disconnect between reality and the rosy Corps forecasts yawns wider and wider."

Latch State Park

South of Weaver Highway 61 returns to the river and the bluffs close in once again. A few miles down the way we come to Latch State Park. Steamboat captains on the Mississippi made use of the park's three bluffs—Faith, Hope, and Charity—for navigation. They tower more than 500 feet above the river. During the 1850s there was a busy steamboat landing and logging town at their base. Today the area is pretty wild. The park was created in 1925 to keep things that way. Ambitious souls can follow a half-mile trail to the bluff-top for a spectacular view of the river valley. It's worth the effort. The park also has seven walk-in campsites.

Winona

The word Winona means "first-born-daughter" in Dakota. The town received this name in 1853 after its original name, Montezuma, had been erased from the official plot. The princess-daughter in question was that of chief Wabasha, who maintained his summer camp in the area. Winona was later the birthplace of Hollywood princess Winona Ryder.

The picturesque bluffs surrounding Winona were noted even by early visitors such as Zebulon Pike. But its prime location on the river rather than its bluffs, helped to make it Minnesota's third-largest town by 1860. It was receiving over a thousand steamboats a year by that time, and thirty years later it solidified its position as a transportation hub by building a bridge across the Mississippi—the only bridge to span the river for hundreds of miles. The bridge had a steam-powered swingspan that allowed steamers and barges to pass when the trains

South of Weaver the bluffs close in again.

weren't running. It served the Burlington Line and also the Green Bay and Western routes for the next 94 years. In its heyday countless freight trains moved in and out of Winona, and the city was also visited by a half-dozen passenger trains every day.

Winona profited greatly from the development of farming in southern Minnesota, and by 1870, it was the fourth largest wheat shipping port in the United States. The city also made the most of the log-rafts moving downriver from the pine forests of the north via the Chippewa and St. Croix rivers.

Winona's population peaked in 1900, and the last raft of timber departed the city in 1915. By that time, the city had already fallen into decline. Its days as a boom town on the American frontier were over. However, unlike other river towns that all but vanished once the timber was gone, Winona retained a degree of vigor, aided by the presence of other industries and also a college. Back in 1858 Winona had become the site of the first Normal School west of the Mississippi. The school later became Winona State University. A Catholic school, St. Mary's College, was established in 1912.

Among the industries that have kept Winona going is the J.R. Watkins Company, which, in 1868, began to manufacture a red liniment with a bewildering array of applications. From its origins in the pharmaceutical expertise and promotional zeal of a single individual, Watkins has grown into one of the largest direct-sales operations in the world. There are still plenty of folks alive who remember the Watkins Man of an earlier time who made door-to-door visits every year, supplying homes with a variety of balms, extracts, and cooking spices. Nowadays mail-order catalogs and internet sales make up a larger part of the still-thriving business.

J.R. Watkins moved his business to Winona in 1885, and its headquarters is currently housed in the majestic Administration Building on East 3rd Street, where the Watkins museum is also housed

The Julius C. Wilkie steamboat sits high and dry on the riverfront in downtown Winona.

(507-457-6095). Winona has several other off-beat museums, including a Polish Museum (102 Liberty Street, 507-454-3431) and the rather stylish Minnesota Marine Art Museum (800 Riverview Drive, 507-474-6626). The remarkable Merchants National Bank (102 E. Third St) designed by Prairie architects Purcell and Elmslie, is definitely worth more than a passing glance.

As you approach the city from the north down Highway 61, with a robust strip-mall to your left and a row of majestic conical tree-covered bluffs to your right, you'll begin to see the lakes that give Winona the name The Island City. Lakeside Park, which runs parallel to the highway, has plenty of picnic areas and bike trails, and the views of the bluffs from there are largely unsullied by highway development. Head downtown to the Julius C. Wilkie Steamboat Center at Levee Park for information about the city's early history, or simply to watch a barge or two pass by (507-643-6849).

In short, Winona is large enough to get lost in, and interesting enough to make the experience worthwhile.

The view downriver from an overlook at Great River Bluffs State Park

Great River Bluffs State Park

South of Winona the bluffs become taller and the islands in the braided river more beautiful. Great River Bluffs State Park makes a good base for exploring the area. (Take County Road 3 up the hill a few miles south of town. Then follow the signs.) From here you can get the feel of the long, deep valleys that remain from a time when glacial melt water thundered through the area. The park has hiking trails, a campground, and several spectacular overlooks. Even the gravel road leading out to the park offers wonderful views down the steep grassy hillsides covered with sunflowers and wild bergamot, with the thin thread of the river passing by in the distance far below.

FURTHER AFIELD

Our trip ends here, though the river remains beautiful well past La Crosse. The Wisconsin hamlet of Trempealeau is charming, and Wyalusing State Park (also in Wisconsin) may have the highest bluffs of all.

A journey up the Root River Valley via Preston will connect you with the trip described on pages 90-103.

THE
SOUTHERN
PRAIRIES

WHEN EUROPEAN IMMIGRANTS FIRST arrived in the Midwest, the landscape was dominated by a vast sea of grass—the prairie. In southern Minnesota the grasses were often more than head high, though further west, in Nebraska and the Dakotas, the land was drier and the tall grasses gave way to shorter, less demanding species. Today, about one-fifth of those western short- and mixed-grass prairies remain, but the tall-grass prairies that first met the eyes of immigrants arriving in Minnesota to farm during the 1850s have almost completely vanished. Only 150,000 acres of prairie remain—less than 1% of its original extent. Therefore, to refer to this area as prairie is largely wishful thinking. We might more accurately call it the Minnesota Cornbelt.

The story of southern Minnesota is largely one of immigrant farmers plowing up the rich tall-grass prairie sod and planting crops. Today Minnesota ranks among the nation's leading producers of sugar beets, corn, soy beans, hogs, turkeys, and winter wheat. In a return to prairie traditions, Minnesota is the nation's number-two producer of buffalo meat. It ranks seventh overall in agricultural output, which is remarkable when you consider that half of the state is covered with woods, lakes, and bogs.

Though we will never again experience the profound expansiveness described again and again by early visitors to the state as they crossed those towering seas of grass, the movement is well underway to preserve remaining pockets of native prairies in neglected corners of the state, and prairie plants are now being re-introduced along highways and in gardens. Such remnants and revivals are well worth visiting, especially for the unusual and colorful plant life, and we'll be highlighting several of them during our driving tours.

Due to its largely agricultural economy, recreational visits to southern Minnesota are undoubtedly less frequent than to other parts of the state. Yet the region is rich in both history and natural beauty, its Native American sites are unparalleled, and its proximity to the Twin Cities metropolitan area make it a perfect destination for weekend getaways. The quarries at Pipestone, the festivals in New Ulm, the wildlife at Lac qui Parle, and prairie remnants and restorations throughout the region are just a few of the highlights that can make a visit worthwhile.

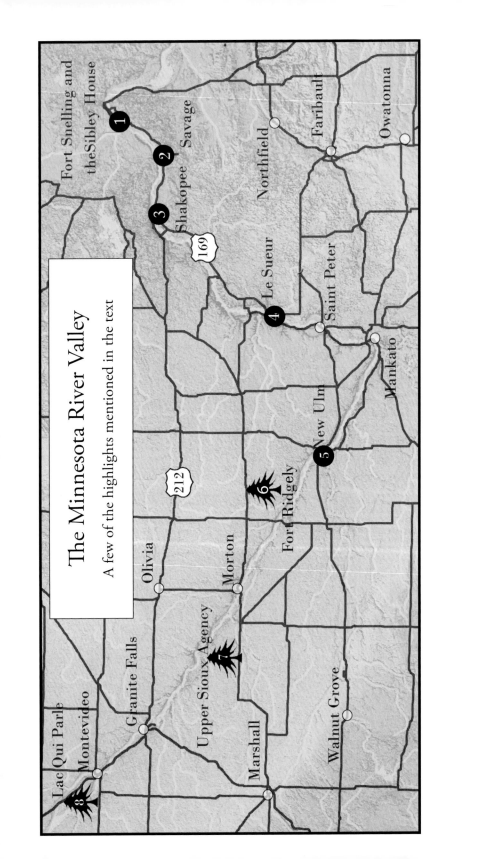

The Minnesota River Valley

A few of the highlights mentioned in the text

Fort Snelling and theSibley House

Savage

Shakopee

169

Le Sueur

Northfield

Faribault

Owatonna

Saint Peter

Mankato

New Ulm

Fort Ridgely

212

Olivia

Morton

Upper Sioux Agency

Granite Falls

Walnut Grove

Marshall

Montevideo

Lac Qui Parle

1

2

3

4

5

6

7

8

I. THE MINNESOTA RIVER VALLEY

As we proceed south and west through the Minnesota River Valley, we'll be passing orchards, dairy farms, feed lots, quaint nineteenth-century churches, sleepy towns, sweeping plains and loping hills, and mile after mile of soybeans and corn, which have a beauty all their own.

1 Fort Snelling

Today Fort Snelling lies in the midst of a tangle of freeways, but when viewed from the far side of the river, it's easy to conjure the time when it was a bastion of civilization amid a seemingly endless wilderness of forests and prairies. To the fur trappers who traded in the area, it represented the authority of the United States Government to curtail the activities of foreign (i.e. British) traders in the region. It also protected the lands belonging to the Dakota Indians whose lived in the area from the incursions of white settlers, and (in theory) helped to ease tensions between the Dakota and their age-old enemies the Ojibwe.

The fort was completed in 1825, and for the next thirty years it was a gathering place for people of all sorts. The land around the fort was soon under cultivation, and various roads and trails were developed connecting it with the nascent milling activities at St. Anthony Falls, the chain of lakes which are now within the boundaries of Minneapolis, and the St. Croix River, where lands first became available for white settlement in 1837. Several fur companies built forts nearby, and the village of Mendota grew up on the south side of the river.

Following the Treaty of Traverse des Sioux in 1851, the rushing tide of immigrant farmers to the newly opened lands of southern Minnesota rendered the fort militarily obsolete, though it later served as the headquarters and supply base for the military Department of Dakota, which was active during the period of the Indian campaigns and the Spanish-American War of 1898.

After serving an important but entirely bureaucratic function during the world wars, Fort Snelling was closed for good in 1950.

In 1960, when the U.S. Department of the Interior designated Fort Snelling as the state's first National Historic Landmark, there wasn't much left of the oldest buildings. Several organizations have been involved in rebuilding the historic structures, and today, through films, displays, and costumed interpretive guides, the fort offers a fascinating look at the early life in the territory that later became Minnesota.

The fort sits at the junction of Minnesota Highways 5 and 55, one mile east of the Twin Cities International Airport. Call 612-726-1171 or visit the Minnesota Historical Society website at www.mnhs.org for more information about hours and programs.

Minnesota Valley National Wildlife Refuge

Minnesota Valley National Wildlife Refuge, one of only four urban wildlife refuges in the nation, lies a few miles upstream from the fort. The refuge was established in 1976 to preserve the river bottom habitat used by ducks migrating across the interior of the continent along the Mississippi flyway and also to support fish and other wildlife species. It stretches for 34 miles from Fort Snelling State Park to Jordan. Bald eagles nest there, and hundreds of thousands of migrating birds pass through the refuge every year. More than 200 species have been sited within its borders. Common mammal sightings include white-tailed deer, raccoon, red fox, muskrat, beaver, and woodchuck. Coyotes are also becoming more numerous.

The Visitor Center is located at 3815 34th Avenue, across from the Airport Hilton Hotel south of I-494. It provides a good introduction to the refuge's features, with an information desk, a bookshop, slide-shows, and four levels of modern exhibits that explore various aspects of the ecosystems contained with the park. Once you've boned up on the science (or even if you haven't) the next step would be take a hike down the Hillside trail just outside the Center. It passes through wetlands, prairie remnants, and forests in the course of its half-mile loop. Although the Mall of America and the airport are right next door, the forests and marshes of the refuge seem hardly changed from the days when visitors arrived by canoe.

Pamphlets are available at the Visitor's Center identifying other points upstream at which the refuge can be more fully explored. For more information call 952-854-5900.

The Sibley House (Mendota)

The tiny community of Mendota sits on the south flank of the Minnesota River across from Fort Snelling, and it retains much of the placid charm it may have had in the early days of white settlement. (Take Highway 55 south across the Mendota Bridge, turn left onto Highway 13, and follow the signs.) Four of the original limestone buildings remain from the era between 1825 and 1853 when the American Fur Company traded here with the Dakota. Among them is the home of Henry Hastings Sibley, the company's young regional manager.

Drawn by a love of outdoor adventure, Sibley gave up a career in law as a young man to take a position with the American Fur Company at Mackinac. In 1834, at the age of 23, he was made a partner in the company and was given control of the trade with the Dakota Indians from the Falls of St. Anthony to the Dubuque River and west to the headwaters of the Missouri River. The division's head-quar-

The Sibley House

ters was in Mendota (then called St. Peters.) Upon his arrival Sibley set to work erecting a warehouse and a large, comfortable residence using locally-quarried sandstone. He lived here for nine years, managing the business and forming lasting friendships with the Indians, missionaries, settlers, and other traders in the vicinity. (His friend Jean Baptiste Faribault build another fine structure that still stands right down the street. It originally served as a tavern.)

Sibley learned the Dakota language and the Indians found him to be a trustworthy individual. They called him "Wah-pe-ton Hanska"—the "tall trader"—and he negotiated on their behalf when the treaties of 1837 and 1851 were drawn up. The incremental expansion of the Sibley house parallels the growth of the community of Mendota itself.

Sibley had a well-stocked library and a piano at his home, and he enjoyed entertaining friends and visiting dignitaries. In 1843 he married Sarah Steele, a sister of Franklin Steele, the sutler at Fort Snelling, and the social gatherings became livelier than ever.

When the State of Wisconsin was admitted to the union in May 1848, the territories beyond its western border continued to be called Wisconsin Territory. Sibley was sent to Washington to represent the truncated territory in Congress, and he worked hard to pass the act re-organizing it as the territory of Minnesota. Sibley insisted that the name "Minnesota" be kept, over the objections of Stephen A. Douglas, who had introduced the bill, and who preferred the name "Itasca." Sibley continued to represent Minnesota Territory until 1853, and during that time he obtained large grants for roads, schools, and public buildings for the territory as well as help for the Indians whom he felt were being driven to desperation by the perfidious acts of the federal Indian agents who handled their annuities. When Minnesota finally became a state in 1858, Sibley was elected its first governor. You can see the office he used as governor here at the house in Mendota.

Three of the four buildings that remain standing from those days have been restored and are now fully furnished, including a warehouse and the home of Jean-Baptiste Faribault. The tour guides will tell you fascinating tales of the fur-trading era, when life was simple, game was plentiful (during one three-year period Sibley shot 1798 ducks) and the influx of settlers had not yet undermined the delicate ethnic balance of the region. For more informations about hours and tours call 651-452-1596. Or stop in anytime to examine the buildings and get a feel for that long-vanished time.

2 Savage

Continuing west along the south bank of the Minnesota River on Highway 13, we eventually arrive in Savage. It's an unprepossessing community today, perhaps, but it was once the home to one of Minnesota's most famous citizens, Marion Savage. Savage was a patent medicine salesman from Iowa who shrewdly shifted his attention to animal feed, devising a special blend and a slogan to go with it: Three Feeds for

One Cent. The product was hugely successful, but Savage's promotional genius inspired him to do more. He purchased a famous Indiana pacer named Dan Patch for $60,000. That was a staggering sum for a horse, (or for anything else) in those days, but Dan Patch proved to be unbeatable on the track, and Savage soon recouped his investment in prize money. Dan Patch became the most famous athlete in America, and you could share in the horse's glory by purchasing not only animal feed, but tobacco, shaving equipment, pot-bellied stoves, stop-watches, and even automobiles carrying the Dan Patch logo. Savage carried on a brisk catalog business, and mailed thousands of free Dan Patch posters to loyal customers. For many backwoods farmers, it was the only color image they had to hang on the wall—and it was a nice one. It kept Savage's product line in the public eye from Connecticut to California and beyond. You'll find the complete story in *The Great Dan Patch and the Remarkable Mr. Savage* by Tim Brady.

The one building in Savage that dates to the era of Dan Patch is the train depot, which has recently been returned to town from nearby Murphy's Landing and lovingly restored. It contains an exhibit of Dan Patch memorabilia and also a coffee shop.

3 Shakopee

Although Shakopee is right across the river from the sprawling Minneapolis suburbs, it retains some of the look and feel of a prosperous small town. During earlier times a Dakota Indian village was located nearby, and there are burial mounds in the town's Memorial Park that testify to a long-standing Native American presence. The village was called Teen-tah-o-tan-wa, "village of the prairie," and Shakopee was its chief. The Indians grew corn on the rich river bottom soil and followed the river upstream in search of buffalo herds. The countryside roundabout was largely prairie.

The sprawling floodplain within which Shakopee is located, and its proximity to the Twin Cities, has made it an ideal location for large-scale entertainments such as Valley Fair amusement park, Canterbury Downs Racetrack, and the collection of pioneer buildings known as Murphy's Landing. These buildings have been relocated to the site from various far-flung locations and arranged chronologically from 1840 to 1890, making it possible to stroll through the grounds on a hot summer day and experience the development of a typical Minnesota pioneer community from rude log cabins to rather genteel dwellings. Various houses emphasize the distinctive life ways of Norwegian, German, Irish, and other immigrant groups. A school, blacksmith shop, and train depot are among the forty-odd buildings. (2187 E. Highway 101: call 763-694-7784 for more details about hours and holiday programs.)

A few miles south of Murphy's Landing, on the outskirts of Prior Lake, lies yet another attraction—Mystic Lake Casino. It's reputed to be among the most successful in the country, and it provides all the eating, lodging, gambling, and entertainment options you might expect from such a place. The Mdewakanton Band who own the massive operation are descendents of the Dakota Indians who were banished from the area following the Dakota War of 1862. In the decades following the conflict, some of them returned to their ancestral homelands. Their numbers were small, but beginning in 1890 the State of Minnesota began to purchase lands for them, and finally, in 1969, a genuine reservation was established.

The best time for non-gamblers to visit Mystic Lake would undoubtedly be during the late summer powwow that's held every year in the hills near the casino. Drumming, singing, and dancing groups from throughout the Midwest and Plains states assemble to perform in an outdoor setting. There are food concessions, a flea market, and a craft fair. As you listen to the powerful sound of chanting and drumbeats echoing across the grassy hills, and stare off toward the trees along the distant bluffs beyond the river, it may be possible to recapture a bit of the flavor of those times when there were more meadowlarks than people in the area, and a thundering herd of buffalo might occasionally be glimpsed on the not-too-distant prairie.

As you leave Shakopee traveling west on Highway 169, you top a rise and the expanse of the Minnesota River Valley—a land of orchards and tree farms—opens itself in front of you. Visitors have often noted that the valley is far more majestic than the river itself, which has little gradient and follows a very meandering path. In fact the valley of the river was created by an older and far more powerful river than the one that now flows between its banks. Geologists refer to the Minnesota River and others like it as "underfit."

Twelve thousand years ago, Glacial River Warren, several miles wide and up to five hundred feet deep, flowed south in a raging torrent from Glacial Lake Agassiz, which at that time covered thousands of square miles in northern Minnesota and Manitoba. Eventually the ice dams at the northern edge of Lake Agassiz melted sufficiently to allow for drainage in that direction, and the flood of water to the south was abruptly reduced to a trickle. By that time, however, the scouring of the mighty river had produced an impressive valley and also exposed some of the oldest rocks ever found on the earth's surface to view.

Following the treaty of Traverse des Sioux in 1851 settlers began to pour into the newly opened farmlands, which proved to be some of the richest in North America. It did not take long for steamboats to begin plying the Minnesota River to service the newly-founded settlements and to transport produce to distant markets. The river was so shallow, however, and the course so full of sharp angles, that it proved impossible to maintain a fixed schedule along the route.

To get a better feel for what the landscape was like in those early days, take the turnoff to Louisville Swamp a few miles outside Shakopee on Highway 169. Follow the gravel road across the railroad tracks to the parking lot. Several hikes begin here, including a 4.5 mile jaunt out across the empty fields past an abandoned farmstead to the river.

Jordan

Take the exit into Jordan, a quaint and still ungentrified town with several antique shops. After poking around, continue through town, then turn right on County 99. Keep on as 99 turns into County 61. This will bring you to some beautiful views of the river valley from the heights.

A few miles further west on Highway 19 you'll reach the village of Henderson, which was founded by Joseph R. Brown back in 1855. The quaint one-street town is home to both the Sibley County Historical Society Museum and The Joseph R. Brown Minnesota River Center (on the second floor of the community building) which houses exhibits about Henderson and early river history.

4 Le Sueur

Approaching Le Sueur from the north gives you the feeling of agriculture as an industry rather than a personal endeavour. On either side of the highway are warehouses, cheese factories, and canneries. You may find yourself whistling a little jingle, "In the valley of the Jolly (ho-ho-ho) Greeeen Giant." Le Sueur is the home of that producer of canned and frozen vegetables, and you'll pass a large billboard representation of the friendly giant himself as you come into town. (The town of Blue Earth, near the Iowa border, has a more impressive 55-foot fiberglass statue of the same figure.)

The Minnesota Valley Canning Company got its start in Le Sueur in 1903 selling sweet creamed corn. The Green Giant was introduced in 1925 to promote the company's peas, and in 1950 the company itself adopted the name. Green Giant is now owned by General Mills, and its headquarters is no longer in Le Sueur. (Incidentally, Minnesota currently ranks first in the nation in the production of sweet peas.)

You can visit a small white frame house at 118 N Main Street, where Carson Nesbit Cosgrove, the founder of the canning company which became Green Giant, once lived. Perhaps a more compelling reason to

---

QUICK STOP: EMMA CRUMBIES

Why not stop at Emma Crumbies, just south of Belle Plaine? Everyone else does. You can eat a meal, buy some bakery goods or a bushel of fresh-picked apples, stock up on candles, greeting cards, and nicknacks, enjoy a malt at the soda fountain, or take a pony ride.

The Mayo House, Le Sueur

visit the house is that at an earlier time the second floor served as the first medical practice of a man named Dr. William Mayo. Mayo actually built the house, and he practiced there for five years before relocating to Rochester. In later years, along with his two sons, Mayo expanded his practice considerably, and the end result was the Mayo Clinic, which is now the largest and most famous medical facility in the world. (See page 98 for more details.) Tours start in the gift shop next door.

Traverse des Sioux

Highway 169 crosses the Minnesota River north of Le Sueur. A few miles downstream you'll come to Traverse des Sioux. Before the era of bridges, this shallow stretch of the Minnesota River was the best place to cross for miles around. Archeological finds in the vicinity date back 9,000 years, and in the era of ox carts and stage coaches the ford was a crossroads for Indians, trappers, traders, and immigrants moving back and forth across the prairie. Its importance to both Indians and whites was underscored by the fact that it was chosen as the meeting site in 1851 for the signing of the treaty that bears its name. By that treaty the Sisseton and Wahpeton Dakota tribes sold 24 million acres of land—most of southern Minnesota—to the United States in exchange for cash, annuities, and the training and provisions necessary to take up an agricultural way of life on a ten-mile strip of land along the Minnesota River Valley upstream from the ford.

The Minnesota Historical Society has placed a series of kiosks on the bank above the river to explain the significance of the site, and the Nicollet County Historical Society has built a Traverse des Sioux Interpretive Center next door. The museum is well worth a stop. It provides pictures and biographies of all the treaty's signers, both white and Indian. A fine collection of prints by Seth Eastman is also on display. Eastman was a military man, and during a brief stint at Fort Snelling in 1830 he married Stands-Like-a-Spirit, the daughter of Cloud Man, the leader of the Dakota settlement at Lake Calhoun. When Eastman returned to the fort during the 1840s he executed a number of sketches depicting the sweep of the river valley and the lifeways of the Dakota people. These sketches, which placed Eastman in the first rank of frontier artists, have been widely reproduced, but the original lithographs on display here are even more evocative, especially after a pleasant drive up the river valley through the countryside many of them depict.

5 New Ulm

Unlike many frontier settlements, the city of New Ulm was established following a rigorous plan. Its founder, Ferdinand Beinhorn, had arrived in New York City in 1852 from the German province of Brunswick, intent on buying a few sections of government land, platting a city, dividing it into lots and then selling them. He formed a land society later that year in Chicago. A cholera epidemic hit Chicago that summer which made many of the members eager to move west.

Beinhorn sent two scouts to Minnesota Territory in June of 1854 to investigate townsites on the Minnesota River. They were favorably impressed by the potential of a location just upstream of the mouth of the Cottonwood River.

The next spring another German, Wilhelm Pfaender, arrived in St. Paul with the intention of establishing a community based on the Turner Movement. The Turners emphasized an unusual mix of liberal politics, gymnastics, and musical training. Many of its followers had lost faith in German politics following the failed revolutions of 1848 and had come to the United States, where they hoped to have better luck putting their ideals into practice. These Germans were often persecuted during the 1850s by settled Americans who were disturbed by the continuing high rate of immigration. Pfaender's mission was to locate a place where Turners could settle without fear of such persecution. He caught wind of Beinhorn's plan to establish a town on the banks of the Minnesota, and the two men joined forces to found New Ulm. A broad tree-lined street was plotted (and still runs) through the center of town, and parks were scattered in every corner of the new city. The next year a Turner Hall was erected and concerts, lectures, dances, gymnastic classes, and court proceedings were soon being held there.

In 1860 only 2 of New Ulm's 635 residents were not of German origin. Although its population has become more ethnically diversified since then, during the middle decades of the twentieth century New Ulm carved out a reputation for itself as the Polka Capital of the United States. Whoopee John Wilfahrt, Harold Loeffelmacher and his Six Fat Dutchmen, and other groups kept the town hopping at several local ballrooms. Even today, the local radio Station, KNUJ, broadcasts polka music for one hour on weekdays and several hours on Sunday afternoons. Is anybody listening? Well, the U.S. Census Bureau reported in 2000 that New Ulm had a greater percentage of citizens of German descent than any other city in the United States.

Visitors to New Ulm today will see plenty of reminders of the city's German heritage. First on the list, perhaps, is the enormous statue of Hermann the German that sits at the top of the hill above town. The statue represents a quasi-mythical Hermann who lead the Germans in battle against the Romans in 7 AD. The Romans were defeated, thus ending their domination of Germany.

The monument was financed and built by the National Grand Lodge of the Sons of Hermann, a fraternal organization with over 300 lodges across the country. Though some of the members questioned the wisdom of spending their local funds to build a monument off in the wilds of Minnesota, the fact that New Ulm was chosen to receive the statue is one further indication of the unusual concentration of Germans in

the vicinity. The views from the top of the 102-foot monument offer a spectacular panorama of the Minnesota River Valley below.

A second monument was erected in 1991 by the German-Bohemian Heritage Society to honor early immigrants to New Ulm from Bohemia. Many of the family names are inscribed in granite slabs at the base of the monument. It sits at 1 North German Street.

To get a sense of the continuing life of New Ulm's German heritage, a visit to the Schell Brewery might be just the ticket. The brewery is the second-oldest family-owned brewery in the country. Its founder, August Schell, arrived in New Ulm from Chicago along with Wilhelm Pfaender's group and found work as a machinist, but it soon occurred to him that what the town *really* needed was a brewery. Schell knew nothing about brewing, so he went into partnership with a brewer from St. Paul, and in 1860 they set up a brewery on a steep hillside above the Cottonwood River two miles outside of town. In its first season it produced only 200 barrels of beer.

Today the brewery is still entirely owned by descendents of August Schell, and it is not only the oldest, but also the largest brewery in the state. It produces 38 different beers, many of which are sold under other names. The buildings are on the National Register of Historic Places, and the elaborately landscaped grounds retain the atmosphere of nineteenth-century European life. You can tour the brewery most days, and sample many of the beers in the sampling room after the tour. The brewery also has a museum and an extensive gift shop (800-770-5020).

Downtown New Ulm has the hodge-podge look of many small Minnesota towns, with facades from many eras vying for attention, but it's livelier than most, and several of its most venerable institutions are located here. The Brown County Historical Society, at Center and Broadway, would be a good place to start any tour. After you've read about the Turner Movement and the early history of the city, head over to the Turner Hall at 100 S. State Street. Though it has been rebuilt several times—the original building was razed during the Dakota Conflict and its successor was flattened by a tornado—it still serves the same functions that it did when it was built in 1857. Perhaps its most interesting feature is the Rathskeller in the basement of the 1872 annex. Here you can enjoy a beer and a bratwurst in the midst of seventy-feet of murals dating from 1873, with rivers, lakes, vineyards, and castles that evoke the romance of the Tyrolian Alps.

For a hefty German meal Veigel's Kaiserhoff (221 N. Minnesota St.) would be a good bet. The ambiance is attractively Teutonic and the ribs are locally famous. For a quick breakfast or lunch, try the Ulmer Cafe, a block west on Minnesota Street.

The back streets of New Ulm are lined with beautiful and interesting homes. Wanda Gag, the author and illustrator of *Millions of Cats* and other books for children, was born and raised here; her childhood home is open for tours during the summer months (226 North Washington St.). The home of John Lind (622 Center St.) Minnesota's fourteenth governor, can also be toured. And even a brief, random excursion through New Ulm's well-kept residential back streets can be fascinating.

Henry David Thoreau in Minnesota

In June of 1861, noted author and naturalist Henry David Thoreau paid a visit to Minneapolis, and in an effort to see more of life on the prairie, he joined in what had become an annual social event of the first order—the riverboat trip up the Minnesota River to the Redwood Agency to deliver the annuities that were owed to the Dakota Indians as part of the treaty agreement. In a letter to a friend he noted that because the water was low, at many places the passengers were required to disembark and walk across an isthmus, while the vessel negotiated the long oxbow leading around the bend to the other side, at which point everyone would re-board the boat.

Thoreau also found the unorthodox means used to steer the boat worthy of comment.

In making a short turn we repeatedly and designedly ran square into the steep and soft bank, taking in a cartload of earth—this being more effectual than the rudder to fetch us about again; or the deeper water was so narrow and close to the shore, that we were obliged to run into and break down at least fifty trees which overhung the water, when we did not cut them off, repeatedly losing a part of our outworks..."

The boat often ran aground and could only be freed making use of a cable and winch fastened to a convenient tree on shore.

Once the party arrived at the agency Thoreau walked several miles out into the prairie without spotting any buffalo. He witnessed the transfer of the annuities and observed that the Indians seemed rather agitated by the proceedings. He also commented on the truth and earnestness of Little Crow's oration, which compared favorably, he felt, with that of the whites. The events concluded with a Dakota dance performed to the accompaniment of twelve drummers and also a piper or two.

A few days later Thoreau was back in Red Wing. The five-hundred mile trip had taken a week.

Though there is plenty to see and do in New Ulm at any time of the year, the city hosts several popular festivals, including Fasching, a series of "crazy days" prior to Lent; a Bavarian Blast in July; and an Oktoberfest on the first two weekends in October. If you're looking for souvenirs of your visit, try Domeier's (1020 S. Minnesota St.), which sells everything from cuckoo clocks and polka CDs to Bavarian chocolates and glass ornaments.

For more information about events, sites, lodgings and restaurants, see www.newulmweb.com.

The Dakota Conflict

The Minnesota River Valley between New Ulm and Redwood Falls contains some of the most beautiful scenery in Minnesota. In 1862 those bucolic fields and hills became the theater for the most violent episode in the state's history.

Much of the valley upstream from New Ulm was designated as Indian land when the Treaty of Traverse des Sioux was signed in 1851. A ten-mile strip of land was set aside on both sides of the river, and two agencies were established to administer the annuities the Dakota were to receive in compensation for their territory. One unfortunate aspect of the treaty was that it did not entirely protect these lands from further encroachment by white settlers, and in 1858 the Dakota signed away their land on the north side of the river—close to a million acres—for a few cents an acre.

Though some members of the tribe did take up farming on their new reservation, the harvest of 1861 was poor, and by the next summer many of the Dakota were destitute. The annuity payments from Washington were late to arrive at the agencies, however—Congress debated for more than a month over whether to send gold or greenbacks. As was then the custom, the agent, Thomas Galbraith, refused to distribute provisions from his warehouse until the money had arrived. On August 4, a force of more than 500 Dakota warriors stormed the warehouse and succeeded in securing some flour. A few days later Galbraith finally agreed to make another distribution of supplies, and the Indians were persuaded to return to their villages.

A similar pattern of events unfolded at the Redwood Agency further upstream. During the heated discussions that took place there between Indians and whites, Chief Little Crow is reputed to have said, "When men are hungry they help themselves." In response Andrew J. Myrick, one of the local traders who had refused to advance further credit to the Indians, remarked, "So far as I am concerned, if they are hungry, let them eat grass."

It was within this atmosphere of animosity and desperation that four young Mdewakanton Dakota who were returning from a deer hunt came upon an isolated farmstead in Meeker County. After engaging the farmer in a seemingly-friendly bit of target practice, the braves murdered the farmer, his wife, two other adults who happened to be visiting, and also a child. They then rode off with the farmer's horses to report their crime to the tribe. Several councils were held, and a number of the Dakota leaders stressed the ultimate futility of engaging the whites in combat, but the views of the young warriors eager to shine in battle prevailed. The next morning the tribe launched a surprise attack on the Redwood Agency, indiscriminately killing both whites and their peace-loving "short-hair" Dakota brothers who had chosen to take up white ways.

Forty-four Americans were killed during the first full day of fighting. Almost two hundred more lost their lives in the next few days. One band of Dakota laid siege to Fort Ridgely and another attacked the town of New Ulm. As word of the uprising spread many settlers left their farms and flooded into the towns. On August 23, the Dakota attacked New Ulm again and largely burned it to the ground. The attack was eventually repulsed, and the next day more than 2,000 refugees, mostly women, children, and wounded men, escaped to Mankato. Three days later, on August 26, Colonel Henry Sibley set out from St. Paul with 1,400 men to lift the siege of Fort Ridgely.

Dakota bands continued to attack white settlements for several weeks. At Birch Coulee Creek, on September 2, Dakota warriors killed twenty soldiers among 170 who were out on a burial detail. But as American forces grew stronger, the Dakota initiatives dwindled in their effectiveness. The decisive battle took place at Wood Lake on September 23, where perhaps as many as a thousand Dakota warriors were forced to withdraw after suffering heavy casualties.

Meanwhile, the divisions among the Dakota themselves began to come into play. The chiefs of the Upper Agency, Sisseton and Wahpeton, had always opposed the fighting, and Chiefs Red Iron and Standing Buffalo threatened to fire upon any Dakota belligerents that entered their territory. During the Wood Lake Battle, Dakotas who opposed the war took many whites captive and brought them into their own camp for protection. In late September 269 of these white prisoners were given over to the control of Colonel Sibley.

As their raids became more sporadic, Dakota food supplies dwindled and morale declined. Many Dakota warriors chose to surrender. By the end of the war the number of Dakota prisoners reached 1,250.

On September 28 Colonel Sibley appointed a five-member commission to try the Indians, and during the next six weeks almost 400 cases were reviewed. Of these 323 led to convictions, and nearly all of the convicted parties were sentenced to death by hanging.

The mood among settlers, politicians, and journalists was overwhelmingly in favor of speedy executions, and the condemned prisoners

were attacked in New Ulm by vigilantes while being transported to Mankato. The single powerful voice crying out for less severe punishment was that of Episcopal Bishop Henry Whipple.

Whipple had lived among the Dakota for many years, and he was well aware of the degree to which government agents were responsible for the plight of the Dakota and other tribes. In the spring of 1862 he addressed an open letter to President Lincoln spelling out the iniquities of the system that was then in place.

Bishop Henry Whipple, 1859

He happened to be in Washington when the Uprising took place, and had recently met with Lincoln to discuss the situation. Lincoln later remarked, "He came here the other day and talked with me about the rascality of this Indian business until I felt it down to my boots."

When the time came for Lincoln to decide about the mass executions, he limited them to those Indians who had clearly participated in the massacres of settlers. Of the 306 who had originally been sentenced to death, 38 Dakota warriors were executed in Mankato on December

26, 1862. In April of the next year Congress passed a law indiscriminately banishing all the Dakota—young, old, peace-loving, and belligerent alike—from the state.

The Dakotas Conflict of 1862 has enough drama, violence, foolishness, and heroism for several Verdi operas, but it is not merely a theater piece. It sent terror through the countryside of southern Minnesota and confirmed the worst nightmares of immigrant settlers, while also spelling the exile of several Dakota tribes from their homeland. But it must also be seen as a desperate attempt by an indigenous people to retain the lifeways that were central to their life and self-esteem. Murderous, yes. Lawless, yes. But those same terms can reasonably be applied to the more genteel methods by which the agents of the American government accrued profits to themselves while squeezing the Dakota off their tribal lands.

The best way to experience these landscapes is along the county roads that run along the north side of the river. Crossing the river on the Highway 15 bridge from New Ulm, turn left onto County Highway 21, which rides the flank of the river valley. The views across the valley to the bluffs on the other side are fine, and you'll often see large colonies of pelicans down on the river during their spring and fall migrations. Many parts of the valley remain uncultivated, because there is little or no soil to cultivate. The rushing waters of River Warren scoured away the soil right down to its Precambrian bedrock. The rocks exposed in some parts of the valley rank among the oldest in the world. It's estimated that Morton Gneiss (which is exposed in several places around Morton) was formed about 3.6 billion years ago, when the earth was in its infancy, and geologists come from all over the world to study it in its native setting. To put that number in perspective, just consider that the rock you see in the vicinity of Morton is five times older than the stars you see in the head of the constellation Taurus.

Harkin Store

A few miles up Highway 21 you'll come upon an old country store nestled in the woods. The town of West Newton was once a bustling riverboat stop between New Ulm and Fort Ridgely, but the railroad bypassed it, and the Harkin Store is all that's left. The store, too, closed its doors in 1901, with much of the merchandise still on the shelves. The Minnesota Historical Society now manages the site, and you can visit it. Call 507-354-8666 or 507-934-2160 for more details.

6 Fort Ridgely

At Fort Ridgely State Park you can wander the ruins of the fort where two pitched battles took place during the summer of 1862. The fort was built in 1853 to insure the safety of the new arrivals who were turning soil and building homes in the area. The fact that it was built without a stockade, and was situated on a piece of land sloping off into ravines on three sides, may be an indication of how unlikely a conflict with the Dakota seemed to the men who built it. The one building that remaining standing houses displays about military life, and if you happen to arrive on the fourth weekend in June, you'll see the costumes, craft demonstrations, music, and other lively foofaraw of the Fort Ridgely Historical Festival. The park campgrounds are nestled in a valley below the fort. Call 507-426-7840 for details.

The Minnesota Historical Society maintains a site at Birch Coolee, a few miles north of Morton on Highway 18, where a heated battle took place in 1862. There isn't much there now but a field and some signs, but the openness of the site gives you a feel for the vulnerability of the besieged troops, who were ambushed by a party of several hundred Dakota warriors while out on a burial detail.

On you way through Morton you'll probably spot some outcroppings of that *very* old rock I mentioned a moment ago. Crossing the river to the south side and backtracking a bit on Highway 2, you'll come to the Lower Sioux Indian Reservation, which was re-established by the government in 1930 to accommodate an informal community of Dakota who had returned from exile to their homeland over the years. The visitor center has excellent exhibits exploring many aspects of traditional Dakota life, the reservation system, and the Conflict of 1862, which started here. Today the reservation covers less than 2 square miles, though it's home to more than 300 Dakota. Further west on Highway 2 lies Jackpot Junction, Minnesota's first casino.

7 Redwood Falls

The Redwood River reaches the Minnesota River at Redwood Falls, and the last mile or two of its descent is truly dramatic. You can visit the impressive gorge at the town's Alexander Ramsey City Park, which also has a campground and six miles of hiking trails. After a robust hike through the park, check out Morgan's Deli downtown. The kitchen prepares more than a thousand meals daily for area nursing homes and schools, and you can enjoy the same tasty, old-fashioned dishes for a very reasonable price at the café.

The Upper Sioux Agency

The Upper Sioux Agency State Park, a few miles beyond Redwood Falls, is located on the site of the old Yellow Medicine Agency, which was established to administer provisions of the Treaty of Traverse des Sioux. The Dakota bands located here were opposed to the conflict raging further south and saved the lives of many white settlers, though when it was all over they were exiled along with their more belligerent neighbors. The park has a small interpretive center and various signs relating to aspects of that unfortunate chapter in Minnesota's history, though only one of the buildings remains from agency days.

The park's natural features are its main draw. It sits on a plateau of gravel left by Glacial Lake Agassiz, upon which wetlands, prairies, and forests have developed over the centuries. There is plenty of camping on the plain and opportunities for hiking abound. (For more information call 320-564-4777.)

The Yellow Medicine River flows down through the park to meet the Minnesota. The yellow medicine for which the river is named is the moonseed plant, a vine that grows in thickets along the shore. The Dakota used the bitter yellow roots for medicine, and the cresent-shaped seeds and flowers are also said to have narcotic properties.

A few miles south of the park a monument memorializes the battle of Wood Lake. It took place on September 23, 1862, with Sibley in command of American forces and Little Crow in command of the Dakota. It was the first in which the whites got the upper hand, and it turned the tide against the Dakota warriors once and for all.

A view of the valley from Upper Sioux Agency State Park

Granite Falls

The city of Granite Falls is best known as the home of U.S. Congressman Andrew J. Volstead, whose name appears on the bill that brought prohibition to the United States for more than a decade. Volstead has been quoted as saying, "Law does regulate morality. Law has regulated morality since the Ten Commandments were given." Yet the fact that he is associated with Prohibition is largely coincidental. He happened to be the chairman of the House Judiciary Committee at the time the bill was written.

Volstead's name also appears on another piece of legislation which is less well known but far more enduring in its impact. The Capper-Volstead Act, signed into law in 1922, established the legal right of farmers to sell their produce cooperatively. At the time there was widespread fear of worker organizations of all kinds. Once the farmers united, it was argued, they would have the nation in a strangle-hold, and food would become exorbitantly expensive.

Volstead saw the matter differently:

> *The objection made to these organizations [cooperatives] is that*
> *they violate the Sherman Antitrust Act, and that is upon the theory*

that each farmer is a separate business entity. When he combines with his neighbor for the purpose of securing better treatment in the disposal of his crops, he is charged with a conspiracy or combinations contrary to the Sherman Antitrust Act. Businessmen can combine by putting their money into corporations, but it is impractical for farmers to combine their farms into similar corporate forms. The object of this bill is to modify the laws under which business organizations are now formed, so that farmers may take advantage of the form of organization that is used by business concerns.

The Capper-Volstead Act even today plays a vital role in protecting farmers who process and market their products collectively from antitrust prosecution.

Volstead also served for many years as the mayor of Granite Falls, and you can visit his house on Ninth Avenue, the main route into town, though there isn't much to see there beyond a few informational kiosks.

Lac qui Parle Mission and Wildlife Refuge

A few miles beyond Montevideo along Highway 7 will bring us into the Lac qui Parle region, which has drawn abundant wildlife to its marshy terrain from time immemorial. Joseph Renville set up a trading post here in 1826, and ten years later a mission was established to convert the local Indians. It was the first church erected in Minnesota, and although the missionary's efforts met with mixed success at best, during their stay Renville worked with them to translate the Bible into the Dakota language and also complete a Dakota dictionary.

In 1841 Eli Pettijohn made his way out to the mission at Lac qui Parle to visit his sister. He left us a vivid record of his arrival at Fort Snelling, a lavish dinner at the home of Mr. Sibley, where he first tasted beaver tail and buffalo hump, and his subsequent journey up the Minnesota on a boat powered by Meti with long poles. Anticipating the laments of future generations of Minnesotans, he observed, "The mosquitoes, even in the daytime were so terrible that it was almost impossible to live."

Upon his arrival at the mission, Pettijohn noted:

*They had a nice little garden and quite a patch of wheat, which I
was told was fine for the climate. The seed came from the craw of
a wild swan that they had shot. It was supposed to have come from
the Pembina country for those people had wheat long before the
missionaries came. It was always called "Red River Wheat."*

A replica of the original mission church now stands on the site,
which even today seems to be out in the middle of nowhere, and it's
well worth a stop, not only for the exhibits inside, but also as a means of
contemplating a long-vanished era of the region's history. During spring
and fall you'll often see pelicans drifting in the water below the dam, and
the nearby state park has both wooded and prairie campgrounds.

From the mission site you can look out across Lac qui Parle itself—
"the lake that speaks." The lake's name refers to the extraordinary din generated by the geese that congregated there in spring and fall. Though the
migrating population had fallen to a mere 150 birds in 1958, since that
time conservation practices have been put in place returning much of
the region to the habitat preferred by the waterfowl, and in recent years
upward of 200,000 geese have arrived during the autumn months. The
lake is definitely "speaking" once again.

Trails lead off in several directions across the valley and along the
sloughs, providing good opportunities for bird watching and wildlife
observation. The park adjoins a 35,000-acre wildlife management area,

and the entire region is a birder's paradise. The newly established upper campground on the east side of the river has a number of prairie sites that make for wonderful stargazing. (To reach the park call 320-752-4736. For the mission call 320-269-7636.)

Milan

The town of Milan lies just north of the park on highway 7. This miniscule hamlet treasures its Norwegian heritage. The Arv Hus Museum, which is open only every now and then, contains an eclectic collection of folk artifacts and historic oddities. The town is also home to the Milan Village Arts School, which hosts a variety of classes ranging from Norwegian knifemaking and rosemaling to paper-marbling and silverwork. It's housed in an old country schoolhouse that was moved downtown for the purpose. For information about classes see *www. milanvillageartsschool.org.*

Big Stone Lake

An oasis in the prairie, Big Stone Lake runs for many miles along the Minnesota-South Dakota Border. The town of Ortonville clings to its banks and a modern development spreads across the upland. Highways 7, 12, and 75 cross outside town, and there are many lodging options in the vicinity.

Ortonville was once a major corn canning center, and it holds an annual Cornfest in midsummer. The big draw is the lake itself, however, which is known for its walleye fishing. Big Stone Lake State Park, seven miles up the shore, offers camping, hiking, and boat rentals. Eleven miles further up the shore the smaller Bonanza Scientific and Natural Area of the park will give you a glimpse of what the area looked liked before settlement.

The habitats found at Big Stone National Wildlife Refuge, just south of town on Highway 75, are even more distinctive. In this region the waters of Glacial Lake Agassiz tumbled down into Glacial River Warren, and vast sheets of granite and gneiss bedrock are exposed. Geese, ducks, shorebirds, and passerines—more than 200 species in all—can be spotted here. Some are on their way north, others nest for the summer.

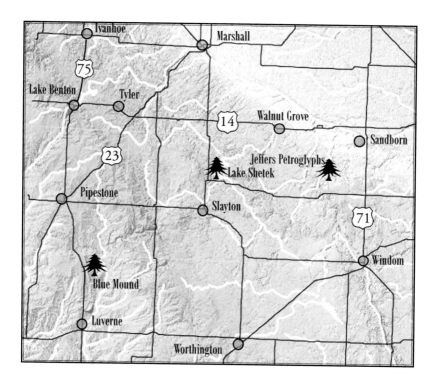

SECTION II: THE COTEAU DES PRAIRIE

As if to provide a rim to keep the contents of the state in place, the extreme southwestern corner of Minnesota is defined by a ridge running southeast to northwest from western Iowa to the northeast corner of South Dakota. In many places the rise is so gentle that it's almost indiscernible, though at others the change in relief is very obvious.

The Coteau was formed by debris left from retreating glaciers. It divides the watersheds of the Minnesota and Missouri rivers. Much of the area has been converted to farmland, of course, but there are pockets that are still redolent of times long past, and as we move up along or across it, we may feel that the true West is almost within reach.

Because it stands above the general level of the surrounding landscape, the Coteau has become famous for its wind turbines. And several of its most distinctive areas display extensive outcroppings of the pink-to-purplish rock known as Sioux quartzite.

Jeffers Petroglyphs

The Jeffers Petroglyphs site is located on County 2, five miles east and three miles north of the town of Jeffers. It lies on Red Rock Ridge, a band of Sioux quartzite that extends for more than twenty miles across the landscape, hardly noticeable in many places, but rising occasionally as much as 300 feet above the surrounding countryside. Deer, raccoon, rabbit, fox, and other animals occasionally visit the banks of the Cottonwood River which winds its way through the ridge.

You can see a wagon trail along the northern border of the site. No one knows for sure who made the ruts: Stagecoach? Immigrant settlers? Looking out across the landscape in any direction you'll see houses, barns, planted fields, and silos in the distance, but the hills around the rock shelf are prairie—some of it original, some recently restored. The site contains one of the largest known populations of the Prairie Bush Clover, and the unusual drainage patterns created by the exposed bedrock make it a showplace for wet, dry, and mesic prairie environments.

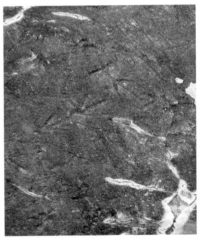

Mysterious images abound, though they're often hard to see.

As you wander across the slab of rock you'll come upon the ripple marks created by wave action when the rock was nothing more than a sandy beach. That was 1.5 billion years ago. Glacial striations can also be easily seen on the rocks dating from the last ice age—relatively recent times, in other words. The most compelling reason to visit this vast sheet of red rock, however, is to see the images that were carved on its surface by Native Americans after the ice sheets retreated

No one knows how old these carvings are, though the presence of atlatls leads archeologists to suspect that the oldest may date back 5,000 years or more. Who carved the figures, and what they mean, is anybody's guess. Nowadays various tribes that inhabited the area in more recent times, including the Iowa, Cheyenne, Arapaho, and Dakota peoples, draw sustenance and inspiration from the images, which bespeak the spiritual life of distant ancestors and a reverent, albeit rather mysterious, relationship with natural forces.

During the 1960s nearby residents cleared the area of trash and field-stones and began to document the carvings and plant life. In 1966 the Minnesota Historical Society bought the parcel. In the following decade the Society began to reconstruct the prairie environment on those acres that had been converted to farmland, so that now the prairie ecosystem spreads across a much wider swath of the countryside. A new visitors' center was built in 1998 to highlight the natural features of the area and place the carvings in a broader historical perspective.

Though there are more than two thousand images carved into the rocks at the site, they're not always easy to see. A visit would be worthwhile at any time of day, but the glancing light of the morning and evening hours highlight the edges of the carvings most dramatically. Among the representations are animals, tools, and human figures. Some of the carvings are emerging from beneath the surrounding turf at the edges of the slab, and there are undoubtedly many carvings that have not been exposed for hundreds or even thousands of years.

Among the more fascinating images are those of the thunderbird, the turtle, and horned figures that may be representations of warriors or religious leaders wearing headdresses. Who knows? Something about the yawning open spaces, the wind in the grass, and the call of a meadowlark may allow us to reconnect here with women and men who spent long hours incising these red rocks with fantastical images.

Sanborn Sod Houses

If you have a hankering to relive the experiences of those immigrants who spent their early years on the largely treeless prairie in houses built of sod, then the Sanborn sod house is the place to visit. The owner, Stan McCone, is descended from such homesteaders, and he has built two sod structures on his property. The larger structure is quite comfortable inside, with whitewashed walls, a plank ceiling, windows, a wood-burning stove, and a good deal of pioneer furniture. McCone

The interior of the Sanborn sod house

estimates that it would have cost $50 to build at the time, largely because of the wood and glass in the windows. The smaller structure, hardly more than a dirty cave, might have cost $5.

Sod did have advantages as a building material. It was easy to come by in those days, and also cheap. It kept folks cooler in the summer and warmer in the winter than log structures did.

The McCones now rent out the larger structure, in case you want to spend the night. It's lit by kerosene and serviced by a genuine sod outhouse. You can fetch your water from a nearby well and cook on the wood-burning stove. The two structures are open for tours on many afternoons, and they definitely convey the feel of life on the Minnesota prairie—both its comforts and its desperation. (For more information call 507-723-5138 or see www.sodhouse.org.)

Walnut Grove

A few miles down the road will bring us to the childhood home of one of the most famous of all pioneer women, Laura Ingalls Wilder. Wilder was born in a cabin near Pepin, Wisconsin, not far from the Mississippi (the cabin is still extant) but for several years her family lived on the banks of Plum Creek near Walnut Grove. Five years later Laura and her family pulled up stakes and moved again, this time to De Smet, South Dakota (then simply Dakota Territory).

Life on the prairie made a deep impression on Wilder, and a half-century later she wrote about it in a series of books that remain popular today. A long-running television program also drew its name and spirit (though not its story-lines), from the Wilder *oeuvre.*

The Laura Ingalls Wilder Museum in Walnut Grove will give you the full story. Fans of Wilder's books will enjoy every inch of it, but even casual visitors will find that the artifacts and memories from the pioneer era come more vividly to life when a specific recognizable individual and her family are the focus of attention. The museum stretches out across several pioneer buildings, and children will have the opportunity to engage in frontier domestic tasks while their parents pound away on an antique pump organ. A separate building is devoted to memorabilia from the TV show, and the adjacent giftshop offers souvernirs and an array of Wilder's books. On the last three weekends in July an elaborate pageant takes place. (For details call 800-528-7280 or see *www.walnutgrove.org.*)

Just outside of town (1.5 miles north on county 5) the Ingalls homestead is also open for visits, though the sod house is long gone, you can still play on the "rock" where Laura played as a child. Inquire at the museum for details.

Lake Shetek State Park

Lake Shetek lies on the uplands of the Coteau, in one of the deposits of glacial till left by the retreating glaciers. Prior to European settlement it was surrounded by a treeless prairie and efforts are being made to bring parts of the park back to that pristine pre-settlement condition. Because it's situated in the midst of arid farms and grasslands, the lake is a hotspot for migrating coots, grebes, ducks, herons, and pelicans, many of which nest in the park in spring and early summer. (In fact, the word "Shetek" is Ojibwe for "pelican.") Birding is especially good out on Loon Island, a 45-acre bird sanctuary reached via a footpath across a narrow causeway.

Though most visitors come to Lake Shetek to fish, its graceful hills make for good hiking. The park has a pioneer cabin, a large campground on the lakeshore, and a smaller prairie campground unit further inland.

Tyler

This small Minnesota town is famous for its Danish heritage. Though Swedes and Norwegians celebrate their traditions in many ways, Danish events are less frequent and less widely publicized. (Well, the Danes emigrated later and in far fewer numbers.) Tyler is unique among the small farming towns of southwestern Minnesota because it was settled largely by Danes, and it retains a measure of its Danish heritage even today.

Danebod Lutheran Church

The area was chosen to serve as a Danish colony following a convention of Danes held in Clinton, Iowa, in 1884. It was one of eight sites chosen to extend the tradition of the Danish folk high school to the New World. That tradition had been established in Denmark generations earlier by the eminent bishop Severin Gruntvig as a means of broadening the humanity of his parishioners. "First a man—then a Christian," was his often-repeated philosophy. In fact, Gruntvig's son Frederik headed the committee that chose the area that eventually became Tyler. Options to purchase 35,000 acres of land were secured from the railroad, and by the turn of the century several thousand Danes, both foreign and American-born, had moved into the vicinity, and a number of co-operative agricultural enterprises had been established.

At the center of the community was the Danebod, a complex of buildings that included a church, a gymnasium, and the folk high school. In keeping with Gruntvig's philosophy, the high school and gymnasium were built first. The church was completed five years later. As the minister in charge of the community put it, "a gym hall can be used temporarily as a church; a church cannot be used as a gym hall."

Today the north end of Tyler looks little different from dozens of other nearby farm communities, except for the rather cute images of *Nissamaend* (Danish elves) peering out from a few of the storefront windows. Once you cross the railroad tracks at the south end of town, you'll see the Danebod off to your left, which consists of a stone hall that now houses a museum; the Gym Hall; the folk school, which is still used for gatherings, retreats, and community events; and Danebod Lutheran Church (1895). The exterior of the prim church has been fitted with vinyl siding, but the interior is sheathed with well-oiled wood panelling, and it's worth a look. A hand-crafted wooden ship hangs high overhead in the nave just inside the doorway.

For an even greater exposure to the Danish side of Tyler, plan to visit during Aebleskiver Days, when there is a parade, a talent show, traditional Danish folk dancing, and plenty of aebleskivers—those delicious round pancakes, sometimes served with jelly.

Lake Benton

Lake Benton is best known for something that's just passing through—the wind. The town is located at a point where Buffalo Ridge—the local name for the Coteau de Prairie—takes a little dip. The energy exerted by the wind as it rushes through that dip and other choice locations nearby is considerable. According to one environmental study, it offers more in the way of wind "resources" than are to be found in the entire state of California. (Minnesota currently ranks fourth among the states in wind-produced electricity.)

There are more that two-hundred windmills operating in the vicinity of Lake Benton today, and as you pass through the area you're likely to see more of these towering giants lying by the roadside, just waiting to be put into place. The towers stand more than 250 feet tall, and the circle cut by the blades can exceed 150 feet in diameter. Once the current plan has been fully implemented, it's possible that more

than 225 megawatts of pollution-free, zero-emission, power will be produced in the area.

That may sound ideal, but there's a catch. The wind blows intermittently, and unpredictably, while energy demands are continuous. It's also rather inconvenient that windy places like these are usually far from the urban areas where the demand for energy is greatest. All the same, a report commissioned by the Minnesota legislature in 2005, concluded that it would be economically feasible for the state to draw upon wind-generated power to supply as much as 25 percent of its energy needs.

Perhaps the best way to approach Lake Benton is from the north down County Highway 1 from Hendricks. This route will take you up and over a few of the more dramatic hills for which the Coteau is named. Arriving from any direction, you'll see how unusual the lake itself is, standing all by itself out in the middle of the prairie. It served as a landmark for generations of nomadic visitors, and more recently for settlers traveling west across the seemingly endless prairies. John C. Frémont gave it the name we know it by. At the time (1838) he was a young and obscure member of Joseph Nicollet's expedition to map the territory between the Mississippi and the Missouri Rivers. Frémont chose the name in honor of his girl-friend, Jessie Benton, though he might also have been thinking of her father, Thomas Hart Benton, the powerful republican senator from Missouri who later sponsored Frémont's exploratory missions across the then-little-known Rocky Mountains.

We can ponder these sidelights to history as we look north across the lake from the town. A less wild-and-wooly aspect of Lake Benton's history presents itself at 225 South Fremont Street, where the opera house built in 1896 has recently been restored. Though it can't compete with La Scala, at various times in its history the building has served as a venue for traveling operatic performers, dances, basketball games, and funerals. It has hosted political rallies and other public events, and extended its life as the local movie theater. Today it once again offers a variety of live entertainment options.

A mile and a half south of town on U.S. 75 will take you to Hole-in-the-Mountain, a small patch of prairie maintained by the Nature Conservancy. It's located in the upper valley of Flandreau Creek, which flows west toward the Big Sioux and eventually the Missouri River. Several rare butterflies species are found in this prairie remnant, including the Dakota skipper and Ottoe skipper—both threatened species—and the Uncas skipper, an endangered species. You probably won't see these species—the entire lifespan of the Dakota Skipper, for example, stretches for only three weeks in June and July. On the other hand, maybe you will. The Dakota Skipper is yellow, about the size of a silver dollar, and has an erratic darting flight. In any case, this tiny valley is a nice place to stop and stretch your legs on the way to Pipestone.

Pipestone National Monument

Stone pipes have been used by Native American tribes for at least two thousand years. The easily-carved red stone found at Pipestone has been a popular pipe-carving material for centuries, and as early as the seventeenth century many Plains tribes quarried here. By around 1700 the quarries had fallen under the control of the Dakota, though the stone was still widely-disseminated through trade.

Carvers prized the stone because it was relatively soft and easy to carve, yet also durable enough to survive repeated use and the rough-and-tumble hazards of a nomadic lifestyle. Its color, which ranged from mottled pink to brick red, only added to its appeal.

Though what we would call recreational smoking was widespread among Plains tribes, the solemn act of passing the pipe was also woven into a wide array of social events, from healing ceremonies and discussions of peace and war to commercial transactions and ritual dances. The pipes themselves were carefully stored in pouches and animal-skin bundles, as was the tobacco, which was similarly revered. In fact, every aspect of ceremonial smoking was approached with a degree of reverence, and even the ashes were disposed of following a time-honored protocol.

The central role played by smoking in the ritual life of Plains Indian tribes naturally made the pipes themselves highly-valued objects, and those who carved them often brought a good deal of creativity to their work. Pipe bowls in various human and animal forms were not uncommon, though most were decorated with simple abstract patterns.

Pipestone was so highly valued that the quarry was one of the few sites in the largely trackless tall-grass prairie of the northwest to develop a reputation even among whites prior to the arrival of settlers. The French explorer Charlevoix mentions a pipe of peace in 1721, which, he adds, "is ordinarily made of a species of red marble, very easily worked, and found beyond the Mississippi among the Aiouez (Ioways)."

One of the first accounts we have of whites actually visiting the area is by Peter Pond, who spent two years in Minnesota at the time of the American Revolution. At one point he describes the approach of five Indians, four of whom carried a beautiful beaver blanket, while the fifth held "a calumet, or pipe of peace—very finely dressed with different feathers and painted hair." Four of the Indians sat with Pond on the blanket while the fifth lit the pipe "with a great deal of ceremony" and took a few puffs. He then pointed the pipe east and west, then north and south, then toward the sky and toward the ground. At that point the pipe was passed to Pond and his companions on the beaver blanket. He concludes, "after which we all smoked in turn and appeared very friendly."

It was not until the 1830s that explorers made detailed reports of the quarry's nature and whereabouts. One visitor, Philander Prescott, described the Indian's methods as follows:

The Indians have labored here very hard with hoes and axes the only tools they have except large stones...[they] clear the dirt then

Catlin's rendering of the pipestone quarry

get stones as large as two Indians can lift and throw it down as hard as they can and in this way break or crack the rock so they can get their hoes and axes in the cracks and pry out piece after piece it is very laborious and tedious.

Prescott himself spent one day quarrying with the Indians, and was rewarded for his labor with rock suitable for "twenty good pipes."

The man who brought the quarry fully to prominence, however, was George Catlin. Catlin, an artist, was fascinated by all aspects of American Indian life, and he has given us some of the most authentic renderings we have of life in the West during the 1830s. In the course of his researches he heard repeatedly of a quarry where "almost every tribe of Indians of the continent" got material for its pipes, and he was determined to visit the site.

Following the usual route from New York to the Mississippi via the Great Lakes and the Fox-Wisconsin link, Catlin arrived at Traverse des Sioux, where he met a party of Sioux who had heard of his plan. They advised him in no uncertain terms to go back where he came from. In his account of the council meeting, Catlin recreated a part of one Dakota oration as follows:

Brothers—I speak strong, my heart is strong, and I speak fast: this red pipe was given to the red men by the Great Spirit—it is a part of our flesh, and therefore is great medicine. ('How! how!')
Brothers—We know that the whites are like a great cloud that

rises in the East, and will cover the whole country. We know that they will have all our lands; but if ever they get our Red Pipe-Quarry they will have to pay very dear for it. ('How! how!')

Brothers—We know that no white man has ever been to the Pipe Stone Quarry, and our chiefs have often decided in council that no white man shall ever go to it. ('How! how!')

In fact, a number of whites *had* visited the quarries before Catlin arrived, but it was his report that brought it to the wider attention of the American people. Two years later the cartographer Joseph N. Nicollet arrived and won favor with the Indians by using dynamite to blast a large chunk of the tough surface layer of quartzite off the underlying soft red rock.

Many early visitors to the quarry recorded elaborate legends associated with it. Drawing on these sources, Henry Wadsworth Longfellow refers to it in his *Song of Hiawatha*:

On the Mountain of the Prairie,
On the great Red Pipestone Quarry,
Gitche Manito, the mighty,
He the Master of Light, descending,
On the red crags of the quarry

Try digging through this with a crow bar and a sledge hammer

Stood erect and called the nations,
Called the tribes of men together.

The Mountain to which Longfellow refers is the Coteau des Prairie, and if it is sometimes hard to spot, the red crags of the quarry itself are still easy to see once you arrive at the site.

As the renown of the red stone grew, elaborately carved pipes for the tourist trade became a source of added income for the Indians who quarried and carved it. But outsiders also arrived to quarry the lucrative stone, and as immigrants arrived in the area to farm, the sacred quarry was in danger of being all but destroyed by encroaching civilization.

When the Sisseton and Wahpeton Dakota signed the treaty of Traverse des Sioux in 1851, they signed away their rights to the quarry as well. The Yankton Sioux, who had not been a party to the treaty, refused to honor its provisions, and when, in 1858, they, too, signed away most of their lands, they insisted in retaining free and unrestricted access to the quarry. A square-mile of land around the quarry became a sort of mini-reservation, and a school was established there in 1892. After decades of legal controversy, in 1928 the Yankton Sioux finally relinquished their rights to the federal government (their main reservation was 150 miles away), and ten years later it became Minnesota's first National Monument. One of the provisions of the legislation establishing the monument preserved for Indians the exclusive right to continue working the quarry.

The popularity of quarrying has increased with time, and there is currently a long list of applicants waiting to receive a permit. Indians come from as far afield as Alaska to quarry and carve here, some of them continuing to practice the arts in much the same way that their grandfathers did. A few of the quarry sites have now passed on to the sixth generation in the same family.

At the Monument's visitor center you can watch a video that will give you an idea of how hard it is to quarry through ten feet of igneous rock using hand tools. Local carvers also demonstrate how the pipes take shape and explain what they mean to the men and women who make and use them. During the summer months you might even happen upon a live carving demonstration.

A well-marked trail leads from the visitor center up across the open prairie vegetation to the quartzite cliffs and an attractive waterfall. At one point you can see the place where Nicollet and Frémont chiseled their names into the stone. The entire landscape carries an aura of beauty and heritage and meaning, and if you buy a pipe at the gift shop, perhaps you can recreate a little of that romantic ambiance while passing it among family and friends on the porch back home. (For added information about the monument call 507-825-5464.)

The town of Pipestone, a few blocks south of the National Monument on Highway 75, developed later than many of its neighbors in the area, due to the proximity of the quarry, but once it had been established it grew with gusto. Many buildings from that early period of growth were constructed of Sioux quartzite, and quite a few of them are still around, including the sturdy Calumet Inn downtown (104 W. Main St., 800-535-7610). It's been taking lodgers since 1888, and it remains popular today. Though currently a little down-at-heel, the rates are reasonable and there's a lot to be said for twelve-foot ceilings and a comfortable wing-backed chair after a long day on the road.

For a meal try Langes Cafe (110 8th Ave SE). No need to list the hours, Langes has been open continuously, night and day, for the last fifty years. The hot beef sandwiches are fine, though for a truly unusual taste try the deep-fried chicken breast on wild rice with an almond-raison sauce!

For nearly sixty years Pipestone has hosted a midsummer pageant on a flooded quarry near the monument site. A cast of several hundred actors in colorful "native" dress dramatize parts of Longfellow's *Song of Hiawatha*. Split Rock Creek State Park, a few miles south on Highway 23, is nothing spectacular but it can be a pleasant place to camp before or after a visit to Pipestone.

Blue Mound State Park

At Blue Mounds State Park we may feel that the West is not that far away. The park maintains a herd of bison, and there are several patches of tallgrass prairie. Its most dramatic feature, however, is a line

THE PRAIRIE POETS

In his book *Roads* the novelist Larry McMurtry remarks, as he speeds down Interstate 35 from Duluth toward the Iowa border, "… how good Minneapolis looks may depend on how far out on the prairies you're coming to it from." Yet many of Minnesota's most interesting writers come from out on the prairies, and it's not Minneapolis they're writing about. Robert Bly was raised on a farm outside of Madison, and later he and then-wife Carol maintained a farm there for many years. (You can visit a recreation of his study in the local museum in Madison.) The poet Phebe Hanson—a minister's daughter, no less—hails from the miniscule town of Sacred Heart out on Highway 212. Read a few of the poems from her collection *Why Still Dance*, to gain some some insight into what growing up rural means.

Bill Holm grew up in tiny Minneota, a few miles northwest of Marshall. The poet and novelist Louise Erdrich hails from Wahpeton, North Dakota, right across the river from Breckenridge. Paul Gruchow was raised on a farm near Montevideo, and as an adult wrote eloquently on prairie subjects in such classics as *The Necessity of Empty Places*. O.E. Rövaag got the feel of prairie life in Elk Point, South Dakota, before settling down in Northfield to write such classics as *Giants in the Earth*. If we add Sinclair Lewis and Garrison Keillor, those bards of small town life, to the list, it grows more impressive still.

of red cliffs that rise 100 feet above the prairie floor. To passing settlers the cliffs looked blue, hence the name Blue Mound. And most settlers did just pass on by, because they had little desire to set their plows into the rocky terrain. This explains why some native grasses are still to be found hereabouts.

Blue Mound also has a few other natural features rarely seen within the borders of Minnesota. It has several outcrops of prickly pear cactus, and if you arrive in late June or July you'll see them flowering on the rocky shelves above the cliffs.

The tale is told locally of large piles of bison bones found by earlier generations at the base of the cliffs, which would suggest that Native Americans once stampeded the creatures to their death here. Archeologists have found no evidence to support such claims, however. A more concrete archeological phenomenon is a 1,250-foot-long line of rocks that stretches across the south end of the park. Strange as it may seem, these rocks are perfectly aligned in an east-west direction, so that they point to the spot on the horizon where the sun rises and sets during the spring and fall equinoxes. No one knows who built this mini-Stonehenge, which only adds to the mystery.

The mysterious rock alignment at Blue Mound State Park

Blue Mound has a pleasantly wooded campground and a man-made lake—the only lake in Rock County. The rock-climbing amid the cliffs is fine (permit required) and there are thirteen miles of hiking trails weaving in and out across the crest of the mound, through the fields, and along the stream and reservoir.

The visitor center (507-283-1307), located in the southern part of the park, was once the home of plains novelist Frederick Manfred. Though Manfred's many novels have never entered the mainstream

Bison grazing at Blue Mound

canon of American literature, several of them are well worth reading. They're set in a region Manfred refers to as Siouxland, which includes the part of Minnesota we've been exploring as well as portions of Iowa, Nebraska, and South Dakota. The best of Manfred's works might well be *Lord Grizzly*, a retelling of the adventures of Hugh Glass, a mountain man who was attacked by a bear and left by his companions for dead. Glass crawled across most of South Dakota before being rescued, all the while vowing to seek revenge on the men who'd abandoned him.

Luverne

Luverne lies just south of Blue Mounds State Park where Highway 75 crosses I-90. It's a prosperous-looking farm community with several motels and such amenities as JJ's Tasty Drive-In (804 S. Kniss Avenue) and the Magnolia Steak House down by the freeway. Luverne happens to be the home-town of acclaimed photographer Jim Brandenburg, and its main tourist draw is the Brandenburg Gallery at 211 E. Main Street. Though Brandenburg is best known for his photographs of boreal subjects, there are plenty of spectacular prairie vistas on display here as well.

Section III: The Rochester Plateau

The region that we're calling the "prairie" actually includes several types of landscape. The large western section is in fact glaciated plain, while the region east of the big bend in the Minnesota River Valley is a hilly moraine where the glaciers dumped the material they'd scraped up during their slow brutal crawl across the face of the continent. The difference between the two areas is reflected not only in the topography but also in the vegetation. Both regions look like farm country today, and they are, but the eastern section preserves a few remnants of both the Big Woods and the oak savannas that once dominated the area. The bluff lands that rise from the west bank of the Mississippi also extend a good ways up into the Rochester Plateau, and some of the most beautiful spots in the state are located within its folds.

The Big Woods

When we speak of the Big Woods, we're actually referring to something that no longer exists, except in a few isolated areas. A few centuries ago an island of deciduous forest stood in the midst of the prairie, stretching across the gentle hills south of the confluence of the Minnesota and Mississippi rivers and east to the Cannon River Valley. The early French explorers referred to it as Les Bois Franc. The phrase Big Woods came into common use during the nineteenth century. It also has a more generic meaning, of course. Laura Ingalls Wilder uses it in *The Little House in the Big Woods* in reference to a forest in Wisconsin, which no doubt appeared much bigger than the family farmstead sitting in the midst of it, though it was not a part of *The* Big Woods.

In its native state the Big Woods may have been 6500 square miles in extent, though most of it has long since been converted to farmland. Much of what we know about its original condition is based on the reports of government employees who surveyed it during the 1850s. The surveyors were required to identify where the sections they were marking out intersected, and this necessitated identifying large trees to help the settlers establish their property boundaries.

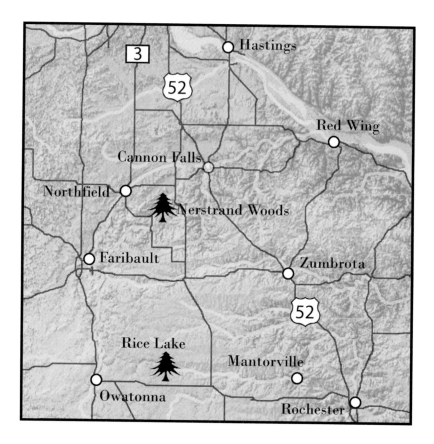

Studies of these records suggest that in those days the region was 80 percent forested, with patches of prairie interspersed here and there. The forests were a mixture of elms, basswood, and sugar maple, with ironwood, ash, and red oak thrown in. The patches of prairie savanna were grassy swards dotted with isolated burr and red oaks, with stands of aspen here and there. A member of the exploratory party that passed through the area in 1839 with Nicollet remarked that the trees were "to be found in a perfection & health & size which is not to compare with any timber at the River [Minnesota] or Afissippi [Mississippi] about St. Peters [Mendota]."

When we come upon one of these impressive blocks of forest today, it may instill us with rapture or studied awe at the beauty, solitude, and stillness they offer. Settlers arriving from worn-out farms to the east after the Civil War, on the other hand, saw lumber, railroad ties, and firewood. This explains why most of that virgin forest has vanished.

Nowadays it isn't the timber, it's the real estate that has so much appeal. As the Twin Cities metropolitan area expands southward beyond Lake City and Farmington, yet more remnants of the Big Woods will continue to vanish beneath asphalt and sod.

Pine Bend Oil Refinery

By night, it looks like a black-and-white rendering of the Emerald City of Oz. By day, it looks like the set for a dystopian science fiction thriller. Odd, impressive, repulsive or dazzling, it's worthwhile reminding ourselves as we drive by it that if the Pine Bend Oil Refinery didn't exist, then we wouldn't *be* driving by it—or by anything else, for that matter. Here is the place where they make crude oil into gasoline and other products that fuel our daily lives.

The refinery (also known as Flint Hills and the Koch refinery) is located in Rosemount where Highway 52 breaks off from Highway 55. It's the fourteenth-largest in the United States, and it can convert 265,000 barrels of oil a day into gasoline, diesel fuel, propane, and butane. It also manufactures asphalt, sulfur for fertilizer, and jet fuel for the nearby airport. During the 1990s the refinery was slapped with $19 million in emissions fines. (In Rosemount and nearby Apple Valley the incidence of asthma is twice the national average). In an attempt to improve its image—and also the environment—the plant had cut its emissions in half by 2004.

Northfield

Northfield is an attractive small town with an architecturally robust town center in a bucolic setting. A hundred years ago it was famous for its milling, and the Ames mill scored a coup in 1876 when its flour received first prize at the Centennial Exposition in Philadelphia. The local economy is still largely agricultural, and Northfield remains the home of Malt-o-Meal (though corporate offices are now in Minneapolis). But the grain elevator was torn down in 2002 and to an increasing degree the town draws its economic vitality from its proximity to the Twin Cities and the presence of two distinguished colleges within its boundaries.

St. Olaf College sits on a hill on the west end of town. It prides itself on its Norwegian traditions and its world-famous choir. Among its intellectual marks of distinction is the Howard V. Hong and Edna H. Hong Kierkegaard Library, which is widely considered to be the greatest center for studying the philosopher's works in the Western Hemisphere. Kierkegaardians from around the world come to Northfield to study the Danish master—recently, guests have arrived from as far afield as Argentina, Australia, India, Japan, and Norway.

St. Olaf is the patron saint of Norway, however (not Denmark), and the heritage of the college is rooted in the needs of the Norwegian immigrants who founded it under the leadership of three Lutheran ministers in 1874. Nowadays St. Olaf is widely-known for its music programs, and its famous choir appears on television across the nation every Christmas. If you're planning to drop by to see the show, you can forget it. Every performance is sold out months, if not years, in advance.

In our more secular times, perhaps O.E. Rövaag might be included among the patron saints of St. Olaf. He taught at St. Olaf for many years. Rövaag is the author of *Giants in the Earth*, which is considered THE classic novel of immigrant life on the prairie. It makes good reading even today. But don't expect anything on the order of *Little House of the Prairie*. Though his rendering of pioneer life is appealing in some ways, Rövaag's novel takes us beyond the romance of western expansion to the solitude and desolation of livelihoods wrested tooth and nail from a hostile and uncompromising environment.

In surveys of liberal arts colleges Carleton, which sits on a hill at the north end of town, frequently appears in the top ten small schools in the nation. It was founded by New England Congregationalists in 1866. If Rövaag epitomizes St. Olaf's Norwegian earthiness, perhaps the Ivy League pretensions of Carleton find their exemplar in famous alumnus Thorstein Veblen. Veblen, also of Norwegian extraction, was one of the founders of Institutional Economics, which explores the ways social habits and legal institutions shape economic transactions. Though the significance of such relationships may seem obvious, this field has only recently received renewed attention, in the face of the manifest shortcomings of the neo-classical theories which have dominated the field for half a century. Veblen's masterpiece, *The Theory of the Leisure Class*, may never become a bedside classic, but it's still in print, a hundred years after it was written, and for an economic treatise, that's rather uncommon. Veblen himself described it as a personal essay. It contains the first detailed critique of consumerism, though his academic colleagues criticized him for neglecting to provide footnotes.

In case all of this seems a little too heady and intellectual, Northfield added considerable luster to its image in 1876 when its citizens thwarted a bank robbery—and they aren't going to let you forget it. After all, it wasn't just any old robbery. Among the outlaws involved were Frank and Jesse James and the Younger brothers, who had ridden all the way up from Missouri, evidently because the bank held the funds of two arch-enemies from Civil War days. After undermining the robbery attempt (two citizens lost their lives), bands of vigilantes chased the gang half-way across Minnesota and captured several of the bandits.

The bank itself still stands at 408 Division Street, though it has long since been turned into a historical museum devoted to that heroic event, (to the virtual neglect of the region's many other historical enticements). For an even heavier dose of action, you can attend the five-day Defeat of Jesse James Days which takes place every year on the first weekend after Labor Day. It includes hourly live reenactments of the heist as well as more benign activities such as a rodeo, a craft fair, and a tractor pull.

When you take into account its riverside setting, youthful academic energy, restaurants, coffee shops, and bookstores, perhaps no town in Minnesota is more quaint and appealing than Northfield. But the nearby town of Dundas, a few miles south on Highway 3, is also worth a visit. Though it's suffering from the same developmental forces that have swept through Northfield, Dundas's core retains a nineteenth-century feel, which is enhanced by the ruins of a mill crossing the stream in the center of town. That mill, the Archibald Mill, was the first roller process mill in the United States. Archibald himself was a member of the Ogilvy family which became the milling barons of western Canada.

For millennia wheat had been ground into flour using stone gristmills. During the mid-nineteenth century technologies were developed to use metal rollers rather than stone millstones to grind the grain. The machines themselves were more expensive and flew in the face of generations of tradition, but the process was faster and it extracted more flour from the grain. Flour produced with rollers was also more uniform, cleaner, and finer than the flour produced by millstones.

Nerstrand Woods

Nerstrand Woods State Park lies a few miles southeast of Northfield along State Highway 246. It contains one of the few remaining large tracts of the Big Woods.

Originally even this small remnant of the Big Woods was far larger than it is today. It consisted of about 5,000 acres, which were sold to farmers as woodlots during the early years of settlement. This patchwork of ownership had the unintended effect of making it difficult for lumber companies to gain access to the timber, though some major clear-cutting did take place during the 1930s. Prescient locals worked with the legislature to acquire parcels of the wooded land to preserve it from destruction, and in 1945 1,200 pristine acres were designated as a state park. It's the only state park in Minnesota endowed with neither a historic site nor a major body of water. This may explain why relatively few people visit it.

The dwarf trout lily

The rolling countryside is beautiful, although the woods, which are made up of elm, maple, and basswood, create a thick canopy of foliage that tends to discourage the growth of underbrush and keeps the litter on the forest floor damp. As a result, the forest can often seem gloomy and uninviting in mid-summer. The best time to visit is in April, when the light is still filtering through the branches of the trees and the woods are alive with wildflowers. Nerstrand Woods is the home to many unusual flower species, including the Dwarf Trout Lily, an endangered species that's found in no other place in the world.

The park has fourteen miles of hiking trails, the most popular being the one that leads to lovely Hidden Falls. It also has a scientific research area managed by the DNR and a functioning eighty-acre dairy farm.

Faribault

Though Faribault looks like any other mid-sized agricultural town from the highway, it's worth a stop just to see the downtown, which has more architecturally significant buildings that any other town its size in Minnesota. Visitors may be especially interested in the interior of Dusek's Bakery (223 Central Avenue N), which offers a wide variety of old-fashioned baked goods daily. Two other structures carry greater historical interest. The Alexander Faribault house, (12 First Ave. NE), built in 1853, is one of the oldest frame structures in Minnesota. Few Minnesotans have had such interesting lives as Alexander Faribault. Raised in Mendota, he was running a trading post in the Faribault area as early as 1826. When it became legal for whites to settle in the area following the Treaty of Traverse des Sioux (1851) he lost little time in establishing the town that now bears his name and building a comfortable residence at the center of it. Though half-Dakota, he fought with the whites during the Dakota uprising and was among the men ambushed at Birch Coolee. Following the war, he succeeding in providing a home for a number of the vanquished warriors, which did not endear him to his neighbors. Several business ventures failed. In the census of 1870 he appears as a white head-of-household and mill-owner. Ten years later he is living with his son William and listed in the category "Indian."

In 1863 another eminent Minnesotan, Bishop Henry Whipple, commenced work on Minnesota's first Episcopal Cathedral (515 2nd Ave NW). A hundred and fifty years later, it's still noted for its classic design and impressive stone tower.

Owatonna

A few miles down the freeway in Owatonna, we have the opportunity to see a splendid building that owes nothing to European or vernacular architectural traditions.

Louis Sullivan's bank in Owatonna

The National Farmer's Bank Building is the work of Chicago architect Louis Sullivan—the largest and most elaborate of eight such banks that he designed during the twilight of his career. A single glance at the facade makes it clear that unusual design principles were at work in the creation of its massive brick block and graceful arched windows sheathed in stained glass. Some parts of the facade are starkly plain, while others are intricately decorated. It stands downtown on the corner of Broadway and Cedar, and its setting across the street from the town square also contributes to its appeal.

Earlier in his career Sullivan had designed such important structures as the Carson Pirie Scott building in Chicago and the Wainwright Building in Saint Louis, often referred to as the first modern skyscraper. Along the way Sullivan founded a new Midwestern school of architecture, the Prairie School, and coined a phrase "form follows function." That phrase doesn't describe his own creations very well, though his name has become indelibly associated with it.

But Sullivan was a heavy drinker and notoriously difficult to work with, and as he turned fifty major commissions were few and far between. It was at this point that he deigned to accept the commission for the National Farmer's Bank. The result was so original that today students and aficionados come from every part of the world to see it.

While the bank's reputation may seem a little exaggerated once you actually see it, the design is clearly both radical and powerful in its effect. Sullivan's local assistant Elmsley designed much of the building's intricate detailing, and Sullivan also worked closely on the design with the bank's president, Carl Bennett. Bennett had studied music at Harvard and was planning to pursue a career on stage in New York when his father yanked him back home to help run the family bank. His aesthetic proclivities reasserted themselves years later when it came time to expand the operation. He had admired Sullivan's earlier work and devoted $125,000 to the new bank's construction—a very large sum for a small-town bank, the equivalent of $25 million in today's dollars. (The bank failed two years later.)

Rice Lake State Park

Rice Lake is one of those out-of-the-way parks that lack dramatic features but make up for it in serenity and natural appeal. The lake is shallow and the marshes, meadows, and forest patches draw a wide variety of birds. The area was originally part of a vast oak savanna extending from the Minnesota River to the Iowa border and beyond. This savanna consisted of large swaths of prairie interspersed here and there with scattered clumps of burr oak. Today some of the oaks are still thriving though the prairie vegetation has long since given way to species introduced by immigrant settlers.

The single bit of remaining evidence of the community that once thrived in the area is the Rice Lake Church, which is located in the extreme northeast corner of the park on Dodge County Highway 20. It was built in 1857 along the Ridge Road that served the stagecoach during the early days of white settlement.

Mantorville

Though Mantorville is not a pretty town, it does have some interesting buildings. There was a fine limestone quarry nearby, and the stone was used in many of Mantorville's buildings, which protected them from the fires that destroyed so many other towns over the years. Mantorville was chosen as the county seat of Dodge County, which allowed it to retain a degree of vitality even after the railroad passed it by. And in recent years residents of nearby Rochester have continued to patronize the many quaint businesses that continue to thrive here. In 1975 the entire twelve blocks of downtown Mantorville were place of the National Register of Historic Places. Its prime tourist attraction is the Hubbell House, which has been providing meals and lodging since it opened as a stagecoach stop in 1854.

Rochester

The prosperous city of Rochester serves as a blunt refutation of any simple-minded theory that geography is destiny. There is no aspect of the city's natural setting, vegetation, or mineral endowment that sets it apart from its neighbors. And there is no logical way to explain why the largest, and perhaps most prestigious, medical facility in the world is located there. Rochester became what it is today because a surgeon and his two talented sons chose to set up practice there. Because a tornado swept through Rochester one summer day in 1883, and in the aftermath of its destruction, the local Sisters of the Convent of St. Francis volunteered to build and operate a hospital, if Dr. Mayo and his sons would agree to manage it.

The hospital opened two years later with twelve beds. Today the clinic covers several city blocks and has fifty-thousand men and women on its staff. More than two million patients pass through its doors each year.

The success of the Mayo Clinic has been attributable largely to the way it was organized. It was the first medical establishment in history to draw upon a variety of medical disciplines and specialties to offer a comprehensive diagnosis of ailments. Before long the sophistication of its methods had become well-known and patients began to arrive from every part of the country, and later the world, seeking cures that had hitherto remained illusive.

The man who is largely responsible for developing these new medical techniques was not a Mayo at all, but a young physician from nearby Racine, Minnesota, named Henry Plummer. Plummer invented the modern system of keeping a dossier of files for each patient. He was also responsible for reshaping the physical layout of a medical facility so that physicians, laboratories, and administrative personal could work well together under one roof. He devised various conveyor belts, telegraph tickers, and signaling systems to facilitate rapid communications.

These days you can take a self-guided tour of the Mayo Clinic (brochures are available at the admissions desk of each hospital) or join the guided walking tour of the clinic that starts each weekday morning at 10:00 a.m. from the Judd Auditorium of the Mayo Building. (Call 507-538-0440 for details.)

Lanesboro

The Root River system is the most extensive of those that cut their way east through the bluffs on their way to the Mississippi. (See map on page 18). In fact, it has several major branches, and on a cool day in April or early May, there may be no better part of Minnesota to set out for than the hill country which the Root River system has created, riddled with ravines, tributary streams, expansive valleys, and attractive farm towns. Spring comes a little sooner to these parts. The warblers may be passing through on their way to nesting sites in Canada. The trout lilies and the Virginia bluebells may be out. Perhaps the morels.

Though there are a number of interesting towns in the region, Lanesboro has become a focal point for visitors. It's nestled in a bend of the south branch of the Root not far upstream from where it meets the north branch, and the impressive bluffs just across the river set off the weathered structures downtown to give the place a quaint and intimate feel. You won't find many fast-food outlets or motels in Lanesboro, but it does have a theater that produces plays throughout the year, an art gallery, a winery, shops, and several bike and canoe rental establishments. Though you could see the town in fifteen minutes, Lanesboro is a place for strolling, lingering, browsing. It also happens to lie on one of the most attractive bicycle trails in the state. More than forty-two miles of abandoned railroad bed have been paved, with the main trail running from Fountain to Houston and a side-trail setting off toward Preston and Harmony. The trail follows the valley of the river and crosses it more than forty times. There are quite a few B&Bs in the vicinity catering to the needs of tourists and outdoor enthusiasts, and the Old Village Hall

restaurant is one among several worthy dining options. Be forewarned that most of Lanesboro's B&Bs are booked months in advance for the summer and fall weekends. It would be risky to arrive in town at these times expecting to find accommodations.

This section of the Root River Valley has been heavily settled by Amish families, and several firms in Lanesboro organize tours. You're likely to encounter Amish folk selling their pies and jam in the parking lot of the city park, and there are also shops in town where Amish furniture and quilts are for sale.

The best place to get an overview of the valley is at the Eagle Bluff Environmental Learning center. (It's two miles west of town on Country Road 8, then north on County Road 21.) From the bluffs here you can see for miles, and the center also has a few displays that identify the forces that continue to shape the countryside.

Forestville / Mystery Cave State Park

The easiest approach to Forestville State Park is from the west via County Road 12, but the better approach is up the valley from the east. The gravel back-roads that take you from Lanesboro to Forestville are among the most beautiful in the state. The section from Lanesboro to Preston (Highway 16) takes you up along the top of a ridge with lobes of

There isn't much left of the town of Forestville.

farm country rising and falling to your right as the South Branch of the Root River cuts its way through them. If you leave Preston on County Road 15, and turn left outside of town on County Road 14, then make another quick right turn onto County Road 12, you'll be following the valley of the Root as it winds its way up into the hills.

This last stretch of fine white gravel can be dusty, but under a pale blue sky in the evening light, the scattered farms, golden grasses, and shadowy woods you pass as you proceed west up the valley, are simply gorgeous. The crickets chirp and the meadowlarks sing from scrubby Chinese elms along the fence-lines.

The walls of the valley close in on either side, and eventually you'll come to a cluster of buildings at the edge of the trees. All that remains of the once thriving town of Forestville are three or four structures standing in a row, but what more do you need to evoke a time when everyone rode horseback, clothing was largely hand-made, and the standard meal was cornmeal mixed with lard? These buildings make an attractive ensemble, nestled in the trees at the edge of the hillside, and there is nary a trace of antique cuteness about them. An iron bridge spans the river just past the general store, and parklands and picnic areas lie beyond it amid the trees.

Fly-fishermen explore the pools and backwaters of the river. Horse-trails lead off in several directions.

The campground at Forestville is nice. You'll often hear coyotes howling at night, and during spring mornings the surrounding woods are alive with thrushes, towees, field sparrows, and passing warblers.

A trail runs through the hills above the campground, with grassy slopes running down to the river, and the entire area—deciduous wood, pinewood, and river bottom—looks as beautiful, well groomed, and yet natural, as any hillside in rural France. If you proceed on foot a mile or two upstream along the riverbank you'll come to the Big Springs, where the river emerges after having run underground for quite a while.

From the picnic grounds near the village, an easy trail leads out across the fields of the valley floor, while longer trails climb up from both sides of the gravel road through open woods to the bluffs.

From May 1 to the end of October the Minnesota Historical Society offers tours of the abandoned townsite that take in the store, the house, the carriage barn, and other structures. (For more details call 507-352-5111.)

Mystery Cave

If you're wondering where the water emerging from Big Springs comes from, why not pay a visit to nearby Mystery Cave, also administered by the park. The limestone within which Mystery Cave developed was formed on the bottom of a shallow sea as much as five hundred million years ago. Rainwater percolating through the soil over very long stretches of time eventually dissolved the rock to create caves and sinkholes.

A tour of Mystery Cave offers an unparalleled look into the subterranean world of stalactites, stalagmites, capacious underground caverns, and more than twelve miles of labyrinthine corridors and silent, mysterious pools. Park naturalists provide tours of the cave throughout the summer and on weekends in the spring and fall, but dress appropriately—the air in the caves hovers around 48° degrees F. throughout the year. (For more information call 507- 937-3251.)

THE HEARTLAND

Minnesota's Heartland is the largest of the seven "states" we're going to explore, and perhaps the most arbitrarily defined. It's a hodgepodge of farms, ranches, forests, hills, rivers, bogs, and lakes. In its northern and eastern sections it shares coniferous forests with the Boglands and Arrowhead. But the Heartland has always been a little easier of access due to the network of rivers and trails that includes the St. Croix, Rum, Mississippi, Crow Wing, and Ottertail rivers, and the Red River oxcart trails. The Itasca and Alexandria moraines make it hilly in many places, though large parts of it are also deadly flat. From Mille Lacs and Gull to Leech and Red lakes, the area has been a home to Native Americans for centuries. Today Minnesota's largest reservations are located within its boundaries. It's rich in lumbering and railroad history, and it holds some of Minnesot'a finest state and national forests. In the Heartland our thoughts don't tend to wander off in the direction of Winnipeg, the Rockies, or New Orleans.

Many parts of the region have been prime vacation destinations for more than a century, drawing tourists from all parts of the United States to its wooded lakes. And there are quite a few resorts still standing from those golden years of leisure. Many Minnesotans, and wanderers from much farther afield, return to a favorite corner year after year, and wouldn't think of venturing much beyond the familiar family cabin or lakeside resort. "It's not far from Jenkins," you will hear them say, or, "If you know where Vergas is...." or "You take Highway 38 toward Bigfork...." Well, if you haven't actually been there, all such descriptions bring the same images to mind: the trees, the glistening water, the wooden dock, and the smells of fish and gasoline.

In the following pages we explore a few of the main arteries into this region, attempting to connect with some of its most attractive landscapes and distinctive towns. Route I will take us up Highway 169 through Elk River, Princeton, Mille Lacs, Crosby, Aitkin, and Grand Rapids. Route II follows Highways 10 & 371 past Anoka, St. Cloud, Collegeville, Little Falls, Brainerd, Walker, Bemidji, and Itasca. Route III takes in a portion of the Leaf Hills, including stops in Sauk Centre, Alexandria, and Fergus Falls. And Route IV offers a brief look at the St. Croix Valley.

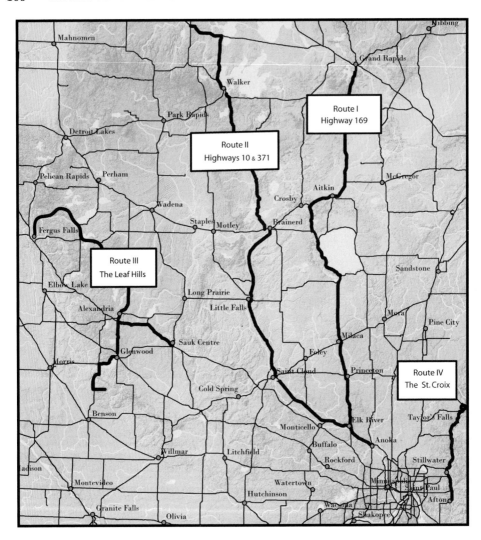

An Overview of the Routes followed in this Section

Route I will take us up Highway 169 through Elk River, Princeton, Mille Lacs, Crosby, Aitkin, and Grand Rapids.

Route II follows Highways 10 & 371 past Anoka, St. Cloud, Collegeville, Little Falls, Brainerd, Walker, Bemidji, and Itasca.

Route III takes in a portion of the Leaf Hills, including stops in Sauk Centre, Glenwood, Alexandria, several unusual state parks, and Fergus Falls.

Route IV offers a look at the St. Croix Valley from Afton to Taylor's Falls.

I: Highway 169

Elk River

Though it's far from spectacular, the hilly countryside around Elk River defines a natural boundary between prairie and woodlands. This region also served for many years as a border between Ojibwe and Dakota hunting grounds. The hills themselves were scraped up from the bedrock more than ten thousand years ago by the forward edge of advancing glaciers. The presence of so much rock in the soil makes it relatively poor for farming, though it also explains why Elk River has so many gravel pits.

Elk River was given its name by Zebulon Pike, who saw herds of elk during his exploratory journey through the area in the fall of 1805. Forty years later David Faribault built a trading post at the point where the Elk and Mississippi rivers meet. Like many early fur-traders, David was a "mixed blood", the son of an Indian mother and Jean Baptiste Faribault, one of Minnesota's earliest fur traders.

David Faribault later married Nancy McClure, the daughter of the Dakota chief Winona. Chief Winona had been sent to Florida by the government when Nancy was only a few months old, and she was raised in mission schools, where she was instructed in European ways. The two were wed at Fort Snelling in 1851, and this propitious match between members of two frontier aristocracies was a gala affair, attended not only by the head chiefs and the principal men of the great Dakota nation, but also by Alexander Ramsey and officials from Washington who had come to Minnesotra Territory to negotiate the treaty of Traverse des Sioux.

By this time Faribault had sold his trading post in Elk River to Pierre Bottineau. Bottineau was also a mixed-blood. He had arrived in St Paul in 1841, served as an interpreter and guide for General Sibley, and purchased tracts of land in both St. Paul and St. Anthony Falls, before establishing a settlement further west known as Bottineau's Prairie—now Maple Plain.

By many accounts, Bottineau was one of the most extraordinary men of his time. He spoke a number of Indian languages, and had guided trips throughout many parts of the region extending from the

Mississippi to the Missouri River and beyond. One man who knew him well later described Bottineau as follows:

He is a large man physically as I remember him, with a prominent face and head, straight black hair and piercing eyes, and a swarthy complexion. An odd contrast to this appearance is his exceeding pleasant smile which nearly always radiates his face. He has the characteristics of the bear and the gentleness of the woman.... He is a noble link of the past, as he combines the French, the Indian and the American, in all his elementary peculiarities. One of the best things which can be said of Bottineau is, he was always true to his trusts, and that of itself is a noble monument to any man.

Pierre Bottineau

Bottineau spent his later years in the Red River Valley, an area that drains to the north, though it was linked to the Mississippi through the famous Pembina Oxcart Trail. That trail also passed through Elk River, adding to its importance as a commercial hub during its early history. Following a pattern that was to repeat itself again and again throughout the region, fur-trading gave way in time to lumbering, which in turn was replaced by agriculture as the base of Elk River's economy. Though it will never become "just another suburb," the city has long since been absorbed in the spreading sphere of the metropolitan Twin Cities area.

In recent times Elk River has developed an enviable reputation as a result of its forward-looking use of energy. It became the location of America's first rural nuclear power plant in 1960. That pilot project was discontinued after a few years, but during the 1980's the plant was redesigned to generate electricity by burning garbage. Elk River was designated as Minnesota's Energy City as a result of these groundbreaking initiatives.

Princeton

The first settler to move into the area of Princeton was a mulatto lumberjack named "Banjo Bill." The town was officially settled in 1854 and named after John Prince, a local fur agent. Two years later the town got its first sawmill.

For many years Princeton was inhabited largely by lumberjacks working seasonally in camps along the Rum River, two branches of which meet in town. As the timber was cut and loggers moved farther north and west in search of virgin forests, Princeton began to cultivate another natural resource—clay. A fine deposit was located two miles north of town, but it was not economically feasible to develop it until the railroad finally arrived in 1886.

The first brickyard was established north of Princeton that year. Soon Princeton, and the newly founded town of Brickton (which has subsequently vanished) was supplying bricks for buildings throughout the Upper Midwest. By the turn of the century Brickton had become one of the largest brick manufacturing towns in the state. In those days 20 million bricks were shipped annually from the area—enough to fill 1800 freight cars. Workers in the brickyard earned from $1.50 to $1.75 per day, and those wages kept the local economy of both cities afloat.

As you drive through Princeton take a look around, and you will see more than a few examples of the local cream-colored brick. The Oddfellows Hall on Main Street is a particularly nice example. A description written at the time the building was completed suggests something of the flavor of Princeton's small-town pride—an attractive sentiment, which has not changed much, perhaps, with the passing decades.

It is a three-story brick structure, imposing in appearance, substantial and enduring, higher than any other building between Minneapolis and Duluth. It is made from the famous cream-colored Princeton brick. The foundation is sandstone granite, the basement is ten feet deep. The store on the north is being occupied by the hardware conducted by B.D. Grant. The store on the south is occupied by the Princeton Roller Mill Company. On the second floor M.S. Rutherford has his real estate offices. Also there are the offices of Judge

C.A. Dickey, County Attorney J.A. Ross, Guy Ewing, insurance
agent, and the dental offices of C.F. Walker. On the third floor are
the lodge rooms for the Odd Fellows and Rebekahs. The building
is steam heated.

In 1929 the last remaining brickyard closed. In thirty-six years
of production more than 800 million bricks had been produced in
the area.

Nowadays Princeton can boast a state-of-the-art medical facility
and a distinguished public library overlooking the river (formerly the
train station). There is a charming park along the banks of the Rum
River within the city limits.

The Rum River

The Rum River, which we have already crossed in Princeton, follows
a lazy course from Lake Mille Lacs to the Mississippi. For centuries it
was a popular route for Native Americans traveling between these two
important bodies of water. It should come as no surprise, therefore, that
the upper valley of the Rum has one of the highest concentrations of
prehistoric sites in Minnesota, some of which date back more than 3000
years. Burial mounds, copper tools, ricing pits, and other artifacts have
been found throughout the area.

Though the river was called the Rum even as far back as 1776, when
Jonathan Carver explored the area, a number of attempts have been
made over the years to change the name, and for brief periods it has
been referred to as the Anoka, the Temperance, the St. Francis, and even
the Volstead, in honor of the Minnesota legislator who introduced the
bill that brought prohibition to the United States (see pages 69-70).

When Father Hennepin visited the area in 1680, he noted that the
natives called it Isaati or Nodouessians. Carver's reference to the Rum
was no doubt a translation of an Indian name, because no whites had
been in the area for about a hundred years. Various interpretations have
been given for what that translation entailed.

In the 1930s, under the auspices of the Minnesota Historical Society, one researcher came up with the following line of reasoning.

Early maps of this territory label the stream "Iskootawaboo," which means "warm water." The Rum is generally a shallow stream running through largely open country, which gives it a warmer temperature than deeper streams flowing through heavily wooded areas or fed by springs. Hence "Iskootawaboo': warm water. The highly alcoholic beverages introduced to the natives by the white traders seemed "hot" to their tastes. Therefore they also referred to rum or whiskey as "iskootawaboo" —a hot liquid. hence the Iskootawaboo became the Rum.

More recently another theory has been advanced. Because the Rum flows out of Mille Lacs Lake, which several local tribes refer to as the Lake of the Great Spirit, the Mdewakanton Dakota called the river Mdotemniwakan, meaning Mouth (of river) + water + Sacred. The early European explorers interpreted the Dakota word for spirit in a somewhat different sense—hence the Rum River.

What may seem like an issue of largely antiquarian interest has become more heated as yet another movement to rename the river gathers force—this time, to return it to its Dakota name of Mdotemniwakan. The movement has been endorsed by tribal organizations far and wide, the Minnesota Historical Society's Indian Advisory Committee, several prominent Christian religious leaders, and even the United Nations' Secretariat of the Permanent Forum on Indigenous Issues. Those who oppose such a change point out that the Mdewakanton Dakota people do not actually name rivers. Rather, they name the land surrounding rivers. Mdotemniwakan is actually the Dakota name for the land surrounding the mouth of the Rum River.

However the current dispute is resolved, it seems doubtful it will alter the speech habits of those who have lived and worked near the Rum River since childhood. In any case, as we drive northward through the forests and farms toward Lake Mille Lacs, it's interesting to ponder the ways that this poky river has been a source of communication, commerce, and conflict over the centuries. We might even be tempted to take a closer look by canoeing a stretch of the largely peaceful river. The entire course of the Rum is navigable, and in 1978 it was designated a Minnesota Wild and Scenic River.

Onamia, Vineland, and Lake Mille Lacs

Lake Mille Lacs has been a Mecca for sportsmen since the earliest days of European settlement in the area, and it retains that distinction to this day. The shores of the lake—the second-largest within Minnesota's borders—are lined with marinas, outfitters, and accommodations of every size and description, though the preponderance of modest cabins, motels, and trailer parks testify to the importance that many of its visitors place on serious fishing. Mille Lacs is a premier walleye lake, and fish weighing ten pounds and more are landed with remarkable frequency. In a good year more than half a million walleye are taken from Mille Lacs, and the lake also contains plenty of northerns, yellow perch, small-mouthed bass, and even a few muskies.

The name Mille Lacs, is once again a misnomer, though in this no one seems to mind. The Dakota referred to the lake and the surrounding countryside as Missi-Saigagon, which can variously be translated as "everywhere lake," "all sorts of lakes," or "great lake." The French voyageurs, following their usual practice, crudely translated the Indian name, and referred to this entire region as the "thousand lakes" region—Mille Lacs. In time it became common to apply the same name to the large lake we are passing, though it would be hard to imagine a body of water that more powerfully exhibits a singularity and unity of water mass.

As you pass along the shores of the lake, you may see advertisements for "launch fishing." Even novices can catch fish on these large vessels, which hold up to fifty people, and are commandeered by veterans who know where the walleye are, and also how to catch them. If you do decide to go out to try your luck, be prepared for some fierce weather. Although Mille Lacs is so big you can't see across to the other side, it is also very shallow, rarely dipping below 40 feet in depth. As a consequence, a little bit of wind can stir up an awful lot of waves.

The abundance of fish to be found in Mille Lacs made it a popular area long before the appearance of white explorers and fur traders. In fact, the Mdewakanton band of the Dakota considered the area between Mille Lacs and the Mississippi to be the heart of their ter-

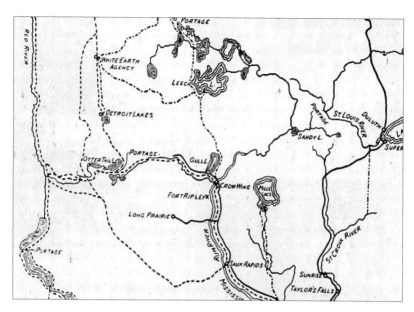

A portion of an early map showing overland and water routes through the interior of what later became Minnesota.

ritory. Not only was the fishing good, but wild rice and maple sugar were also relatively easy to come by. The proximity of the plains made buffalo hunting another attractive option for the Dakota. When the first white explorer, Daniel Graysolon, Sieur Dulhut (Duluth), arrived in 1679, the shores were lined with Dakota villages. In the recount of his visit Dulhut claimed the territory for France, stating that he "had the honor to set up the arms of his Majesty in the great village of the Nadouessioux called Izatys." This is the village we now know as Kathio.

The French may have claimed the territory, but it was the Ojibwe who were threatening to overrun it. The Ojibwe's traditional territory had been in the vicinity of Sault Ste. Marie, and they were the first Great Lakes tribe to participate as middle-men in the French fur trade. The Dakota allowed them to travel and hunt on their lands because the Ojibwe brought the French trade goods with them—the pails, the knives, the clothing—that the Dakota found very useful and attractive. In time the French themselves began to build trading posts further inland, however, and this undercut the Ojibwe's privileged position. Of greater concern to the Dakota, however, was the fact that the

French could now trade directly with the Dakota's enemies—the Cree and Assiniboine. In 1736 the Dakota killed some Frenchmen near Lake of the Woods, and the Ojibwe, hoping to win favor with the French, attacked the Dakota in turn, opening a period of hostilities between the two tribes that would last for half a century.

With the aid of European firepower which the Dakota largely lacked, the Ojibwe skirmished with the Dakota repeatedly over the years. The final blow to the Dakota came in 1740, when, according to Ojibwe tradition, a three-day battle took place at Kathio (Izatys), the largest of the Mdewakanton villages, which was located near the present town of Vineland. During the battle, the Dakota villages were overrun, and they were forced to move their encampments further south.

During the last fifty years a good deal of archeological work has been done at the attractive Dakota village sites on the river south of Mille Lacs, yet strange as it may seem, no evidence of a serious battle has ever been unearthed. The fact that the Dakota themselves have no tradition of being removed from their home turf by force also lends support to the theory, which has become increasingly popular in academic circles, that the famous Battle of Kathio never actually took place.

Though the reasons are now obscure, it remains clear that the Dakota moved their encampments to the south during the mid-eighteenth century, but found the area around Mille Lacs so bountiful that they were reluctant to abandon it entirely. In 1768—almost thirty years after their defeat at Kathio--various bands located in southern Minnesota gathered at the Falls of St. Anthony, and once they'd finalized their plans, 400 braves started up the Mississippi in a flotilla of more than a hundred canoes toward the Ojibwe village at Sandy Lake, near the present-day town of Palisade. Rather than approach the village from the south, this large force headed up the Crow Wing River, planning to take a circuitous route through Gull, Leech, Cass, and Winnepegoshish Lakes, and come upon the village unexpectedly from the north. Though scholars dispute the details of their route it was an impressive itinerary by any stretch of the imagination. The war party was eventually spotted by Obijwe scouts, however, who returned to their village to warn the tribe....only to find that many of their braves had departed to the south in search of the Dakota. The remaining Ojibwe were able to hold off the Dakota and avert a massacre, although the village was all but destroyed and the Dakota took thirty Ojibwe women captive before retreating downstream on the Mississippi.

The Dakota braves were greatly pleased with their efforts, but had the misfortune on their return journey of running into a trap laid by the Ojibwe warriors, who had spotted the remains of one of their camps at the mouth of the Crow Wing River, and suspected that they would soon be returning that way. The battle raged for three days, with the Dakota having the advantage in numbers and the Ojibwe in position. The Dakota finally withdrew in the night and continued down the Mississippi, completing their 600 mile circuit with only half the men they'd started out with. In the end, the campaign had not produced the massive levels of destruction for which the Dakota had hoped, and they resigned themselves to moving their villages further south into the Minnesota River Valley. Since that time the region has been the home of the Ojibwe, and they still live there today.

To get a feel for the landscape that these Native Americans found so appealing, pull into Mille Lacs Kathio State Park (320-532-3523), which contains the site where the village of Kathio once stood. The park is Minnesota's fourth-largest, and it has plenty of hiking, camping, swimming, and even horseback riding. You can rent a canoe and paddle just a bit of the Rum River, which runs through the park as it leaves Mille Lacs. At the interpretive center, which is open year-round, you can get information about the park's recreational opportunities and the history of the village of Kathio. There are three shallow lakes in the park which still produce wild rice.

A little ways beyond the park entrance on the right is the impressive Mille Lacs Indian Museum. It's run by the Minnesota Historical Society, and has a number of permanent exhibits relating to the Mille Lacs Band. In February of 2005 the band celebrated the 150th anniversary of the Treaty of 1855, which created the Mille Lacs Reservation through which we are now passing. They were also celebrating the perseverance of their forefathers who successfully resisted repeated

HARVESTING WILD RICE

Wild rice is not actually a form of rice. It's a grain. The Ojibwe call it Mah-NO-min, which means spirit-seed. It is traditionally harvested in early September, and the full moon of that month is called Manoominike Giizi, or "wild rice moon."

It grows from eight to twelve feet tall in shallow waters of varying depths, and it often grows so thick that a harvester using traditional methods will pole his or her way through the reeds from the stern of the canoe, while a companion sits in front knocking the reeds with two long sticks so that the grain falls off into the canoe. It can take anywhere from two hours to an entire day to fill a canoe, depending on the thickness of the reeds, the ripeness of the grain, and the energy of those who are collecting it. Once the rice is harvested, it must still be dried, pounded, and winnowed.

Much of the wild rice we find in stores today was commercially grown and mechanically harvested on farms in California and Canada, but there is little doubt that the naturally-occurring grain, harvested by traditional methods, is far superior in taste. Minnesota has well over sixty-thousand acres of natural wild rice—more than any other state—and the plant can still be found in more than half of Minnesota's counties, though Atkin, St. Louis, Itasca, and Cass counties have the most.

Anyone can harvest wild rice. All you need is a license, a canoe and a pole, some knocking sticks, a familiarity with the regulations, and confidence that the bed you're harvesting is in public waters. Reservation lands may also be open to public harvesting once the proper permits have been obtained. Many wild rice harvesters process the rice themselves—the first time—and then hire an expert to do the dirty work, paying for the service with a percentage of the finished product.

attempts by the U.S. government to move the tribe to the nearby White Earth Reservation.

Tourism mushroomed on Lake Mille Lacs during the 1920s, following the completion of the highway we've been traveling. Yet family resorts have declined considerably in popularity in recent years. For example, there were once at least a dozen resorts on the shores of Wigwam Bay. Now there is only a single campground located there. Many resorts are being razed to make way for luxury condominiums. Others are being supplanted by large full-service resorts like Izatys, which offer golf, tennis, swimming pools, spas, live entertainment and other amenities that mom-and-pop motels and resorts do not provide.

Another relatively recent development in the area has been the surge in ice fishing, which began to gain in popularity during the 1950s. There are times when the population out on the lake, which can number more that 8,000, is greater than that of any town nearby on dry land.

The recent change with the greatest impact to the area, however, has undoubtedly been the arrival of Grand Casino. Its presence was made possible by passage of federal legislation in 1988 outlining the rights of Indian tribes, as sovereign nations, to regulate gaming on their own land. The purpose of the law was to promote economic development, self-sufficiency, and stronger tribal government on the reservations.

The Grand Casino Mille Lacs opened in 1991, and it has been a success from the first. In 1990, the Mille Lacs Reservation had a poverty rate of 81%—one of the worst in the nation. Today, the number has dropped to less than 17%. The casino has also alleviated poverty in the surrounding area. Ninety percent of the casino's 3,000 employees are non-Indian.

With casino-generated revenue, the band has recently built two schools, three ceremonial buildings, a language and culture center, two health clinics, four community centers, a government center, a center for the elderly, a water treatment plant, and more than 200 new homes. They've also been able to spend money on road maintenance, the renovation of older homes, and other projects and services. The band has also invested in many non band-owned hotels, resorts, and businesses.

Aitkin

Long a Dakota hunting ground, the area around Aitkin has at
various times in its past been claimed by Spain, France, and
England.

Hoping to tap into the bounty of furs in the area through trade
with the Indians, the North West Company established a post on the
north shore of Cedar Lake (a few miles west of modern Aitkin) during the 1780s. We may consider this odd, in light of the fact that the
North West Company was British, and the territory had come into
the possession of the United States at the conclusion of the American
Revolution. The United States had no real means of securing the vast
territories of the interior, however, and in 1784 a group of British businessmen founded the North West Company in Montreal and began
to exploit its commercial potential, establishing their headquarters at
Grand Portage, on the northern shore of Lake Superior.

It was not until 1805 that the United States government sent Zebulon Pike with an expeditionary party to find out what was actually going
on in the area. Pike came upon the British fort at Cedar Lake on January
2, 1806.

Pike's journal entry describing his first contact with the British conveys the flavor of a time when chaos and confusion reigned in the wilderness of northern Minnesota, but also courtesy and good judgment:

*Jan. 2d. - Fine warm day. Discovered fresh sign of Indians. Just as
we were encamping at night, my sentinel informed us that some
Indians were coming full speed upon our trail or track. I ordered
my men to stand by their guns carefully. [The Indians] were immediately at my camp, and saluted the flag by discharge of three
pieces; when four Chipeways, one Englishman (Mr. Grant), and
a Frenchman of the N. W. Company, presented themselves. They
informed us that some women, having discovered our trail, gave
the alarm, and not knowing but it was their enemies, they had
departed to make a discovery. They had heard of us and revered
our flag. Mr. Grant, the Englishman, had only arrived the day
before from Lake De Sable, from which he had marched in one*

day and a half. I presented the Indians with half a deer, which they received thankfully, for they had discovered our fires some days ago, and believing it to be the Sioux, they dared not leave their camp. They returned, but Mr. Grant remained all night.

Pike spent some time at the North West fort as the guest of the English commandant, and he also conferred with the local Dakota leader Babesigaundibay (Curly Head).

At the time of Pike's visit the presence of the British fort was not illegal, but after defeating the British in the War of 1812, the Americans reversed their position, enacting a law in 1816 that forbade foreign commercial interests on American soil. The North West Company grudgingly abandoned their forts in the region, and soon were replaced by forts run by John Jacob Astor's American Fur Company.

Astor's firm had divisions stretching throughout the Northwest, and eventually extended to the Pacific but at that time the Northern Outfit, which encompassed most of what is now northern Minnesota, was considered to be the most richly endowed. Its headquarters was on Sandy Lake until 1822, when that post was abandoned and a new one was built near the portage connecting the Lake Superior region with the Mississippi. That post was put under the supervision of a man named William Aitkin, and it served as the headquarters of the district until about 1838.

Aitkin had begun his career working for a trader by the name of Charles Ermatinger, and eventually he married the man's half-Ojibwe daughter Madeleine. Thus Aitkin became both the son-in-law of an influential trader and the husband of the Ojbiwe Chief Broken Tooth's granddaughter. These family ties served Aitkin well during his career as chief factor of the Fond du Lac division of the American Fur Company and also during his later career as an independent trader. His Ojibwe friends and relatives called him Sha-gah-naush-eence, which means "Little Englishman."

Aitkin was abruptly fired by the American Fur Company in 1838, after a change in ownership. No one knows why, but his great influence in the region, and the fact that he had installed his sons in several outlying posts, may well have been seen as a threat to the sovereignty of the firm. As luck would have it—bad luck for the giant firm, but good luck for Aitkin himself—the demand for beaver pelts was declining, As raccoon replaced beaver as a fashionable fur, so the independent trader began to play an increasingly important role in the fur trade. Aitkin continued to do well, establishing trading posts at various strategic points along the Mississippi, including one on the mouth of the Mud River, where the town of Aitkin later grew, and just a few miles from the rival American Fur post at Sandy Lake. The American Fur Company collapsed in 1842, but Aitkin continued to do business until his death in 1851.

The town of Aitkin did not really come into being until the railroad reached the Mississippi from Duluth in 1870, as part of Jay Cooke's ambitious, and ultimately successful, plan to run a rail line from Duluth to the Pacific Ocean. Once the rail link to Aitkin had been established, the town almost immediately began to play a key role in the lumber industry, transporting men and materials to lumber camps by means of steamboats up the Mississippi. For nearly half a century, until the 1920s, these steamboats would operate between Aitkin and Grand Rapids, and the remains of the ones that sank can still be seen on the river bottom during periods of low water.

Aitkin became a supply center too, and industries related to lumbering, including sawmills and cooperages, sprang up. It also developed a reputation for rough living, as lumberjacks arrived in town following a long hard winter and spring in the lumber camps with their pockets full of cash. Five years after it was founded, Aitkin had a population of 165, and all but 20 were men.

As the forests retreated north, however, settlers arrived to cultivate the cut-over land, and Aitkin developed a veneer of civilization, with church socials, public lectures on erudite subjects, and even an opera house.

Though its importance as a hub of civilization is far from what it once was, Aitkin remains a pleasant town and a regional center for tourism. You can explore its early history in a museum located in the well-preserved train station downtown, and if you're lucky enough to be passing through on the day after Thanksgiving, you can take part in the festivities associated with its annual Fish House Parade, when a succession of fancifully-decorated ice houses proceed slowly down Minnesota

The local theater in Aitkin

Street on trailers, and the American Legion hosts a Chili Cook-Off. You can shop at the day-long craft fair, sample the Fish House Stew provided by a local bank at the Moose Lodge, witness the ceremonious coronation of the Crappie Queen, and finish off the evening dancing to live music.

Francis Lee Jaques Museum

The landscape and wildlife painter Francis Lee Jaques was a long-time resident of Aitkin, and at the Jaques Art Center downtown (121 2nd St NW; 218-927-2363) you can take a look at several of his works. Jaques is best known for a series of dioramas he did for the Museum of Natural History in New York City—or perhaps *not* so well-known. Not long ago the following remarks appeared in the *New York Times*:

> *The painted backgrounds of the dioramas at the American Museum of Natural History have a curious place in the hearts of almost everyone who has grown up in New York City during the last century. They are some of the most elaborate landscape paintings in the city and some of the most frequently viewed pictures anywhere, but almost nobody knows who did them or, in a sense, even seems to notice them when they're staring straight at them.*

Yet in Minnesota several generations of outdoor enthusiasts have cherished Jacques (pronounced JAY-Kweese) illustrations for the wilderness canoeing books of Sigurd Olson, and also the books he did with his wife Florence, including *Canoe Country*, *The Geese Fly High*, and *Snowshoe Country*. Jaques was also responsible for the diorama paintings at the Bell Museum of Natural History at the University of Minnesota, and children beyond counting have stared into the scenes of elk on Inspiration Peak, of moose on Gunflint Beach, and of timber wolves on the rocky cliffs of the North Shore, as if they were real.

Jacques was raised on farms in Illinois and Kansas, though when the chores were done he would often go hunting with his father in nearby wetlands. The boy became entranced by the plumage of the birds he shot, and began to work at depicting them realistically.

In the spring of 1903, after yet another unsuccessful year of farming, the family pulled up stakes once again and headed north in search of fertile, inexpensive soil. They ended up in a log cabin on a plot of land just north of Aitkin, with an oxbow of the Mississippi River wrapped around it. As a young adult, while working at various occupations—lumberman, railroad hand, taxidermist—Jacques continued to draw and sketch, and he also spent a good deal of time exploring the forests and lakes of the northern Minnesota border region by canoe.

In December 1917, Jaques was drafted. He was stationed first in San Francisco, and later New York, and in both cities he visited the local museums, drawing inspiration from the complex and yet "scientific" diorama exhibits he met up with there, the like of which he had never seen before.

After the war, Jaques returned to Minnesota and found work in the Duluth shipyards, but his interest in nature stayed with him, and in 1924 he sent a painting of a black duck to Dr. Frank Chapman, a curator in the Ornithology Department at the American Museum of Natural History. To his surprise, the musuem took Jaques on as a staff artist and he suddenly found himself working in the company of some of the country's leading scientists. In time Jaques himself was recognized as one of America's foremost wildlife artists.

Perhaps due to his years spent as an untrained but avid observer of nature, Jaques had developed the ability to render an animal's posture and flair without resorting to the painstaking depiction of every piece of fur or feather. He was especially adept at capturing the form of birds in motion. Yet he was no less adept at integrating the elements of the surrounding environment into a pleasing whole—thus satisfying the requirements of art and science at a single stroke.

He once remarked:

The shape of things has always given me the most intense satisfaction. Everything one sees and senses. Geese in a storm, a landfall after a long period at sea, horses in a fence corner, the first glimpse of the 'shining mountains' across the plain, the eroded bank of a stream winding through a pasture. With me the keenest interest of all has been in wildlife, and that includes its habitat.

Jaques' deft handling of such scenes is in full view in the museum in Aitkin, which contains several of the painter's works and also displays exhibits by local artists.

Rice Lake National Wildlife Refuge

To get a look at an unusual natural environment that Jaques must have enjoyed exploring, take a sidetrip to Rice Lake National Wildlife Refuge, located on Hwy 65 five miles south of McGregor. Its greatest claim to fame is as a seasonal home to one of the largest populations of migrating ring-necked ducks in North America. The refuge is also known for its wild rice, the Kettle River runs through it, and you can take a nine-mile self-guided interpretive drive that will expose you to several different habitats. (800-877-8339)

The region north and east of Aitkin has very few towns but lots of interesting countryside to explore. Parts of it are hilly and wooded, due to the presence of the St. Louis Moraine, but much of the terrain consists of tamarac bogs. Savanna Portage State Park, on the east side of Big Sandy Lake, is rich in history, being located at the height of land between the Great Lakes and Mississippi drainage systems. The park's hiking trails weave their way between several small lakes, and it also offers a variety of camping options.

Further to the north and east the landcape becomes less inviting, though the bogs do attract rare bird species. The Sax-Zim Bog in particular has become well-known for unusual sightings. It's located north of the intersection of County Roads 52 and 7. And while you're roaming the bogs in search of a stray sharp-tailed grouse, great gray owl, boreal chickadee, or LeConte's sparrow, why not pay a visit to nearby Elmer, the childhood home of pulp fiction author Frank Gruber?

The Lumber Industry

As you drive the lonely miles between Aitkin and Grand Rapids, it may be well to ponder the lumber industry that continues to thrive in this part of the state. Grand Rapids is the home of the Forest History Center (run by the Minnesota Historical Society), and also home to the Blandin Paper Company, which continues to process timber—though both the trees being used and the products being produced are different from what they were during Minnesota's golden era of logging a hundred years ago.

Back when Minnesota was covered with first-growth forests, lumbermen developed an almost religious affection for *pinus stobus*, the white pine. That tree is arguably the most beautiful of all the evergreens, with its soft, thin, five-needle clusters and its tall statuesque outline

The noble white pine

made up of irregular but harmoniously out-thrust branches. But what the lumbermen liked about the tree was its wood. The tree frequently rose to more than a hundred feet in height, with a diameter of two feet or more. Its grain was so straight that planks could be severed with an ax, and to top it all off, the tree was light enough to float cooperatively downstream to the lumber mills without any of the fuss or bother often associated with denser species. The white pine, in short, was the lumberman's dream, and the only complaint that could be made against it was that it often grew in the midst of other, lesser, species. This not only made it more difficult to harvest, but also left huge piles of unsightly debris behind, which greatly increased the danger of forest fires.

The lumber industry in Minnesota began in the vicinity of the St. Croix, but it made its way north and west as the forests were cut one by one. In time Minneapolis became the state's chief lumber city, milling logs that had been rafted down the Mississippi to supply the planks that built the cities of the Midwest—Bismarck, Omaha, Sioux Falls—as well as the small towns burgeoning on Minnesota's own western prairies. A large portion of the timber was rafted all the way to St. Louis before being cut. In 1882 St. Louis received 160 million board feet of uncut white pine from the Upper Mississippi. By 1890 the population of the Twin Cities itself had skyrocketed to a quarter of a million people—and that also required a lot of new boardwalks and housing.

But two technological innovations also had an effect on the industry. During the 1870s steam power was introduced into saw milling, and this made it possible to build mills closer to the forests, and farther from the hydro power that had previously been needed to cut the logs. The invention of new circular saws, and later the band saw, also helped the mills to increase their production. During the 1880s Little Falls, Duluth, Crookston, Cloquet, Brainerd, and International Falls became saw-milling towns. Lots of money was being made in the lumber business, and names like Pillsbury, Washburn (of General Mills fame), T. B. Walker (of Walker Art Center fame), and Weyerhauser, made their fortunes largely by means of the white pine.

The golden age of Minnesota lumbering extends roughly from 1890 to 1910. During this period, as rail lines probed deeper into the forests, the railroads assumed an ever-increasing role in moving logs to market. Over 20,000 lumberjacks were employed in the northern parts of the state in those days, and twice as many worked in the state's sawmills and other wood-production factories. The industry peaked in 1918, when 2.3 billion board feet of Minnesota lumber was cut and processed.

Such rampant deforestation was not without its disastrous side effects, however, and deadly forest fires raged through Hinckley, Chisholm, Baudette, and Cloquet at one time or another, often as a result of the waste trees and scrub that the lumbermen left in their wake. Historians estimate, in fact, that more forest lands were destroyed by fires than by logging during that bustling age. Eventually the virgin forests gave out entirely and sawmills closed down one after the other. The last log drive in Minnesota went north down the Little Fork River in 1937. You can watch it on film at the Forest History Center in Grand Rapids.

But that's not the end of the story. Following a half-century of decline, the timber industry regained momentum during the 1980s as a result of changes in the wood fiber industry. A variety of products made from softwood chips and improved synthetic glues became widely used in the construction of houses and other structures. The market for paper products also increased, and capital investments in lumber mills, which in Minnesota had been less than $600 million between 1975 and 1985, more than doubled to nearly $1 billion in the five years between 1985 and 1990. The state's timber harvests increased during the same period from 2.2 to 3.7 million cords.

Long gone, of course, are the winter harvests of impressive stands of virgin white pine using hand tools and horses. Nowadays the forests being harvested are more likely to be aspen groves, which lack the nobility and lumber value of the white pine, but have the advantages of being fast growing and also self-regenerating. Where lumberjacks used to fell the trees by hand and to move them to the riverbanks or rail lines using horses and chains, workers now use "feller-bunchers" to bring down trees. While safely ensconced in a cab, the operator of this machine directs a long arm equipped with a saw toward the top of the desired tree. Once the tree's upper vegetation has been removed, an arm with several clamps seizes the trunk. The trunk is severed from its base near the ground, and then it is gently lowered to a horizontal position and stacked in a pile on the ground along with other severed trees. There will usually be a grapple-skidder nearby to grab the logs and move them to the landing for transport. A more advanced machine called the feller-forwarder will both cut the trees and load them onto a bunk which it can then easily transport to a nearby loading area, landing, or truck.

Loggers still do much of their work in the winter time, when the branches "pop" more cleanly from the trunks and the frozen ground is less sensitive to the weight of the heavy machinery.

The lumber industry now ranks third among Minnesota industries, with over 8 billion dollars in annual wages. In an effort to maintain forests and keep the industry healthy, in 1995 the legislature passed the Sustainable Forest Resources Act and created a Forest Resources Council to establish guidelines for the industry.

Blandin Paper

The career of Charles K. Blandin, who has played a prominant role in the development of Grand Rapid, reads like a Horatio Alger story. The son of a Wisconsin farmer, he was largely self-taught. He pursued a career as a school teacher, later worked on a weekly newspaper, and eventually became the manager of the St. Paul Pioneer Press/Dispatch Printing Company. When the owner of that company died Blandin bought half of it and took control of the entire operation, including the newly-purchased Itasca Paper Company in Grand Rapids. He soon turned his attention to paper manufacturing, and eventually developed innovative ways to make high-quality coated paper stock. In 1927 Blandin sold off his interest in the newspaper to concentrate on the paper mill itself. Two years later he renamed it the Blandin Paper Company.

The Blandin Paper Company continued to prosper, and the city of Grand Rapids along with it. To insure that the relationship continued, Blandin stipulated in his will that profits from the company be distributed by a foundation to meet the needs of the community. The Blandin Company has been so successful, however, that the foundation has broadened the scope of its concerns far beyond the borders of Grand Rapids, though it continues to focus on issues related to the economic viability of rural Minnesota communities.

In 1997 Blandin Paper was purchased by the Finnish company UPM-Kymmene, becoming its first North American mill. Today Blandin employs 850 workers, with more than 2000 local jobs attributable to its operations, making it one of northern Minnesota's largest employers. It also maintains its long-standing reputation for paper quality and innovation. In 2001 one of Blandin's operations set a 24-hour world speed record for paper-coating, and its employees

The lumber camp at the Forest History Center

were given UPM-Kymmene's award for "Best Lightweight Coated Productivity Improvement." Blandin also manages over 200,000 acres of forest lands.

You can tour the mill, which looms over the city of Grand Rapids, at selected times, and watch the processes by which logs become pulp, which in turn is spread out, heated, dried, and rolled into enormous cylinders of glossy paper. (218-327-6682)

The Forest History Center

The Minnesota Historical Society, with the help of the Blandin Foundation, has established a forest history center in Grand Rapids to bring the era of the early industry to life. The center contains a number of interpretive displays and a logging camp has also been recreated in the woods nearby, where "living history" loggers, cooks, blacksmiths, and other workers give you the feel of the camps by performing humorous and dramatic skits that evoke the tenor of those rugged times. You can tour the logger's floating dining room and join the "river pugs," those daring men who used long poles to keep the logs floating free as they made their way downstream to the mills. You can climb a hundred-foot fire tower and look down on the sea of forest below.

Of even greater interest, perhaps, are the exhibits in the interpretive center that focus on modern lumbering techniques. You can listen to brief video interviews with the men who run the machines and work in the mills, and you can try your hand at felling trees yourself inside the cab of a complicated logging trainer-simulator. (Call 218-327-4482 for details.)

The Lost Forty White Pine Stand

There is one chunk of forest land north of Grand Rapids that was never cut, though to get there will require a bit of extra driving. It was surveyed in 1882 but erroneously recorded, so that it appeared to be at the bottom of a lake. The loggers ignored it, and it remains today perhaps not much different from the way in appeared to the men who surveyed it more than a hundred years ago. It's referred to nowadays as the Lost Forty, though the tract encompassed 144 acres. The red and white pine on its eastern end are as much as 350 years old, and can measure up to four feet in diameter.

To get there from Grand Rapids, head north on Highway 38 to Bigfork. Turn left (west) on Highway 14 to County Road 26. Turn right (north) and go for two miles to Forest Road 2240. Turn left (west) and go 1.5 miles to the Lost Forty. You'll find a picnic area and a one-mile self-guided hiking trail through the majestic pines. There is a campground nestled into a birch grove nearby at Noma Lake.

If you do make the trip to the Lost Forty, you'll see some very large trees, though most of them are widely spaced. In fact, its curious history notwithstanding, much of the hilly area looks a lot like other white pine forests in northern Minnesota. A visit to the Lost Forty may remind us of a world we have lost, but it also leaves us with the impression that there are still some mighty fine forests around to explore.

Judy Garland Home

Grand Rapids is more than just paper and trees. It's a bustling tourist center with plenty of lodging options along the highways and a pleasant residential sector north of Highway 2. It also happens to be the birthplace of one of America's most beloved entertainers—Judy Garland. Judy's parents were former vaudeville performers who chose Grand Rapids as a pleasant place to settle down and raise a family. They bought the New Grand Theater and ran it for twelve years. In fact, Judy made her first public performance there in 1924, when, at the age of two and a half, she sang several choruses of "Jingle Bells" to an appreciative audience. Her two older sisters were already performing locally at the time, and before long she had joined their duo to form the Gumm Sisters.

The family moved to the Los Angeles area two years later, where opportunities for the young group to perform were far greater, and that was the last that Grand Rapids saw of "Baby" Gumm (as Judy was known then) except from the seat of a darkened movie theater. Judy appeared in her first film at the age of seven, and went on to a remarkable career as a movie star and nightclub entertainer.

Though the connection between Grand Rapids and Judy Garland is not, perhaps, deep-rooted, the actress's appeal was always based not only on her magnificent voice, but also on her sweet, somewhat vulnerable girl-next-door quality and her sincerity and heart. These qualities struck a chord in small-town audiences through the 1930s and 40s, and there is more than a little poetic justice in the town of Grand Rapids celebrating her life, career, and family, during its yearly Judy Garland Festival.

The city started the festival in 1975, and it includes various film memorabilia swaps, repeated showings of *The Wizard of Oz*, and an occasional appearance by one of the Lollipop Kids. The festival is held on the last week in June.

You can tour the Judy Garland Museum just about any time of the year. It houses thousands of items associated with the star, including the carriage in which Judy rode down the final spiral turns of theYellow Brick Road in *The Wizard of Oz*. The museum is housed in the home where Judy lived until the age of four, at 2727 Highway 169 S. (1-800-664-5839). The memorial garden adjacent to the house contains a field of poppies.

II. Highway 10 and 371

Anoka

Anoka sits at the mouth of the Rum River. The countryside round-about is sandy, and has always been considered mediocre farmland. In fact, a vast triangular area north of Anoka stretching west to St Cloud and east all the way to the St Croix River is known to geologists as the Anoka Sand Plain. Yet settlers arrived in the area relatively early in the region's history, largely because the Rum River was such an important conduit between the Mississippi and Lake Mille Lacs.

Father Louis Hennepin was probably the first white man to visit the area. He was captured by the Dakota in 1680 near Lake Pepin and taken to the Dakota Camp at Lake Mille Lacs. He later accompanied one of their hunting parties down the Rum River to the Mississippi.

In those days battles took place from time to time between the resident Dakota bands and the Ojibwe bands that were moving into the area from the Great Lakes region. Our knowledge of that time is scanty, but in the spring of 1839 a skirmish took place between Ojibwe and Dakota braves on the shores of Lake Harriet in what is now Minneapolis. A Dakota brave was killed, and the Dakota, seeking revenge, stalked the retreating Ojibwe to their camp on Round Lake, just north of Anoka. On the morning of July 4th the Dakota attacked the Ojibwe as they slept, and many Ojibwe were killed. Seven years later a lumberman came across the bone-strewn battle site and counted more than fifty skulls in the vicinity.

The first white settler, Joseph Belanger, arrived in the Anoka area a few years after this disaster had taken place and set up a trading post at the mouth of the Rum River. With the onset of lumbering a few years later a genuine town began to develop. At the time many thought that Anoka, rather the St Anthony, would become the metropolitan center of the region. Yet Anoka lacked both the hydro power of St. Anthony Falls and the cultural energy of Fort Snelling, and it never approached the pace of development set by its rival a few miles downstream.

Nevertheless in 1853 a dam was constructed on the Rum River at its present location and Anoka began its own milling operations. A shoe factory and a potato-starch factory kept the town's economy afloat after the timber gave out, and in 1898 Anoka was chosen as the site of a major medical facility, now known as the Anoka-Metro Regional Treatment Center.

Today Anoka calls itself the Halloween capital of the world. It held its first community-sponsored Halloween celebration in 1920, and has maintained the tradition to this day, though the festivities now stretch out for several weeks in late October, and include parades, bingo, a horseshoe tournament and other athletic contests, costume contests, and block parties.

The Oliver H. Kelly Farm

Just south of Highway 10, a few miles west of Anoka, you'll see the turn-off to the Oliver Kelly Farm (763-441-6896). But be forewarned! You could spend half a day here enjoying the countryside and learning about how farmers farmed back when Minnesota was still a territory.

The park is managed by the Minnesota Historical Society. Its designers have wisely set the farm off from the road and parking area, and as you approach the farmhouse on foot, you also step back in time, to the days when oxen, horses, women and men did the work, and most of the food on the table had been grown very near at hand. Members of the staff at the site wear period costumes, and they can introduce you to the ingenious techniques by which the hard-working settlers coaxed a living out of the soil. In its efforts to make the park authentic, the staff is dedicated to a program of developing heirloom seed varieties, and it's also engaged in breeding a type of horse very similar to the Morgan breed that was widely used in those days.

The Kelly Farm allows us to experience what the life of a typical farmer might have been like during the early years of white settlement in Minnesota, but Oliver Kelly himself was not a typical farmer. When he bought the land in 1849, he knew almost nothing about farming. Before long he became an expert on insects, debt-management, weather, and soil, largely by reading books and through correspondence with other farmers. In 1853, Kelly was among the first to suggest that wild rice be harvested commercially—an idea that came to fruition a century later.

Kelly's enterprise, creative thinking, and expertise eventually got him a job with the U. S. Bureau of Agriculture, and he was sent to other parts of the country to report on farming conditions and methods. During his travels Kelly frequently noted the loneliness and isolation of farm life—which he had also experienced himself, no doubt—and in 1867 he and six associates formed the National Grange of the Patrons of Husbandry. The purpose of the ostensibly "secret" organization was to foster communication between farm families and to educate them in the latest advances in farming technique. The movement spread rapidly during the early 1870s, and by 1875 more than twenty thousand Granges had been set up across the country, with total membership surpassing 850,000. It was at Grange meetings that farmers first came to recognize the need for a political party to advance their common interests. Several parties were formed in due course, and in a number of states, including Minnesota, California, Iowa, Wisconsin, and Illinois, "Granger" laws were passed that helped to regulate railroad and grain storage rates. The Granges also set up their own co-operative stores, banks, grain elevators, and distribution centers. As the movement toward regulation developed strength, however, the role of the Grange itself diminished, and new parties and organizations arose to continue the fight, including the Greenback Party and the Populist Party. Meanwhile, many of the institutions that had developed on a local level failed, due simply to the farmers' lack of business expertise. Within a few years many of the Granges had collapsed, but others survived by returning to the social and educational functions for which they had originally been created. Kelly himself continued to serve as the organization's secretary until 1878.

The Grange played a seminal role in the political battles of the late nineteenth century. And we ought not to refer to it exclusively in the past-tense, either. Today it has 2,800 chapters and over 300,000 members in 37 states. It pursues an agenda of which Oliver Kelly would approve, in which energy issues, the limits of public domain, and the continuing economic health of family farmers and ranchers all figure prominently.

Sauk Rapids and the
Red River Oxcart Trail

As we proceed north on Highway 10, we pass through a flat sandy area following a route that at an earlier time was used as an ox cart trail. The trail was known as "The Woods Trail" which may suggest how the landscape looked at the time. Another trail, "the East Plains Trail" ran in the same direction along the other side of the Mississippi.

The Ox Cart era has not captured the public imagination in quite the same way that the railroads, the steamboats, or even the voyageurs have, yet it marks a fascinating, albeit brief, chapter in the history of the region.

The wooden carts had originally been designed and used locally in the Red River Valley to transport the hides gathered by the French and Indian mixed-blood workers called Metis at their annual buffalo hunts. In the period between the 1840s and the 1860s, the ox cart trails fanned out as a broader network across the prairies to the north and west of the Mississippi.

Furs from the forests and plains of the Canadian hinterlands would be collected at Fort Gary, on the shores of Lake Winnipeg, and brought to St. Paul in long caravans, some reaching more than 200 carts in length. Many of the drivers were Metis, French-Canadians, or Scots. Having deposited their valuable freight, the carts were re-loaded with tobacco, liquor, guns, and other manufactured goods that were hard to come by on the distant outposts to the west.

It was a long journey, and also a noisy one. The carts were usually made entirely of wood, and as the caravans moved slowly across the prairie the squeaking of the axles could be heard five miles away. All the same, it was far easier and cheaper for the inhabitants of the Red River Valley to travel along this route than via a complicated chain of lakes to the Great Lakes, or to proceed north along often-treacherous rivers to Hudson's Bay and thence by ship through arctic waters to the Atlantic. In those days the border between American and British territories had never even been surveyed, much less marked, and one renowned Minnesota trader, Norman "Commodore" Kittson, made a fortune in trading between St. Paul and that part of Canada then known as Prince

Rupert's Land. One of the principle reasons that Minnesota has a border with Canada today, rather than stretching westward laterally into the prairies, is that civic leaders were convinced that the rich forest lands to the north would someday become a part of the United States, rather than Canada, and they wanted Minnesota to partake of the bounty.

Among the most difficult parts of any ox cart journey were the river crossings, and the Mississippi presented one of the greatest challenges. Towns frequently sprang up at the fords. One such crossing was at Sauk Rapids. A trading post was established here as early as 1805, just below the mouth of the Sauk River. In 1850 steamboats began to ply the waters of the Mississippi between Sauk Rapids and St Anthony Falls, and a year later W. H. Wood built a large mansion in the vicinity and named it Lynden Hills. Other settlers arrived, and a store, a hotel, and a jail soon followed. The prominence of the town as a transportation center in Minnesota's early history may be suggested by the fact that its newspaper, the *Sauk Rapids Frontiersman*, was the state's second newspaper.

Sauk Rapid's growth was slowed somewhat when the railroads proceeded westward out into the prairies; it suffered a major setback when most of the downtown area was wiped out by a tornado in 1886, and Saint Cloud eventually overtook it as a regional center.

St. Cloud

The city of St. Cloud bills itself as a crossroads, and it's true that highways of every description pass through or nearby on their way to other places. St Cloud itself draws much of its vitality from the four colleges and universities located there, and it has plenty of coffee shops and restaurants that cater to the student crowd. The downtown area has a long and interesting history, and efforts have recently been made to restore more of the nineteenth-century flavor to its streets and buildings. Brochures are available locally that describe walking tours of various neighborhoods and also the central business district, which has been included on the National Register of Historic Places.

Though there is nothing especially French about the city today, St. Cloud owes its name to the town of the same name on the Seine

River just downstream from Paris. The man who platted St. Cloud, John L. Wilson, happened to be reading a biography of Napoleon at the time, and he was impressed by the fact that the Empress Josephine often paid extended visits to the royal palace there. He thought St. Cloud would be a fine and grandiose name for his riverside town.

In the early days St. Cloud was actually three communities, not one, and they were anything but grand. The central town was inhabited by settlers from the East, but the northerly one had a population made up largely of Southerners, some of whom kept slaves. When editorials began to appear in the local paper lambasting this barbaric practice, the newspaper office was ransacked and the press was destroyed.

St. Cloud is most famous nowadays for the granite that has been quarried in the vicinity since 1868. The granite is still popular with

An abandoned quarry pit

builders—it was recently used to make the F.D.R. and Korean War Memorials in Washington, D.C, for example. At Quarry Park, on the west side of town, you can follow hiking and bike trails past dozens of abandoned quarries, most of which are now filled with water. A few have even been turned into trout farms. With rusting twenty-foot saw blades, old wooden derricks, giant iron scoops, and enormous blocks of rough-hewn granite scattered in piles here and there along the paths, the entire park has the look of an environmental art installation set in the midst of a French Barbizon forest. One of the pits has been outfitted with a swimming hole, and both scuba diving and rock-climbing are allowed at designated sites (320-255-6172).

At the nearby Strearns Counry Historical Museum (320-253-8424), you can learn more about the granite industry, and also hear the tale of St. Cloud's unusual contribution to the auto industry. The museum is top-flight, and the mini-biographies of various nearby towns, from Avon and Freeport to Paynesville and Brooten, may leave you with the impression that they are all worth visiting.

For an excursion closer to the highway, the Munsinger and Clemens Gardens are a good bet. The grounds of the two gardens are located along the east bank of the Mississippi. The Munsinger Gardens were laid out in the 1930s in an informal American pattern, with a lily pond and a bank of pines included. Across the way, the Clemens Gardens are set out in six formal, geometrically shaped plots, with a fountain, myriads of roses, and a traditional English-style "white garden." John L. Wilson probably never imagined, on the day he gave the city of St. Cloud its name, that one section of it might actually take on the appearance of a European palace grounds. Then again, considering how optimistic and even visionary many early settlers in the area were, maybe he did!

Saint John's Abbey

Somewhat further afield, but definitely worth a detour if you have the time, is Saint John's Abbey in nearby Collegeville. The abbey is located on the beautifully wooded grounds of Saint John's University, which was founded by the Benedictine brothers in 1858. When the Benedictines arrived in the area, they'd planned to establish their abbey on the banks of the Mississippi, and in those days the entire area was pretty wild. One of the fathers describes their journey north along the Mississippi River as follows:

The boat left St. Anthony on May 19, and by evening arrived at the point where the Crow River enters the Mississippi. Here a stop was made until the next morning. The craft was merely a boat for transportation of freight, had no conveniences whatsoever for passengers, furnished no meals, not a chair to sit upon—still 50 passengers entered at this place. For two days and one night we sought comfort among the trunks and other freight, and were exposed to ferocious attacks of mosquitoes and had nothing to eat.

On the afternoon of the 20th the boat was moored about two miles below St. Cloud; orders were given to have freight unloaded at this point while passengers were to step out at St. Cloud. About half of the freight was unloaded. Father Bruno and one of the lay brothers were on shore attending to their baggage and the other lay brother remained on board keeping guard over our cask of mass wine for the little cask was an attraction to the deck hands. Before we who were on shore could realize our situation, the boat pushed off and made for Sauk Rapids. Now find a human habitation or even St. Cloud without roads or guides! The lay brother remained with the baggage and Father Bruno set out to explore.

To find St. Cloud was then a rather more difficult task than it would be today, comprising as it did one house and four less dignified edifices and these far apart. On the prairie Father Bruno met a Catholic German, a Mr. Lodermaier, who showed him the direction in which he would find St. Cloud ...

Up to the date of our arrival St. Clouders had not dreamt of making land claims—all looked so hopeless. But our appearance turned the tables and that very night the inhabitants of St. Cloud claimed and staked out the entire prairie between St. Cloud and the crossing of the Sauk River not leaving a single spot in the vicinity for us to locate upon."

On the next day, May 22, Feast of Corpus Christi, the Benedictines held church service for the first time in the attic of a local man.

The altar was placed at one end under the apex of the gable to enable the celebrant to stand upright, but it was necessary, especially at the Elevation, to look upward lest he strike the roof. The narrow space could not contain all who had come for services and so many were compelled to remain on the lower floor and that was fortunate. In the course of the solemnities they noticed that the ceiling—our floor—was giving way and improvised supports with fence rails. Otherwise we might have had a sad accident.

The monks had soon established both a church and a log cabin seminary in St. Cloud, though two years later they moved to their present location in St. Joseph to avoid possible litigation regarding their claim to the building site. The school originally had five students. It has grown considerably since those days, and St John's Abbey is now the largest Benedictine monastery in the Western hemisphere. On the grounds at St. Joseph, you can visit the famous abbey church, designed by the Hungarian architect Marcel Breuer, and described by one art historian on its completion in 1961 as "a milestone in the evolution of the architecture of the Catholic Church in this country." You can also take a look at illuminated manuscripts at the Hill Museum and Monastic Library, which now houses the world's largest collection of manuscript images. The abbey also has a bakery and gift shop, and it can be pleasant to stroll through the woods to the lake nearby, while taking in the ambiance of a pioneer Minnesota institution that's steeped in Old World traditions.

The campus of the College of St. Benedict, in nearby St. Joseph, has an altogether quieter tone, but it's also worth a stop if you're in the mood. The Sacred Heart Chapel has an exquisite interior, and the nuns in attendance both at the chapel and at the museum/gift shop across the street will tell you everything you may want to know about their order, early times in St. Joseph, and the Ojibwe missions further north they may have served at. In fact, they may well be the sharpest and most courteous people you meet on your trip.

Once you've wandered the gardens ajoining the chapel, step across the street to the Local Blend Coffee Shop and Wine Bar (19 Minnesota St. W.) to read the local papers, enjoy a cup of coffee, eavesdrop on the

The childhood home of Charles Lindbergh.

student gossip, and admire the fine paintings on the walls. (The last time we were there some colorful European streetscapes by Father Tupa were on display.)

Little Falls

L ittle Falls is a small town with a large reputation, based on its role as the boyhood home of Charles Lindbergh, who became an international celebrity after flying solo across the Atlantic Ocean from New York to Paris in 1927. The falls after which the town is named has been obscured by a dam ever since 1849, but the drop in water level made the area active in both lumber and flour milling throughout the second half of the nineteenth century. The Old Woods Oxcart trail passed nearby, and Ojibwe chief Hole-in-the-Day also had a camp in the area.

Until Lindbergh made his historic flight, however, his father, Charles Sr., had been the most eminent man in town. The elder Lindbergh served as a U.S. congressman and later ran for the senate, though his stanch isolationism during World War I did not appeal to the voters, and he was defeated. Charles Jr. spent many summers on the Lindberg farm, which still stands on a handsome site south of town, and he lived there year-round from 1917 to 1920. The family eventually donated the site to the state for use as a State Park, and the house was later transferred to the Minnesota Historical Society. The park is small but the campground is wooded and attractive. Most visitors, however, come to see the beautiful old house where "Lucky Lindy" lived before going off to college and eventual world-renown. (For further park info call 320-616-2525.)

The childhood homes of many celebrities are objects of slight curiosity, but with Lindbergh the appeal runs deeper, because he projected an image of sincerity and purpose that seemed to have its source in his Scandinavian Minnesotan small-town upbringing. Though Lindbergh was among the world's most famous men, fame didn't really appeal to him, yet it's easy to image him sleeping on the screen porch of his home in Little Falls, with the summer breeze blowing in through the screens, looking up at the stars and dreaming about flight.

There is a visitor's center (320-632-3154) alongside the house that reminds us of the various pursuits Lindbergh engaged in following his historic solo Atlantic crossing—his work with the airlines designing circumpolar traffic routes, his controversial enthusiasm for the German Luftwaffe, his research in the area of organ transplants, and his later work on environmental issues.

Though Little Falls and Charles Lindbergh are inextricably linked in the public consciousness, the town has several other interesting sights.

At the Charles A. Weyerhaeuser Memorial Museum you can take in the history of the area in a series of displays. It's located at 2151 South Lindbergh Drive, just south of the Lindbergh Historic Site. (320-632-4007). Of even greater interest, perhaps, are the two mansions standing nearby. They're furnished with antiques and original Weyerhaeuser heirlooms, and though they're not always open for inspection, even the exterior and grounds are well worth a look. During the later decades of the nineteenth century the forests to the north and east of Little Falls were filled with lumber camps, and the timber was floated down the Mississippi every spring to mills at various points along the river. The men who managed these vast enterprises, Charles Augustus Weyerhaeuser and Richard Drew Musser, lived in high style in these mansions.

Charles Weyerhaeuser was the son of lumber baron Frederick Weyerhaeuser. As a youth, under his father's aegis, he familiarized himself with various aspects of the family business, and in 1890, when he was 25, he was put in charge of the newly-formed Pine Tree Lumber Company in Little Falls, along with family friend Richard "Drew" Musser. At first, the company made use of an old mill on the east bank of the river while a massive new plant was being built on the opposite shore. The new mill employed almost four hundred workers and produced millions of board feet of lumber annually. After ten years of operation, the debt associated with the company's development had been retired, and the two men built their mansions side by side on the riverbank. They lived here with their families until the timber ran out twenty years later.

Life wasn't quite so comfortable for the two during their early years running the firm, however. You can visit the office building on the east side of the river where daily business operations were conducted. Weyerhaeuser and Musser lived in the attic of this building for several years while running the business. The conditions were cramped...but the daily commute to their offices one floor below perhaps made up for it.

The most interesting place to eat in town is the Black and White Hamburger Shop, 116 SE First Street. The restaurant, located in a former hardware store, has wood floors, an enormous mural on one wall, and memorabilia from the early days of Little Falls on display here and there. The back room has plenty of comfy chairs and a modest used bookstore. And the menu lists plenty of interesting sandwiches, from classic burgers and egg salad to *noveau* vegetarian specialties.

Camp Ripley

At Little Falls we leave Highway 10 for Highway 371, which is fairly new and sometimes all but deserted. The highway follows the path of the Mississippi, though at a distance. We soon come upon the turn-off to Camp Ripley. There is no better place in Minnesota to take in the varied roles played by the military in the state's history.

Fort Ripley was built for a purpose that may seem rather bizarre to us. In the period before Minnesota became a state, violence erupted intermittently between the Dakota and Ojibwe living in the area, and it was thought that tensions would be eased if a third group of Indians was introduced as a buffer. To this end, the Winnebago Indians were moved from their ancestral lands in northern Iowa to a newly-established reservation, and Fort Ripley was constructed in 1848 to oversee the area. In May of the following year a garrison of soldiers from Fort Snelling arrived to man the fort.

The original fort was a three-sided structure, with the open side facing the river. Blockhouses were built at every corner. An enormous amount of land—ninety square miles—was set aside for use in growing food for the soldiers, and also to keep settlers from encroaching too closely on the military defenses. Much of this land was later auctioned off, and homes and farms were soon dotting the countryside.

The Winnebagoes were miserable on their new reservation, however, and they were removed to Mankato a few years later. Life at the fort was drearily uneventful. The mosquitoes were bad, winters were harsh, the soldiers were bored, and to many it must have seemed they had been posted to the very ends of the earth. Few complained when, in 1857, the entire fort was shut down. Once the soldiers were gone, however, conflict increased between the farmers who had settled nearby and the resident Ojibwe, and the fort was hastily reopened.

With the outbreak of the Civil War in 1861, the soldiers at Fort Ripley were immediately transferred to the east, and a volunteer regiment was sent to man the fort. The next summer the Dakota Conflict erupted in southern Minnesota, and when the local Ojibwe chief, Hole-in-the-Day, threatened to initiate a similar conflict on the Upper Mississippi, settlers poured into the fort from far and wide for protection.

Hole-in the-Day's threats of attack never really materialized, but for the next three years Fort Ripley served as a headquarters, supply base, and staging area for military campaigns against the Dakota. During the winter of 1863-64 nearly 500 cavalry troops were quartered there.

By the 1870s the Ojibwa had been moved north to a new reservation on Leech Lake, and the fort's role in frontier life came increasingly into question. When the laundry, commissary, and officers quarters burned down in January of 1877, the War Department decided to close the post permanently, rather than rebuild it. By 1878 Fort Ripley had been abandoned for good.

Today the ruins of the powder magazine are all that remain of Fort Ripley. The grounds lie within the Camp Ripley Military Reservation, which is considered one of the nation's premier National Guard facilities. Sixty thousand troops train here annually, hailing not only from Minnesota, but from states throughout the Midwest, as well as from the Netherlands, Norway, and Great Britain. The camp is the United States official winter combat training center, and it's equipped with state-of-the-art combat simulators that allow instructors to gauge a recruit's prog-

ress using computers and lasers, without endangering anyone or wasting valuable ammunition. Guard members are also trained to patrol airports and power plants for suspected terrorist activity. Many of the men trained at Camp Ripley in recent years have been stationed in Iraq, and it's a strange footnote to history that a facility originally built to maintain peace between warring tribes of Indians 150 years ago, is now training soldiers to maintain peace between warring factions of Iraqis in the far-off Middle East.

You can't actually visit the site of old Fort Ripley, though a few miles up the highway you can gaze across the river from an overlook to the area where it once stood. However, you can stop in at the modern camp to visit the Minnesota Military Museum (320-632-7374). It offers a variety of exhibits focusing not only on the whiz-bang technology and heroic detail of modern warfare, but also on the history of Minnesota's military personnel and how military life relates to the larger social fabric. The old tanks and helicopters in the yard are fun to climb around on even if the musuem happens to be closed.

The Ripley Esker

A mile or two north of Camp Ripley on Hwy 371, turn right onto County 48 and follow it east for 0.7 miles. You'll see a low hill stretching across the horizon in the distance in front of you. That's the Ripley Esker. When you reach County Road 282, you can take it north to drive along the top of the esker for a mile or two.

An esker is a large snake-like pile of rocks left by a glacier. Fifteen to twenty thousand years ago glaciers covered the entire area. As the atmosphere began to heat up, melt water started to drain through and under the retreating sheets of ice. Over time enormous piles of sand and gravel were deposited on the beds of these sub-glacial rivers. When the glaciers finally disappeared entirely, rocky ridges remained to identify where those rivers had once flowed.

The Ripley Esker is not dramatic. It varies in height from ten to fifty feet above the surrounding plain, and is often two to three hundred feet wide. It runs across the countryside for more than six miles, though at several places more recent geologic activity has obscured its path. The rocks that make up the Ripley Esker, true to their origins in the Lake Superior basin, include Lake Superior agates and other rocks from that region. The esker is most easily seen in the spring and fall, when the absence of leaf cover make the landforms more pronounced. It may be interesting to imagine, as we scan the countryside, that at the time the Ripley Esker was emerging from beneath the retreating wall of ice, the region was inhabited by woolly mammoths, saber-toothed tigers, and enterprising hunters who stalked and killed these enormous beasts with hand-made stone tools.

Crow Wing

Following the highway north past Little Falls, we come upon two communities—Crow Wing and Brainerd—that exemplify the changes that took place when the railroad arrived in the area in 1870.

The name Crow Wing, which has been applied to a county, a city, a river, and a state park in this area, is actually a slight misnomer. The Ojibwe name for the river was "Raven Feather," as several early explorers in the region noted. Scholars reason that most of the settlers com-

The abandoned townsite at Crow Wing State Park is a good place to ponder the early history of the region.

ing into the area were from the east, however, where the raven is a far less common bird than the crow. This might explain the name-change, though it might also have come about simply because "crow wing" is easier to say than "raven-feather."

Under whatever name, the river had been one of the most important avenues of travel for Dakota and Ojibwe moving back and forth from the Mississippi to the prairies for generations, and as early as 1826 a trading post was built where the two rivers meet. Ten years later a more substantial fort was built and Crow Wing became a trading center for the upper Mississippi. In 1866 seven white families lived in the village along with twenty-three families of Ojibwe and mixed-bloods. One early historian of the period estimated that when the trappers and traders passing through the area are taken into account, the population of Crow Wing might at one time have risen as high as 600 souls.

Very little remains today of that once-bustling town. In 1870 the Northern Pacific Railroad decided to cross the Mississippi at a point eight miles upstream, and the town of Brainerd was born at that point. Brainerd was also chosen as a supply and repair center for the railroad line, and the city grew rapidly, soon eclipsing its neighbor to the south.

In fact, many of the houses in Crow Wing were simply moved to Brainerd, and the others were eventually torn down. The one house that stands there today, that of the trader Clement Beaulieu, was moved to a nearby farm and altered several times. It has only recently been returned to its original site.

In 1768, long before the first white traders set foot in the area, the confluence of the Crow Wing and the Mississippi was the site of a major confrontation between Ojibwe and Dakota warriors. A vast contingent of Dakota braves had came north from the Minnesota River Valley in a flotilla of more than a hundred canoes to regain the rich territory in the vicinity of Mille Lacs that they'd lost more than thirty years earlier to the Ojibwe. As they were returning downstream after attacking the Ojibwe camp, they fell into an ambush laid by Ojibwe warriors at the confluence of the two rivers. The battle raged for three days before the Dakota finally withdrew in the night and continued down the Mississippi, completing their 600 mile canoe trip with only half of the men they'd started out with.

A visit to Crow Wing State Park (218-829-8022) will amply reward both the historian and the nature-lover. You can review that famous battle of 1768 while strolling the now peaceful environs in which it took place. You can examine the wagon ruts created by the Red River oxcarts that once moved their loads of buffalo hides and trade goods back and forth through the area along the Big Woods Trail. And you can take a look at the Greek Revival house built by Clement H. Beaulieu, who was in charge of the American Fur Company operations at Crow Wing during the twilight years of that industry. The local graveyards tell the tale of a village that grew and died on the spot.

The muskrat and beaver that once drew trappers to the area are still around, and you might catch a glimpse of a passing deer or coyote. The placid waters of the two rivers beckon even the inexperienced canoeist, and considering the beauty and abundant natural charm of the place, it's fair to say that Crow Wing not only lost, but also gained, when civilization up and moved to the railroad river crossing eight miles upstream.

Brainerd

To take the measure of Brainerd's sudden appearance on the face of the land, it would be enough for us to consider that in 1870, it consisted of a single log trading post surrounded by a few tents and lean-tos. Three years later it had 21 stores, 18 hotels and boarding houses, 15 saloons, 5 churches and the Northern Pacific railway station. The town's name was chosen to honor the wife of the first president of the Northern Pacific, whose maiden name was Brainerd, and the choice may well have been apt, considering the bounty brought to the locale by the rails running through it. The first train arrived from Duluth on March 11, 1871, and regular passenger service commenced not long afterward. Rail connections to the Twin Cities were completed seven years later.

The tenor of life was not entirely genteel in those early days. Most of the hotels and saloons in town catered to the needs of the workers employed at the repair yard of the Northern Pacific Railroad or at the lumber mills that processed the timber floating downstream from the pine woods to the north. The pace of town life became even more vigorous when the lumberjacks themselves came into town, flush with cash after a long hard winter in the woods. The economy of the region was given added buoyancy by the iron mining operations taking place at the Cuyuna Range to the east. And by 1910, when the timber to the north had been exhausted, a new industry was already getting a grip on the area—tourism.

A visitor to Brainerd today is likely to drive right past the Potlatch paper mill on the banks of the Mississippi and the Northern Pacific railyard on the east end of town. Both of these historic institutions, though still functioning, have relatively little impact on the life of the community. Yet it might be worthwhile to take a look at that railyard, much of which remains just as it was when Brainerd was the headquarters of the Northern Pacific Railway. Many East Coast investors blamed this railroad line for the failure of the New York branch of Jay Cooke and Company, which led to the financial crash of 1873.

The nation, and the railroad, did survive the crash, and by the 1880s the Northern Pacific was expanding its facility in Brainerd. Much of the railyard burned to the ground in 1886, and a reporter for the Brainerd

The Northern Pacific railyard in Brainerd.

Dispatch described the event in vivid detail, seemingly oblivious to its destructive nature:

> *The flames lighted up the country for miles around and in the darkness of the night, with the flames roaring skyward, and the clouds of sparks and cinders being carried by the wind out over the city, [it] made a grand sight.*

The Northern Pacific rebuilt the rail yard, and by 1890 it was employing more than a thousand people locally. During the 1930s the operating and engineering headquarters for the line were moved to Livingstone, Montana, which stood near the center of its expanse, and the Brainerd facility fell into decline. It finally closed up shop in 1981. Nowadays some of the buildings have been refitted for use by light industry, and the entire complex is on the National Register of Historic Places.

Visitors are more likely to be drawn to Brainerd by the more than 400 lakes within a 50-mile radius of the city, and the 150 resorts and campgrounds lining their shores. This fascinating confluence of the old and new, the industrial and the leisurely, finds it fitting symbol in the outsized icon of Paul Bunyan.

What many children remember best about their first family vacation is the candy in the shop at the resort, the gooey worms their dad or mom helped them put on their fish-hooks, and the towering statue of Paul Bunyan they visited in Brainerd along the way.

Everyone knows that Paul was a lumberjack. Most of us know that he had a big blue ox named Babe. Walt Disney made a movie, after all, though the tales we learned at school have that element of fantastic exaggeration that does not always appeal to children. Whatever the entertainment value of the stories may be, it remains an intriguing question—Where did they come from in the first place?

No one knows for sure, though most explanations sound as generic and far-fetched as some of the stories themselves. One interesting theory holds that the Paul Bunyan stories originated in Canada, in events associated with the Papineau Rebellion of 1837, a movement on the part of the citizens of Quebec province to resist the union of upper and lower Canada. When the movement's requests for reform were summarily rejected by the British authorities, open rebellion broke out, and a series of battles took place in the vicinity of the Ottawa River. Eventually the two Canada's were merged into a single state, though in Quebec, Pabineau's Rebellion is commemorated as the Journée nationale des patriotes (Patriots Day) on the day set aside by the government for Victoria Day.

What does all of this have to do with a statue in Brainerd, Minnesota? Many of the skirmishes of the Papineau Rebellion took place near the Ottawa River, which was a main highway used by the forest industry to move logs. Legend has it that a group of loggers participated in the rebellion against the British, and among them a giant of a man named Paul Bonjean, who was also referred to as Bonyenne. "Bonyenne" is a colloquial French-Canadian expression of astonishment meaning "Oh my God!" or something of the sort. A set of stories dealing with lumber camp life was also going around in those days, centered on the larger-than-life exploits of a real lumberjack named Big Joe Mufferaw. These two bodies of narrative were conflated and made their way westward with the advancing tide of the lumber industry. In northern Michigan the name was Anglicized and Paul for the first time began to operate with a Blue Ox as a sidekick.

Though historians have attempted to identify this or that famous logger with Paul Bunyan, many elements of the Paul Bunyan stories could easily derive from a stock of trickster tales centered on "Ti-Jean" or Little John, that were told at French fur trading outposts as far back as the seventeenth century, and also from Native American folklore. In short, the Paul Bunyan legends combine a variety of perspectives on woodland life during the frontier days in the Great Lakes and Mississippi Valley region.

In 1906 a Michigan news-paperman named James Mac-Gillivray collected a few Paul Bunyan stories from the lumber camps and wrote an article about them. The Red River Lumber Company made use of Paul in a series of advertising campaigns during the 1920s. The novelist John Dos Passos further enhanced the mighty logger's stature in the 1930s by making use of him to describe the independent American worker during a

Bemidji's Paul Bunyan

time of labor unrest. And poet W. H. Auden and composer Benjamin Britten found it worthwhile to collaborate on an opera devoted to the lumberjack hero. Paul had entered the cultural mainstream.

As tourists and outdoorsmen gradually replaced the lumberjacks in the forests of Northern Minnesota, Paul's popularity actually increased, and eventually statues of him were erected not only in Brainerd, but also in Bemidji and Akeley, Minnesota, in Eau Claire, Wisconsin, and in various cities in California, Maine, Idaho, Washington, and Oregon. Of course, the tales themselves are localized wherever they're told. It's said in these parts that the ten-thousand lakes of Minnesota are Paul and Babes footprints. In the Southwest the story goes that Paul created the

Grand Canyon by dragging his ax, and in Oregon it's said that Mount Hood is really just a pile of rocks Paul used to put out his campfire.

Brainerd's statue of Paul has him sitting down, and children delight in the fact that as they approach, the giant lumberjack greets them by name! The statue is located on Highway 18 seven miles east of town, at This Old Farm, which has a variety of other exhibits, frontier buildings, and antiques for sale.

Brainerd does have a downtown area, and the Front Street Cafe (616 Front Street) would be a good place to grab a bite while reflecting on the town's early history. If you stop at the Crow Wing County Historical Museum at 320 Laurel Street, you can see one of the ox carts that once passed back and forth through the area carrying buffalo hides. West of the Mississippi at 801 W. Washington Street, you may be impressed by the pies at the West Side Cafe, where "coffee is served by the hour, rather than the cup." Brainerd's famous racetrack is located seven miles north of town on highway 371. But so much development has taken place along the highways leading through Brainerd, Baxter, and Nisswa, that many visitors can hardly wait to proceed out into the woods and lakes of the surrounding area. Brainerd is known as Minnesota's premier golfing town. In fact, with more than 30 golf courses in the area, designed by the likes of Arnold Palmer and Robert Trent Jones, *Golf Digest* recently ranked Brainerd a surprising 40th best in the world as a golfing destination.

As the pine forests of Northern Minnesota fell to the saw and ax, Brainerd's rail connections and convenient position on the edge of the northern lakes district made it a popular tourist destination. A traveller could board a train in Minneapolis in the morning, arrive in Nisswa by 2:30 in the afternoon, and continue on to resorts on the nearby lakes via steam-powered launch. Once the roads were improved and automobiles became more widely available after World War I, the tourist industry grew by leaps and bounds.

Today the countryside roundabout is strewn with resorts, many of them still owned and operated by the families that started them up several generations ago. The oldest is Ruttger's Bay Lake Lodge south of Deerwood, which opened in 1898 and is still going strong. Madden's and Craguns are both sprawling places with recreational facilities to meet almost any need, from fishing and golf to bird-watching and badminton. To get a flavor of these charming resorts, make a visit to Grandview Lodge, on the northeast end of Gull Lake. The central lodge sits amid towering white pines on a hill overlooking the broad expanse of the lake. It's listed as a National Historic Site. Its restaurant, Sherwood Forest, is housed in a 1920s lodge a few miles down the way.

A fifteen minute detour up Highway 210 will bring you to the town of Crosby, which lies in the heart of the Cuyuna Iron Range. This range was much smaller than the Mesabi Range to the east, and the deposits appeared in deep-running veins rather than on the surface, making the ore more difficult to extract. But the manganese content of the ore was unusually high, which made it a valuable commodity, especially during the world wars, when imports of manganese were restricted. As you drive toward Crosby, you can see the lakes and hills created by the mining activity, and a visit to Croft Mine Historical Park (218-546-5466) will fill you in on the local history of the industry.

Leech Lake Reservation

On the journey north from Brainerd to Leech Lake along Highway 371 we move by imperceptible degrees into a more rugged sphere. The strip-malls of Baxter seem but a distant memory, and the larger wilder lakes ahead—Leech, Cass, and Winnebegoshish—seem manlier and more remote. The territory was considered a sort of paradise by the Dakota and Ojibwe tribes that battled for possession during the eighteenth and early nineteenth centuries. Much of the land is now a part of the Leech Lake Indian Reservation.

The region has been inhabited by Native Americans since at least 1000 AD, and by the 1600's, the Dakota Indians had several communities at Leech Lake. The Ojibwe began to move west into the region during the mid-to-late 1700's and established settlements on a few of the lake's small islands.

The reservation was created as part of the treaty of 1855, by which the Ojibwe ceded much of their land in northern Minnesota to white settlement. The original plan was to consolidate all the Ojibwe bands at

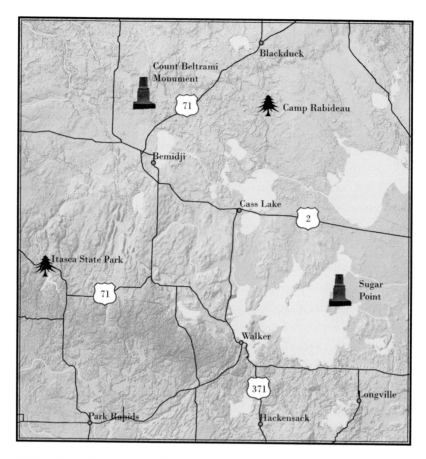

White Earth Reservation, but this proved unworkable, and Leech Lake Reservation remained active. The reservation is made up of eleven communities, with Cass Lake serving as tribal headquarters.

The area that encompasses Leech, Cass, and Winnebegoshish Lakes is actually a broad shallow drainage area (yet another remnant of Glacial Lake Agassiz) and many parts of it are swampy. You'll notice that, unlike other resort areas, some sections of lakeshore remain undeveloped, and there are plenty of bullrushes here and there. This does not make for good swimming beaches but the migrating ducks love it, and wild rice also flourishes in this environment.

The entire area was logged at the turn of the twentieth century (in the midst of much legal chicanery in the handling of logging rights on the reservation) and the upland regions are now mostly second-growth forest, with a smattering of hardwoods and pines in a sea of aspen.

In the early 1990s the Leech Lake Tribal Council contracted with the Bureau of Indian Affairs to participate in a pilot program that granted it a greater degree of self-governance. The State remains responsible for criminal and some civil jurisdiction over Indians on the reservation, but the Leech Lake Tribe controls hunting, fishing, and ricing activities. It issues its own automobile license plates, has its own ambulance service, and operates its own day care facilities, schools, and junior college. It also operates two casinos in the area, one in Cass Lake and the other in Walker, which make the tribe the largest employer in the county. Restaurants, gift shops, motels, and convenience stores have also been established with the help of capital generated by the casinos.

At one time wild rice made up as much as 25 percent of the Ojibwe diet, and later it became an important cash crop, though the market for naturally grown and harvested wild rice has been undercut in recent years by commercially grown rice from Canada and California. Yet market fluctuations notwithstanding, harvesting wild rice has remained not only a practical necessity for the Ojibwe, but also a sacred undertaking. In fact, their origin myth relates that in earliest days the Ojibwe were told to live "where the food grows on the water." And as the rice develops in the course of the summer, sections of Leech, Cass, and Winnebegoshish Lakes begin to look more like prairie lands than bodies of water.

If you explore the backroads around these beautiful lakes in the late summer, you may come upon drying areas for the rice and roadside stands selling the native product. The stuff isn't cheap, but it isn't easy to harvest either, and if you're interested in unusual flavors, or in indigenous cultures, why not purchase some of this genuinely "wild" wild rice and try it?

Walker

The hills on which Walker sits were formed by debris left by the glaciers during their most recent visit to the area, about 10,000 years ago. The region was highly prized by both Ojibwe and Dakota tribes, and skirmishes were not uncommon in early times.

The Ojibwe referred to Leech Lake as Ga-sagasquadjimekag sagai-igun, which means the-place-of-the-leech-lake. Evidently early visitors to the area had seen an enormous leech swimming in the waters near shore. French fur traders visited the area during the eighteenth century, and once the British had defeated the French in the Seven Years War, British traders moved in to set up a post on Otter Tail Point in Leech Lake in 1785. A year later they built another one on what is now known as Oak Point.

In 1805 Zebulon Pike visited the British fort on Leech Lake, where he and his men were well-housed and cordially entertained. Before continuing on his exploratory journey, however, Pike ordered his men to shoot down the Union Jack from its flagpole, as a reminder to the British that since the War of American Independence, they had been operating on American soil.

The next white explorer of note to pass this way was Lewis Cass. He arrived in 1820 with a party of forty men in search of the true source of the Mississippi. Cass didn't find what he was looking for, but one member of his party, Henry Schoolcraft, was taking very good notes. But more about that later. At the time of the Cass expedition the area was a part of Michigan territory, and Cass was the territorial governor. Evidently the requirements for high office in those days included wilderness survival skills. Well, Lewis Cass was a man of unusual qualities. By the time he arrived in northern Minnesota, he had already risen to the rank of Brigadier General in the War of 1812, and served as governor of Michigan Territory for eight years; he was later chosen by President Jackson to fill the post of Secretary of War, which embroiled him in the violent Black Hawk War of 1832 in southern Wisconsin; from 1836 to 1842 he was minister to France, and for the next twelve he served in the U.S. Senate, with a short break to run for president in 1848. James Buchanan appointed him Secretary of State in 1857.

When cartographer Joseph Nicollet passed this way during his scientific expedition of 1836, he described Leech Lake in the following terms:

> *The perimeter of the lake is at least 160 miles. Twenty-seven rivers empty into it coming from every direction on the horizon.*

There are plenty of open horizons in the Leech Lake area.

One river flows from it to join the Mississippi: its name is Leech Lake River. There are nine large bays...and six large capes...The population exceeds 1,000 inhabitants, more than 200 of which are warriors.

Most of the nine large bays Nicollet refers to were submerged into a single larger body of water in 1882 when a dam was built on the river flowing out of the lake. At the time Minneapolis was the nation's largest flour producer, and it was imperative that a steady flow of water be maintained to operate the mills. The Leech Lake Dam was only the second ever to be built by the Army Corp of Engineers to control the Mississippi, and at 3,500 feet from end to end, it remains the longest. It had the effect of raising the water level at Leech Lake by four to seven feet, which effectively connected several distinct bays to form the lake we know today.

As the railroad followed the lumber companies north in search of new trees to fell, a small settlement developed on the west shores of Leech Lake. In 1896 it was incorporated under the name Walker, in honor of the Minneapolis tycoon T. B. Walker, who owned large tracts of land in the area and operated lumber mills in Crookston and other river cities. Once the rail connections had been established, resorts sprang up around the lake, and Walker almost immediately became a hunting and fishing hotspot—a role that it continues to play today.

The Battle of Sugar Point

Things were not entirely peaceful during those early years of white settlement, however. In fact the Leech Lake area was the site of the last true Indian battle in American history.

The background to the story is interesting, in that it allows us a glimpse of how the transition from forest lands to tourist mecca took place, and what was gained and lost in the process. Once the Ojibwe had given up much of their land in northern Minnesota, the government found it expedient to set up Indian agencies to accommodate their neighbors. These agencies distributed the annual payment that had been agreed upon in the treaties, and they often had schools, farms, blacksmith shops, mills, and other accoutrements of "civilization." The local Indians found their presence troubling, to say the least, and often agitated to have them removed from the reservations. One such agency was built at Leech Lake in 1855, immediately after the treaty establishing the reservation had been signed.

The first step was to build a road for sixty-five miles through the woods from the then-bustling town of Crow Wing up to the lake. Hitherto the area had been accessible only by canoe or dogsled.

Congress appropriated funds for the agency the following year, and a missionary was sent to buy land and clear it for cultivation. He also started work on a mission house and a blacksmith shop.

The white settlers found it prudent to evacuate the agency during the Dakota conflict of 1862, but by 1865 a sawmill had been built, land had been cleared, and the agency was once again up and running.

During the following decades, as shady timber deals and heavy-handed law enforcement became the norm, the Ojibwe became increasingly irascible. The dam that was built at the outlet from Leech Lake in 1882 may have been a good thing for the millers in Minneapolis, but it flooded more than forty thousand acres of the local wild rice supply, which did little to improve the Ojibwe diet.

Tensions came to a head in a series of events centering on the figure of chief Bug-O-Nay-Gee-Shig (often referred to simply as "old Bug"). In 1896, two years prior to the Battle of Sugar Point, Bug-O-Nay-Gee-Shig, had been called to Duluth to testify in a bootlegging trial involving another member of the tribe. The charges were eventually dropped for lack of evidence and Bug-O-Nay-Gee-Shig was let go, though for some reason the court neglected to pay his witness or mileage fees, and he was left to walk a hundred miles through the winter snow back to his home on Leech Lake. Bug-O-Nay-Gee-Shig vowed that he would never again respond to such a court summons.

It was common practice in those days, however, for U.S. Marshalls, some of them Ojibwe mixed-bloods, to arrest local Ojibwe and bring them to court on drinking charges or to summons them as witnesses in other cases. It was inevitable that Bug-O-Nay-Gee-Shig would be summoned again, and shortly thereafter he was. He and his band, secure in their community out on Bear Island, ignored the summons. He was therefore held in contempt of court by the white authorities, and when, in September of 1898, he arrived at the Onigum Agency to pick up his annuity payment, he was arrested for a second time. He cried out for help, and with the assistance of more than twenty braves he succeeded in escaping to Bear Island, which lies at the opposite side of the lake from the agency. Warrants were in due time issued for all the Ojibwe involved, and twenty soldiers who had been dispatched from Fort Snelling were sent out to Bear Island to confer with the Indians. The wary Bug-O-Nay-Gee-Shig was not interested in meeting with the soldiers, however, so another eighty were dispatched with more forceful intent.

On October 5th these soldiers were clumsily towed on a large barge to the shores of Bear Island by two steamers loaded with officers and newspaper reporters. The island was deserted. The flotilla moved on to Bug-O-Nay-Gee-Shig's cabin on Sugar Point, which lies at the tip of a peninsula on the mainland extending down from the north toward Bear Island. The cabin was empty. The soldiers paused to eat lunch, and while they were thus at their ease a rifle discharged by accident. Thinking that the battle had commenced, the nineteen Ojibwe braves hiding in the woods nearby opened fire with their Winchesters. The commanding officer was killed, and the reporters on board the steamers turned tail, with the Indians firing on them from shore as they made a hasty retreat back to Walker.

With the departure of the steamers, the troops no longer had a means of escape, and they entrenched themselves at Bug-O-Nay-Gee-Shig's cabin to await the attack. The next day a rescue operation arrived from Walker, but was repelled after saving only a single wounded soldier. That evening, with a note of rising hysteria in the air, more than two hundred national guardsmen arrived by rail from the south with a Gatling gun in tow. It was expected that a general uprising of the Ojibwe was imminent, and troops were set off to Deer River, Cass Lake, and the Winnibegoshish dam. Perhaps word of the soldier's arrival reached the Ojibwe in the night. In any case, the next morning, appeased by the entreaties of a white priest named Father Alyosius, whom the Indians trusted, and with no further objective in mind than to protect their chief from being arrested, the braves allowed the soldiers to depart in their ungainly barge, and the guardsmen met the retreating men out on the lake. The battle of Sugar Point was over. Seven soldiers had been killed and sixteen had been wounded. The Ojibwe had suffered no casualties.

Bug-O-Nay-Gee-Shig never was arrested, though thirteen of his compatriots served a few month's time in prison before being pardoned by President McKinley.

The Battle of Sugar Point does not rank among the more heated or bloody in the long-running feud between natives and whites, but it is often referred to as the last true battle of the Indian Wars.

Chippewa National Forest

The Leach Lake Reservation is entirely contained with the Chippewa National Forest, which was the first such forest established to the east of the Mississippi River. Many factors were at play in Theodore Roosevelt's decision to create the forest, but one played an especially important early role—the Minnesota Federation of Women's Club. The wives of some of the state's most influential political leaders were members of the federation, and when it took up a cause, it was a force to be reckoned with. The federation was disturbed by the encroachment of lumber operations into what one member described as "the last remaining public white pine forest in America."

The forests had long been preserved by the existence of the Ojibwe reservations, but with the passage of the Dawes Act in 1887, tribal lands were divvied out in eighty-acre parcels to individual Ojibwe families. The remaining reservation land—more than 80 percent in all—suddenly became available for public sale, as if by magic.

The Women's Federation and its allies first proposed to make the area into a national park, and one wealthy sportsman from Chicago even financed a junket to the area on the Great Northern Railroad for 100 congressmen. The congressmen were not convinced, however, that the region had enough dramatic features to justify such an enormous forest set-aside, and to local congressmen it was obvious that the financial gain to be got from lumbering far exceeded anything a national park might bring in.

The Federation did, however, succeed in forestalling the immediate sale of northwoods timber. Lowering their sights, the group began to work in concert with the Agricultural Experiment Station in Grand Rapids to develop a more modest proposal for preservation along with a "rational cut" of timber, with added provisions for reforestation.

This new plan had greater appeal for Minnesota lumber companies, and after some serious lobbying it received the blessing of Gifford Pinchot, a friend of Theodore Roosevelt and head of the newly created National Division of Forestry (later renamed the U.S. Forest Service).

To modern-day conservationists, it may be obvious that the basic provisions of the plan favored the lumber interests, as 95 percent of the newly-available forests were to be sold to them, with only five percent to be preserved along lake shores and highways for aesthetic reasons. Meanwhile, the Ojibwe who actually owned the land were not only being forced by law to turn it over, but were also forced to accept whatever price-tag the federal government happened to put on it.

On the other hand, the creation of Chippewa National Forest was historic, being the country's first congressionally-mandated national forest, and also the first established with a view to preservation and regeneration. Reviewing the act that created the forest, Forestry Chief Pinchot would later say, "Here was the first application of Forestry to

Government-owned forests in America. . . . Without the farsighted and patriotic support of the Minnesota Federation of Women's Clubs, it would have been impossible."

Today the Chippewa National Forest spreads itself across 1.6 million acres of the state, with aspen, birch, pines, and maples forests, 1,300 lakes, more than 900 miles of rivers and streams, and 400,000 acres of wetlands. It has 23 campgrounds, nearly all of which are on or near a lake, and more than 400 backpacking sites. It has become famous in recent times for the large stretches of relatively undisturbed wetlands it contains, and also as home to the largest population of bald eagles in the lower 48 states. As you drive along you're likely to see one soaring above you with its white tail and head flashing in the sunlight.

At their low ebb during the 1960s, there were fewer than 12 known pairs in the entire Chippewa National Forest. Today the number has soared well past 150 pairs. This dramatic turnaround has been made possible by the federal ban on DDT, and a careful monitoring of habitat. Eagles mate for life and return to the same nest year after year, making it imperative that established nests remain undisturbed.

In the Chippewa National Forest, a management plan is developed for each breeding pair, and buffer zones have been created to further increase the likelihood of breeding success. The results of this care have been impressive, although the number of breeding pairs seems to have reached a plateau in recent years, suggesting that the forest is approaching its proper "carrying capacity" for the species.

You might happen to see an eagle overhead at any time or place in the forest, but your best chance would be at dawn and dusk, and the open expanses of the big lakes offer the best viewing opportunities. Don't forget to scan the trees along shore, too. You might see an eagle perched on a branch enjoying the sunshine or waiting for a fish to surface in the water below.

A Detour West of Walker

There are plenty of places to eat in Walker, but if you're in the mood for a little more driving, take Highway 34 southwest past the towns of Akeley, Nevis, and Dorset. Each town has an unusual claim to fame.

Akeley sports the largest statue of Paul Bunyan in the state—it's hard to miss as you pass through town. Just west of Nevis you'll come upon the Heart of Minnesota Emu Ranch, where they let you hug the fuzzy creatures, and explain the role played by emus in a variety of skin-care products. Dorset lays its claim to fame on its four restaurants. (Here's where the eating comes in.) With a population of 22, Dorset is perhaps more well-endowed with eating places, per capita, than any other city in Minnesota, and maybe the world. While digesting your meal, you can wander over to Sister Wolf Books and do a little browsing, or cap things off with a cup of espresso.

Cass Lake

The town of Cass Lake was once a major rail yard for the Northern Pacific Railroad and also the center of lumbering activities, with a population that exceeded 7,000 people. Today fewer than a thousand people live in Cass Lake, though at Lyle's Logging Camp downtown you can take a step back in time to a more vibrant period in the region's history. The entire museum was built by a man named Lyle Chisholm, who became a logger at the age of 11, and after a long career spent largely in the woods, felt that the way of life he'd experienced ought to be preserved for future generations.

The largest island in Cass Lake, Star Island, is also noteworthy, though you'll need a boat to get out there. There is a second lake contained within the island. Star Island was once the home of Chief Oziwindib, the man who guided Henry Schoolcraft to the source of the Mississippi in 1832 (see pages 169-175).

The headquarters of the Chippewa National Forest

Cass Lake is the headquarters of the Consolidated Ojibwe Indian Agency, which oversees the administration of seven reservations stretching across the northern part of the state from White Earth and Red Lake in the west to Grand Portage on the shores of Lake Superior to the east.

The headquarters of the Chippewa National Forest is also located in Cass Lake (200 Ash Ave, 218-335-8600). The three-story log headquarters building is notable itself, being constructed in the Finnish style from materials gathered entirely within the borders of the state. The hand-crafted details in the interior are also worth a look, as are the exhibits devoted to the natural history of the area.

The CCC and Camp Rabideau

The forestry building was built in 1936 by young men who had signed up for the Civilian Conservation Corp. In fact, impressive stone bridges, pavilions, walls, and other structures can be found at many state parks, courtesy of the CCC. To get a better idea of what that program was all about, take a detour along the east shore of Cass Lake and north on County 39 toward the town of Blackduck. You'll pass several attractive campsites, Norway Beach (check out the visitor's center) and the Knutson Dam, a beautiful campground and picnic area and also a good place for bird-watching. Ten miles further up the road you'll come to Camp Rabideau. Of the more than 2,500 CCC camps that were established across the United States during the 1930s, this is the best preserved of only three that are still standing.

The CCC was created in 1933 by President Roosevelt to revitalize the economy during the darkest days of the Depression. Roosevelt's idea was a simple one. Men needed work, the woods needed to be tended to—so, put the men to work in the woods. During its years of operation the CCC provided jobs and training for almost three million workers. Trees were planted, fire towers were constructed, bridges were built, trails were cleared, and recreation areas were established, often with sturdy stone buildings and shelters. Today when we see a handsome stone visitor center in a park that's been built to massive proportions, we're likely to say, 'It looks like the CCC was here." Perhaps a more significant contribution is something we're less likely to attribute to the Corp: enrollees in the program planted an estimated three billion trees from 1933 and 1942.

Camp Rabideau

The nation's economy was in deep trouble when Roosevelt assumed office, and he went to work immediately devising schemes to revitalize it. The CCC was among his pets. The president called an emergency session of Congress to authorize the program, which he promoted as a plan to combat soil erosion and rebuild America's forests. Labor leaders were opposed to the program, which they feared would undercut the employment that was available, but the bill flew through Congress all the same, and arrived on the President's desk a mere four days later. The first enrollee was inducted on April 7th, not much more than a month after Roosevelt had assumed office. Such rapid implementation of a program had never before been seen during peace time.

The most immediate problem facing the CCC was that most of the unemployed youths were in the East, while most of the projects were to be found in the forests of the West. Therefore, the U.S. Army was put to work on a massive scale ferrying inductees to their appointed tasks. Meanwhile, the Departments of Agriculture and Interior began hastily to devise the specific tasks that were to be performed by the workers, while the Department of Labor shouldered the task of finding and enrolling participants. It was a rare example of coordinated effort between four federal agencies with a minimum of red tape and a maximum of results.

All would have been for naught, however, if no one had stepped forward to participate. As it happened young men signed up in droves, eager to earn some money and see a bit of the world without actually joining the army. The public was wildly supportive, and even the Soviet Union found the program commendable.

Under one of the unusual provisions of the plan, the workers received $30 a month, though $22 dollars of it was sent home each month to their families. This helped to stimulate the economy around the camps, and also in more heavily populated parts of the country that were equally hard pressed for funds.

Although the primary objectives of the program were work-related, educational opportunities were also a part of the mix, and more than 40,000 enrollees were taught to read and write under the CCCs auspices. Though they were excluded from the program at first, eventually more that 80,000 Native Americans also took part.

By the time the program was finally terminated with the coming of World War II, the Corp had built 97,000 miles of roads and more than 3,000 fire towers. Erosion had been arrested on more than 20 million acres of farm land. Grazing land had been improved, streams had been restocked, and flooding averted on a massive scale.

As the economy gained strength and employment prospects improved, enrollment in the CCC fell off, though more that 200,000 were still at work. After the Japanese attack at Pearl Harbor, the war effort made attempts to improve wildlife habitat rather beside the point, though the vote to finally abolish the Corp was a very close one, as the program had always been popular and not all young men were fit to fight for their country overseas.

The first contingent of young men to arrive at Camp Rabideau were from Missouri. Later that year the Missourians were trucked out to California and a crew of Minnesota boys was brought in. That company remained at work until the program was terminated in 1941. During that time they built the Blackduck ranger station and several fire towers, and they also became adept at hunting up the folks who got lost every year during berry-picking season.

Today fifteen of the original twenty-five buildings are still standing, and interpretative displays shed light on both the camp and the broader history of that fascinating era. Guided tours are conducted during the summer months.

Bemidji

Bemidji is a town that seems to have everything one might want in a northern Minnesota community. It has a college, and also a giant statue of Paul Bunyan. It's located on the shores of a beautiful lake, and the Mississippi River flows in and out of the lake within the city limits. In fact, the Ojibwe name for the lake is "Bemiji-gau-maug" which means "cutting sideways through or diagonally" which was a reference to the path the Mississippi River takes through the lake.

The Pembina Ox Cart Trail that we've been following throughout our journey passed nearby. Bemidji is home to Minnesota's oldest summer theater company, The Paul Bunyan Playhouse (what else?). Other cultural highlights include International Days, which takes place twice each summer under the auspices of Concordia Language Villages. During these festivals you can learn about Concordia's language immersion programs, or simply enjoy the foods and music of other lands. You can stop in at Northern Depot downtown any time of the year. It houses the Beltrami County History Center and is interesting in its own right as a relic from the golden era of rail transportation.

On the far side of the lake sits Lake Bemidji State Park, which still holds a few acres of virgin forest. This is surprising, when we consider that at one time the south side of the lake was lined with lumber mills, and Bemidji was one of the premier lumber-producing towns in the Unites States. The park contains a variety of trails through the woods, and some even snake their way along boardwalks through conifer bogs, where you may spot orchids and other unusual plant species.

Itasca State Park

Many visitors to the area, however, bypass Bemidji State Park on their way to another, more famous park a few miles south of town. Itasca State Park (218-266-2100) was Minnesota's first, founded in 1889.

The headwaters of the Mississippi

The record of human habitation in the Lake Itasca area extends back for more than 8,000 years, to an era when Indians using stone-tipped tools stalked bison, moose, and deer. Visitors who take the Wilderness Drive can examine the archeological site where some of these tools have been unearthed. A second group of Indians entered the area a few thousand years later. They're known today as the Woodland Indians. Their settlements were more substantial and their material culture was more elaborate. At the Itasca Cemetery some of the mounds they built can still be seen.

There are more than 100 lakes within the borders of the park, but one in particular has grabbed the imagination of generations of Americans—Lake Itasca. The lake is lovely considered on its own terms, though it's rather narrow and surprisingly modest in size. The name takes on added luster, of course, as the source from which the Mississippi River begins its 2,500 mile journey to the Gulf of Mexico. Both children and adults get a special thrill from wading across the Mississippi as it leaves the lake.

The effort to find the ultimate source of the Mississippi had been a favorite objective of explorers throughout the early decades of the nineteenth century. In 1820 the Governor of Michigan Territory,

Lewis Cass, led an expedition from Detroit up the Great Lakes to Duluth, then up the St. Louis and Savanna Rivers, portaging to the Mississippi at Sandy Lake. Two months after setting out, he arrived at the lake now called Cass Lake and proclaimed it to be the headwaters of the Mississippi.

Henry Schoolcraft, who had accompanied the party in the role of mineralogist, noted in his journal that day that "this lake may be considered the true source of the Mississippi," then added immediately afterward that there were two rivers flowing *into* the lake, one of which came from a lake lying a six-day canoe journey to the west-northwest. He further noted the intriguing fact that the French-Canadian voyageurs in their party referred to one of the incoming rivers as "Mississippi." It would seem that the ultimate source of the mighty river lay further off in the forest.

Twelve years later Schoolcraft got an opportunity to return to Cass Lake and pursue this hunch.

In the meantime, in 1823 Major Stephen H. Long was sent on an expedition up the Minnesota River, the ultimate purpose of which was to determine at what point the Red River crossed the forty-ninth parallel. Long was accompanied on the journey by a flamboyant Italian count named Giacomo Constantino Beltrami, whom he had met up with by chance at Fort Snelling while he was preparing for the expedition. Beltrami, inspired by the discoveries of his countrymen Marco Polo, Cabot, and Columbus, had dreamed since boyhood off discovering the Mississippi's source. The party reached Pembina and determined the border between the United Sates and Canada without unusual incident, at which point Long and his men continued northward to Lake Winnipeg. Beltrami, on the other hand, struck off up the Red Lake River, moving east through the wilderness in search of the Mississippi's source. He was accompanied at first by a white guide and several Ojibwe, but the guide returned to the Red River after a few days, and the Ojibwe vanished into the woods after having been fired upon by a party of Dakota, leaving the Italian count on his own. Unable to paddle his canoe upstream single-handedly, Beltrami was obliged to walk along the shore towing the vessel by the painter until he met up with an Ojibwe who agreed to guide him to Lower Red Lake.

From that point, with the help of Ojibwe guides, Beltrami proceeded up the river now known as the Mud to a heart-shaped lake that still bears the name he gave it, Lake Julia. Beltrami proclaimed confidently that this lake was the source of both the Mississippi and the Red River systems. Filled with grandiosity as a result of his accomplishment, Beltrami later wrote, "Like Aeneas I have roamed through the unknown world and have discovered the well-spring of the Mississippi."

If you drive from Bemidji a few miles north on Highway 15, you'll come upon Lake Julia, where there is a roadside marker on a hill honoring Count Beltrami. The area may seem rather obscure to us today, but the flamboyant count was not really so far off. Lake Julia lies near the point considered by the indigenous people since time immemorial as the best, and almost the only, place to portage from the Mississippi to the Red River watersheds, as Lake Julia, which Beltrami reached from Red Lake, lies but a short walk from the Turtle River, which flows southeastward into Cass Lake. In fact, as early as 1806 Zebulon Pike had been told by British traders at both Leech and Sandy lakes that the Turtle River was the ultimate source of the Mississippi. The Leech Lake Trail also passed nearby, serving for many years as a major transportation corridor for the Ojibwe people between the two drainage systems.

One of the early homesteaders in the area describes her childhood as follows:

I was five years old when my folks, Charley and Katherine Durand, took a homestead two and a half miles north of what is now Puposky, on Mud Lake. We were the first ones in there and it was wild country.....

The Indians used to go by our house, long strings of them on the trail going between Red Lake and Cass Lake. This trail went through our homestead and past the house. The squaws would walk with big packs on their backs and the men riding on little ponies with a gun laying across the horse. I can see them yet. They never stopped at our house, just went past.

I remember the first time I saw an Indian close up. My dad had built the barn down the hill from the house. One day there were just the three of us little kids and Mother at home. We kids saw an Indian standing by the corner of the barn, and were scared to death! We ran to tell Mother there was an Indian down by the barn. Finally he started walking up toward the house. When he got to the top of the hill he asked for Charley. After he mentioned Dad's name Mother wasn't afraid of him any more. We never had to be afraid of Indians; they were good.

Though the old Leech Lake Trail has been covered over by a county road between Puposky and Julia, in many places the modern roads follow a different line, and traces of the trail can still be seen in the ditches here and there, though the trail itself has not been used for more than seventy-five years.

Count Beltrami wrote a best-selling book about his "discovery," but Henry Schoolcraft was not convinced. In 1831 he received a commission from the government to travel the region between Lake Superior

Henry Schoolcraft

and the Mississippi River in an effort to quell the incessant warfare between the Dakota and Ojibwe peoples. He travelled more than 2,000 miles by canoe that summer, and one historian remarks that "much good tobacco and eloquence was wasted" cajoling the enemy tribes to live in peace with one another. The next summer he set out again with a smaller party, consisting of a few soldiers, a priest, and a doctor (to vaccinate the Indians against various diseases), ostensibly to further his peace efforts, though there can be little doubt what was in the forefront of his mind. Upon reaching Cass Lake, he ran by chance into a party led by Oziwindib. The following day Schoolcraft's party proceeded along with Oziwindib and five other canoe loads of Ojibwe toward Lake Bemidji.

It would be easy to imagine that by simply following the Mississippi upstream from Lake Bemidji the party would arrive at Lake Itasca straightway. In point of fact, on Oziwindib's recommendation, the party proceeded up a *different* creek, now called Schoolcraft Creek,

In its upper reaches the Mississippi can be rather unprepossessing.

which comes into Lake Bemidji to the east of the Mississippi. After two days of paddling and portaging though very rough terrain, the party reached the headwaters of this creek, and then made a portage of six miles across a series of sandy ridges, before at last coming upon what Schoolcraft later described as "a transparent body of water... it was Lake Itasca—the source of the Mississippi."

As the preceding remarks should make clear, at the time of the discovery there was no way for Schoolcraft to know that the lake that had suddenly come into view was connected with *any* river, much less the Mississippi, except that Oziwindib told him it was. But after lingering for an hour or two and planting an American flag on one of the islands, the party did proceed downstream and eventually arrived back at Lake Bemidji, confirming, more or less, that Itasca was, indeed, the Mississippi's source.

Oziwindib and his men called the lake Elk Lake, and the French, who were also familiar with it, called in Lac la Biche. But Schoolcraft had concocted a new name for the lake well before he ever set eyes on it. During the journey from Detroit he had asked the priest for a few Latin words that might suggest "true source." The best the priest could come up with was "veritas" for truth, and "caput" for head. Schoolcraft removed the first syllable from Veritas and the second from Caput, and came up with Itasca. Though the name is artificial, it is also unique, and it does have a poetic ring.

Nowadays historians sometimes berate the efforts of white explorers to expose the origin of things, and point out that Schoolcraft could not have "discovered" the Mississippi's source because the Ojibwe knew where it was all along. Such views perhaps expose the strange warp of our own era as much as the ethnocentricity of former times.

To the Ojibwe of Leech Lake, who travelled at will up streams and across divides throughout the Upper Mississippi drainage system, the idea that the Mississippi River started at a single place might well have seemed absurd. In any case, it didn't seem terribly important. To European-Americans, who lived in a society committed to private property, treaties, and boundary lines, the precise location of rivers was highly useful information. In fact, the Northwest Angle of Minnesota, the only part of the contiguous forty-eight states that juts oddly up above the forty-ninth parallel into Canada, exists only because the authors of the Treaty of Paris in 1783 mistakenly placed the headwaters of the Mississippi too far north on the continent.

It would be fair to say, in other words, that the Mississippi with which Schoolcraft was concerned was somewhat different from the one Oziwindib and his companions knew. It had a French-speaking city at its mouth, and frontier cities were developing on its banks from Memphis to Minneapolis. It had tributaries pouring in from either side, and was the center of a vast drainage system extending from the Appalachians to the Rockies. Though the Ojibwe of the Great Lakes region were certainly familiar with long-distance travel, the band at Leech Lake was perhaps only dimly aware of how great the Father of Waters really was. In any case, when we say that Schoolcraft "discovered" the headwaters, what we're saying is that he introduced that item of information into the European world-view.

The itch Schoolcraft harbored to uncover a secret that had been hidden from whites since they had come upon the Mississippi more than three hundred years earlier, may also be a peculiarly European-American quality. Schoolcraft served as an Indian agent for many years, and during that time this same curiosity also drove him to collect a large number of Native American folktales from the Great Lakes region. While participating in a treaty council in Chicago Schoolcraft had noted how eloquent and serene many of the Indian leaders were, and it occurred to him that the customs, legends, and manners of these folk ought to be recorded and preserved. While serving as an Indian agent at Sault Ste. Marie, he had the opportunity to do just that. Though not actually an ethnographer himself, Schoolcraft's researches won international acclaim from scholarly and linguistic societies. Their greater cultural impact, however, may be felt in the works of Henry Wadsworth Longfellow, whose book-length poem *The Song of Hiawatha* is considered a world classic. Longfellow once described his magnum opus in the following terms:

> *...I have woven the curious Indian legends drawn chiefly from the various and valuable writings of Mr. Schoolcraft to whom the literary world is greatly indebted for his indefatigable zeal in rescuing from oblivion so much of the legendary lore of the Indians.*

Perhaps few visitors to Minneapolis who board its gleaming new Hiawatha light-rail line on a trip to the lovely falls at Minnehaha, are aware that they are living in the faint afterglow not only of the Ojibwe Indians who once peopled the area, but also of Henry Schoolcraft's early ethnographic researches at Sioux Ste. Marie.

As you enjoy the natural wonders of Itasca State Park, it might be interesting to ponder the career of a second hero of the area. Jacob V. Brower was an explorer and archeologist, and he is also considered the father of Itasca State Park. He grew up on a farm in the vicinity of Long Prairie, and at the age of nineteen, he served under General Sibley in the Dakota War of 1862, and later fought in the Civil War. Returning to Long Prairie, he married, and was later appointed the first auditor of Todd County. In the course of time he served as the president of a railroad company, the owner of two newspapers, and plotted the city of Browerville.

But Brower is best known today as a result of his efforts to establish Itasca Sate Park. Brower was sent into the area as a surveyor and archeologist in 1890 to confirm and clarify the true source of the Mississippi River. While engaged in the project, he was struck by the fact that the area was in danger of being utterly destroyed by logging operations. He urged the state legislature to establish a park there, and eventually they did, though the measure passed by only a single vote.

Thanks to Brower's determination, Itasca Park now contains more than 25 percent of Minnesota's old growth forest outside the borders of the Boundary Waters Canoe Area Wilderness, including a 5,000 acre chunk that's the largest contiguous block to be found anywhere in the state. One fine stand of pines lies north of the visitor's center at Preacher's

Grove. It can be reached on foot, by canoe, or in a car. There are also several fascinating ruins from the homesteading era nearby. The ten-mile Wilderness Drive will take you past other unusual features of the park, from the Bison Kill site to the largest white and red pines still standing in the state. The park includes 157 lakes in all and several stands of virgin Norway pine that are more than 200 years old. If we add to this the many rustic lodge buildings built in the park beginning in 1905, including Douglas Lodge, then Itasca begins to look like our own little Yellowstone. Considered all in all, it brings together much that is unusual and fine about the north woods—its peoples, its history, and its enduring natural beauty.

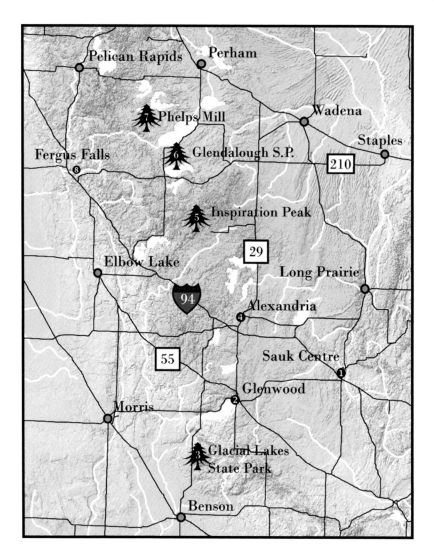

III. THE LEAF HILLS

A massive moraine runs northwest to southeast through western Minnesota, separating the flat and largely dry drainage of the Red River Valley from the woods and lakes of the Upper Mississippi. The area is sometimes referred to as the Leaf Hills, though you don't hear the phrase used much. From a mean elevation of 1,350 to 1,400 feet, the countryside rises in some places as much as 350 feet higher. Inspiration Peak is the highest point in the area at 1,750 feet. Though somewhat off

Sinclair Lewis's father practiced medicine above this drug store in Sauk Centre.

the beaten track, the views of the surrounding lakes and fields from the top is fine, and whatever meandering route you take to get there is sure to lead you across some of the lovely countryside for which the region is famous. All in all, this graceful area contains both the heaviest concentration of lakes in the state and also some of its hilliest country. Yet the presence of farms and pastures and the scarcity of evergreens allow it to retain a lower profile than other places further north and east.

Sauk Centre

In 1931 Sinclair Lewis became the first American writer to win the Nobel Prize for literature. Lewis was born in Minnesota and lived in Sauk Centre until the age of seventeen. Though he traveled widely in later years, Lewis's fiction continued to draw upon impressions that he'd formed during his years in Minnesota, and at his own request his remains were brought from Rome to Sauk Centre for burial when he died in 1951.

Lewis's reputation as a writer was founded on his novels of small-town life, which captured the foibles and petty vanities of its residents, and also a few hints of their restless aspirations. When Lewis won a Pulitzer Prize for *Arrowsmith* in 1925, the committee underscored what it took to be the novel's outstanding presentation of "the wholesome atmosphere of American life." Lewis refused the award on the grounds that his intention had been precisely the reverse.

The citizens of Sauk Centre were not entirely pleased with the light in which they'd been cast in *Main Street*, and it's said that the descendents of some of the individuals portrayed in that novel are still a little upset. Yet no one could deny that Lewis had put Sauk Centre on the map. During the 1920's it was among the most famous small towns in the United States. And even today the best reason for stopping is to visit the Sinclair Lewis Boyhood Home at 820 Sinclair Lewis Avenue (320-352-5359) and the Sinclair Lewis Interpretive Center (320-352-5201), which sits just off the exit ramp from I-94.

The house has been restored to look just as it did when Lewis was growing up there during the 1890s. The museum is a slightly tattered enterprise, though it's definitely worth a stop. Pictures from every phase of Lewis's life have been enlarged and hung on the walls, and the accompanying text is often illuminating. Facsimiles from the Yale library document Lewis's meticulous methods of elaborating the myriad details of his fictional worlds, and a ten-minute video presents us with an overview of both Lewis's early years in Sauk Centre and his later career. Perhaps a few aspects of the museum's interpretation betray the same small-town mentality that Lewis sometimes ridiculed in his famous works, but the city's pride in Lewis's achievement comes through loud and clear. And the significance of the achievement itself is worth pondering, even if we've never glanced at one of Lewis's novels. Works of imagination have the power to transcend the mundane details of daily life from which they draw by focusing our attention on both their emptiness and their significance. We all live on *Main Street*, after all, and there's beauty, enrichment, and perhaps even wholeness to be found there.

In downtown Sauk Centre the Palmer House Hotel, though nothing fancy, retains something of the atmosphere of the days when Lewis was a clerk there. The staff is friendly, the lobby and bar are expansive and inviting, the rooms are small but affordable and well-kept, and the adjoining restaurant is more than decent. Looking south out the lobby window you can see, above the Main Street Drug Store, the offices where Lewis's father practiced medicine, and beyond it, the storefronts and marques from a bygone era. The town makes a convenient stop for cyclists planning to do the Lake Wobegon Regional Bike Trail which runs east-west for forty miles from Sauk Centre to St. Joseph.

Glenwood

One early settler, perhaps more romantic than many soldiers of his era, described his first encounter with Lake Minnewaska as follows:

During the month of June, 1864, in company with a detachment of United States troops en-route for the west, I visited the site on which the village of Glenwood now stands. I can never forget the impressions that came to my mind as we approached the brow of the hill and beheld for the first time the magnificent grandeur of the scenery before us! It was a perfect June day. The air was laden with the perfume of spring and the poetry of nature was written on every tree and shrub. I withdrew from the noisy clamor of my companions to the shade of a spreading oak, that I might gaze, and ponder and dream.

The same view awaits visitors approaching Glenwood from the north today along Highway 55 as Lake Minnewaska appears amid the distant trees, surrounded on three sides by impressive bluffs. The best views out across the lake are from Mount Lookout, just off Highway 55 at 14th Avenue NE. If you continue through town and proceed west on Highway 28, turning right on County Road 24, you'll come to Indian Mounds Park within half a mile on your right, where the view is also very fine. (The obscure Dakota Chief White Bear is buried here.)

To get a better sense of the vanished native culture of the area, plan to visit the Pope County Historical Society (809 S Lakeshore Drive) which houses a collection of artifacts gathered by Cleora Helbing, long-time director of education for the Bureau of Indian Affairs. The Society also maintains the Ann Bickle Heritage House (214 E Minnesota Avenue) a modest Craftsman-style home with a pleasant garden.

Glacial Lakes State Park

Few places in Minnesota provide such an interesting ensemble of natural features as Glacial Lakes State Park (320-239-2860). It's nestled in the moraines of the Leaf Hills, and it's covered with prairie vegetation, some of it native. Small but beautiful Mountain Lake is nestled in the woods at the west end of the park, and trails lead out in several directions across the hills and dales to the east. There is a campground beside the lake and a more appealing one up on the ridge. Most of the features associated with the advance and retreat of glaciers are on display somewhere within the park, including kettles, drumlins, eskers, kames, and erratics. Some of them are identified on trailside markers. Prairie wildflowers are widespread during the summer months. But matters of science and nature aside, the park offers a splendid opportunity to relax in an unusual setting, take a hike, fish, or simply watch the sun set across the rolling fields.

The park is located a few miles south of Starbuck, which sits on the south end of Lake Minnewaska.

Alexandria

Alexandria sits in the midst of a region of lakes and resorts that draw millions of fishermen and vacationing families during the summer months. Its most notable draw for the passing tourist is the Kensington Runestone, which has been a source of controversy for more than a hundred years. The slab of rock is on display at the Runestone Museum, (206 Broadway) along with maps, interpretive displays, and a number of allegedly Norse artifacts that have been unearthed in the region over the years. The Runestone is now widely considered a fraud, though the controversy has never been entirely put to rest. Depending on your point of view, the museum present a remarkable story of fourteenth-century Norse exploration or a fascinating exhibition of modern chauvinistic chutzpah. Either way, it makes a good stop along the highway.

The story behind the stone, in brief, is as follows. On November 8, 1898, Olaf Ohman and his ten-year-old son, Edward, were pulling up stumps on their farm a few miles from Kensington. Edward noticed a large stone under one of the trees that was covered with strange markings. They were runes, the symbols used by the Vikings many centuries ago. The message, when translated, read as follows:

8 Goths and 22 Norwegians on exploration journey from Vinland over the West We had camp by 2 skerries one days journey north from this stone We were and fished one day After we came home found 10 men red with blood and dead Ave Maria Save from evil.

Ohman brought the stone to Kensington, where it was displayed in a bank window, but word of the discovery spread, and a year later it was sent to Chicago to be evaluated by Scandinavian scholars. They declared it to be a fake.

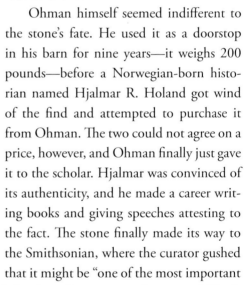

Ohman himself seemed indifferent to the stone's fate. He used it as a doorstop in his barn for nine years—it weighs 200 pounds—before a Norwegian-born historian named Hjalmar R. Holand got wind of the find and attempted to purchase it from Ohman. The two could not agree on a price, however, and Ohman finally just gave it to the scholar. Hjalmar was convinced of its authenticity, and he made a career writing books and giving speeches attesting to the fact. The stone finally made its way to the Smithsonian, where the curator gushed that it might be "one of the most important pieces of evidence for pre-Columbian European exploration of North America."

The Smithsonian later backed away from their endorsement, and the Minnesota Historical Society, after a careful study of the stone, also challenged its authenticity. They noted, for example, that several of the runes on the stone were unknown during the fourteenth century. Such technical matters aside, it was difficult for many scholars to accept the notion that a party of Norse explorers had made their way to the middle of the North American continent at a time when even Columbus had not set foot in the hemisphere. It was far more likely that a very clever immigrant farmer had made use of his school-boy knowledge of runes to cook up a hoax.

The folks who run the museum in Alexandria have no trouble imagining that Norsemen had paid the area a visit seven hundred years ago—and in their museum they will show you how it might have happened. And in recent years the tide of scholarly opinion has very slowly begun to shift in their favor. For example, at the time when scholars originally debunked the artifact, there was no evidence that the Norse had ever set foot *anywhere* in North America. Since that time, the village at L'Anse Aux Meadows in Newfoundland has been excavated, and there is no longer any doubt that Norsemen once lived on the east coast of the Atlantic. Similarly, since the era when scholars in Denmark and Norway challenged the runestone on linguistic grounds, every one of the supposedly anachronistic runes has been found repeatedly in carvings of the period.

At an convention at the University of Minnesota in 2000 it was reported that "Recent discoveries support a 14th-century explanation for the Kensington Rune Stone's apparent oddities: pendatic numbers and the 1362 date, origin of the runes, and Old Swedish...The language is entirely Old Swedish, of which over a dozen words on the Kensington Rune Stone have been published in the Old Swedish Dictionary (1925-1975) only after the finding of the Rune Stone in 1898."

It would seem, then, that if Olaf Ohman did carve the stone, he had somehow developed a knowledge of medieval Norse far superior to that of the scholars in Scandinavia who were critiquing his work.

Meanwhile, on another front, a recent geological analysis of the weathering on the incised surfaces of the runes suggests that they were carved at least 250 years ago—well before Olaf Ohman or any other Scandinavian farmer had appeared on the scene.

And why did it happen that these Norsemen were venturing so far from home in the fourteenth century? It's well-known that they ranged far and wide across western Russia during that period, hauling their ships for miles overland as conditions required. The historian and archeologist Alice B. Kehoe has pointed out that following the Novgorod Treaty of 1323, which put an end to direct trading with

Byzantium, the Norsemen were on the lookout for new trade routes and also new sources of furs. She also notes that scholars who question the likelihood of a Viking presence in the interior of North America at that early date may be in the grip of an ethnocentric prejudice that the "New World" was a trackless wilderness prior to white settlement, whereas in fact by the fourteenth century trade routes had long been established from coast to coast by the indigenous inhabitants.

A hundred years after its discovery, serious scholarly interest in the Kensington Runestone is only beginning to take shape. It cannot be said that "the debate continues," because there has never been much real debate. The locals have championed the rune's authenticity rather uncritically, while scholars, after hazarding a few dismissive remarks, have steered clear of it for fear of tarnishing their academic standing.

Regardless of whether the runestone is real or fake, it looks "cool," and a visit to the museum in Alexandria (206 Broadway, 320-763-3160) gives us an opportunity to see it, to study the movements of Scandinavian peoples in medieval times, and to ponder the methods, prejudices, and enthusiasms of scholars. The novelist Evan S. Connell once mused that perhaps the Vikings not only visited Minnesota, but continued on down the Minnesota and Mississippi Rivers—far easier than returning to Hudson's Bay. Perhaps they eventually headed out into the Gulf of Mexico. He writes:

> *The Mexican Indian legend of Quetzalcoatl says that a bearded white man appeared out of the east on a raft of snakes and later departed in the direction from which he had come, promising to return in five hundred years.*

Inspiration Peak

In 1942 a Minneapolis newspaper asked Sinclair Lewis to name his favorite outdoor Minnesota sights. After reminding his readers that his Minnesota youth was before the days of "motor cars, good roads and the noble maps issued by the gasoline vendors..." Lewis presented his top ten. First on the list was the Saint Croix Valley, especially the area around Taylor's Falls. His second choice was much closer to his boyhood home—Inspiration Peak. "You leave the car in a wood-encircled picnic ground," he wrote, "and climb what would amount to a couple of city blocks, to a bald top from which there is to be seen a glorious 20-mile circle of some 50 lakes scattered among fields and pastures... I pray that the state park authorities will never, never permit the roadway to be pushed through to the very top."

Lewis would be happy to learn that a visit to Inspiration Peak still requires a short but steep hike up the hill through the woods. The view from the top remains outstanding, though the trees are more mature than they were in Lewis's time. Plenty of shimmering lakes can still be seen amid the greenery, and what the site itself lacks in drama is more than compensated for by the small delights of the countryside you must pass through to get there. The back roads wind around and over the hills past farm fields, lakes, and quiet streams edged with reeds. (The peak lies 4.5 miles west of Urbank on County Highway 38.)

Glendalough State Park

Glendalough State Park (218-864-0110) offers us an even more intimate look at the same landscape. The property, which encompasses several lakes and borders several more, served as the private vacation retreat for the family of F. E. Murphy, who owned the *Minneapolis Tribune*. Murphy started a game farm there, raising thousands of pheasants and ducks. When the Cowles Media Company purchased the *Tribune* in 1941, the property came along as part of the deal. The Cowles family expanded it while continuing to make use of it as a vacation spot. Among the important guests that were entertained there in those days were former presidents Eisenhower and Nixon. In 1990 the Cowles family donated the property to the Nature Conservancy and two years later the state took it over to be developed into a state park.

In developing the park, the state made efforts to preserve its pristine condition. Several of its lakes remain closed to all motorized watercraft, and electronic fish-finding devices are also prohibited. These and other restrictions are designed to insure that the lakes continue to provide "heritage" fishing for the park's visitors, and bass and northern of legendary proportions continue to be landed here from time to time.

The campground on the western shores of Annie Battle Lake are shady walk-in sites, though you might experience the peaceful atmosphere of the park even more profoundly at one of the paddle-in campsites on the far side of the lake. Motorized recreation is available on Lake Blanche at the upper end of the park, and a number of hiking trails meander through the woods and fields and along the quiet stream that connects several of the park's lakes. Lake Emma, on the park's eastern fringe, is accessible only on foot, and it provides outstanding wildlife viewing opportunities for birders during spring and fall migrations.

Battle Lake is the nearest town to Glendalough State Park. The name stems from the fact that in 1795, bands of Dakota and Ojibwe Indians engaged here in one of their recurrent territorial skirmishes, perhaps because the territory lies at the head-of-land between the Ottertail and Crow Wing river watersheds. It may seem odd that a large fiberglass statue of the vanquished Ojibwe chief Wenonga, rather than a trimphant Dakota, now stands on the shores of the lake, but there it is. You can ponder this and other historical enigmas as you enjoy a well-made hamburger at the Shoreline Lanes just south of the statue.

The Phelps Mill

The Ottertail River ranks among the best naturally-regulated rivers in the state, flowing strong and clear in a generally southerly direction from its headwaters near Detroit Lakes through a long succession of lakes. In fact, more than a third of the Ottertail's length upstream from Fergus Falls consists of lakes and marshes rather than river *per se*. The river is so clean that not so long ago Japanese entrepreneurs harvested 32 tons of mussel shells from its gravel bottom to seed their oyster industry back home.

A good place to sidle up to the Ottertail is the Phelps Mill, located a few miles north east of Fergus Falls, just off County Road 1 on County Road 45. The mill served the needs of local farmers between 1889 and 1939. It was later restored, and much of the machinery inside the mill is just as it was a hundred years ago. It sits picturesquely on the river alongside the dam that powered its millstones for

The Phelps Mill

half a century, with a grassy park spreading off along the riverbank downstream. The mill's hours are irregular, but when it's open you can wander at random amid four floors of antique milling equipment, much of it made of wood, and watch a 6-minute video explaining the role played by the mill in the life of the community. It's interesting to consider that the man who designed and built the mill (according to an article that appeared in a local newspaper at the time) never drew up a blueprint or marked a single stick of limber, but simply worked from a plan he carried in his head.

At one time the village of Phelps had a blacksmith shop, a cheese factory, a restaurant, and a repair shop. Now the old-fashioned general-store is all that's left of the once prosperous town of Phelps, aside from the mill itself.

Fergus Falls

There isn't much to do in Fergus Falls other than stroll its pleasant downtown streets or visit the excellent Ottertail County Historical Society on Lincoln Avenue on the west end of town. Several motels out near the freeway make it a good base for exploring the region, and a half-mile river walk along the tree-lined Ottertail River will give you a better sense of the community's past.

IV. THE ST. CROIX RIVER VALLEY

The Saint Croix River Valley is one of the most picturesque regions in the state. This is true not only of the wooded and often bluff-lined course of the river itself, which is best seen from the seat of a canoe, but also of the rolling lake-dotted countryside to the west of the river. The lower portions of this upland region were originally prairie and oak savanna—the more northerly stretch was a part of the pine and hardwood belt that stretched all the way to Maine. The entire area was shaped by roaring rivers that drained south out of Glacial Lake Duluth following the last Ice Age.

The Indians who inhabited the region considered it an easy paddle from Lake Superior up the Brule River, over the height of land to the headwaters of the Saint Croix and downstream to the Mississippi. The same route became a major transportation artery for the French fur traders who began to arrive in the area during the seventeenth century.

The land between the St. Croix and the Mississippi was the first part of the region we now know as Minnesota to be ceded to the United States by its Ojibwe and Dakota inhabitants. In 1837 a triangle of territory defined by the Mississippi, the St. Croix, and a line cut between the two rivers from the mouth of the Crow Wing River, was opened to settlement, and at the time it was considered the finest white pine forest on the continent. Lumbermen began to drift into the area from Maine and Michigan, and mills sprang up at Marine (1839), Saint Croix Falls (1842), Stillwater (1844) and other towns further downstream. In the next half-century ten billion board feet of timber was harvested and shipped down river, some of it traveling to mills as far south as Saint Louis. All in all, there were more than 130 lumber mills on the Saint Croix alone at one time or another—not to mention the operations on the Mississippi further downstream.

As the area in the vicinity of the St. Croix was cleared, homesteaders began to arrive, many of them from Sweden. Flour mills were soon operating alongside the lumber mills, and villages grew into towns. However, when Wisconsin became a state in 1848, the territory to the west of the Saint Croix was not included as part of it. There was considerable discussion at the time as to where the boundary of the new state

should be, with many local residents on the east side of the river express-
ing the desire to be *excluded* from the State of Wisconsin, so as to preserve the St. Croix Valley intact. The west side of the St. Croix became
part of a much-diminished Wisconsin Territory, but local activists had
soon convened in Stillwater (under the dubious auspices of John Catlin,
the former secretary of Wisconsin territory), and elected Henry Sibley
to petition Congress to create a new territory called *Minnesota*, (from a
Dakota expression meaning "Water with clouds in it.") Sibley's mission
was successful and the following spring Minnesota officially became a
territory. It is on this grounds that Stillwater claims the title as "birthplace of Minnesota."

But with the depletion of the timber resources in the St. Croix
Delta, and the growth of St. Paul and St Anthony, both of which stood
on the banks of a much larger river commanding far more forested territory to the north and west, the river towns on the St. Croix sank into
obscurity. When the grand institutions of the newly-established State
of Minnesota were being divvied up a few years later by the territorial
legislature, St. Paul got the capitol, St. Anthony got the University...and
Stillwater got the prison!

Nowadays Stillwater and other towns along the St. Croix River ben-
efit from their proximity to the Twin Cities metropolitan area. Their
quaint streets have long-since acquired a patina of history, and the fact
that their hardware and variety stores have often been replaced by restaurants and boutiques also contributes to their allure as an easy day-trip.
Meanwhile, the river itself, which was once choked with logs during the
spring break-up every year, is now often choked with pleasure craft. Yet
here too, a balance seems to have been preserved between recreation,
historic interest, and natural beauty. The St. Croix was one of the eight
American rivers chosen by the federal government for inclusion in the
original phase of the Wild and Scenic Rivers program.

Hudson

Residents on the east side of the St. Croix Valley showed remarkable judgement in resisting attempts to incorporate their communities into the state of Wisconsin, and it would be only fitting to

point out that several enticing towns on the St. Croix now lie on the Wisconsin side. Prescott has some impressive riprap and a classic railroad line running right through town, and Hudson is the perfect destination for both hard-drinking teens and more mature Twin Citians in search of the exotica of upscale small-town life. There may be no more satisfying experience of genuine Americana in the region than the Fourth of July concert on the grass in front of the Phipps Center for the Arts in Hudson, with the Minnesota Orchestra playing Sousa and Gershwin and maybe a little Charles Ives, and the lights on the pleasure boats out in the river beyond the park shifting here and there like fireflies as darkness descends, and children shouting in the distance like a long-forgotten dream…

Afton

The town of Afton has a population exceeding 2800 people, but it isn't really a town. It has a marina and an inn, and a restaurant which has been in operation continuously since 1867. The first farm in Minnesota was established a mile west of town in 1839.

In any case, the most interesting place in Afton is the state park. It's a walk-in park. You must hike down to the river, and the campsites on the ridge are a mile or so from the parking lot. But those who make the effort find solitude and landscapes that are rarely encountered so close to a major city. Remnant prairies are being expanded and oak savannas are being restored. There are fireflies in the trees and whippoorwills down in the ravines throughout the night. But campers should be forewarned—on weekend nights during the summer the peace and solitude of the place is marred by the roaring of unseen motorboats tearing this way and that across Lake St. Croix down in the valley below.

Stillwater

Arrive early on a sunny summer weekend to fully enjoy the amenities that Stillwater has to offer. Take a walk along the grassy riverfront, admiring the lift bridge and the forests on the opposite bank, then head down Main Street, where you'll find shops of every size and description. Stillwater is well-known for its antique malls, art galleries, recreational outfitters, cooking stores, and restaurants. It has a tea shop, a wine co-op where you can sample a few of the local products, and an array of eateries ranging from the downhome saloon atmosphere of Brine's Meat Market to upscale wine bars and restaurants.

One of Stillwater's special attractions is its collection of used bookstores. Loome Antiquarian Bookstore and St. Croix Antiquarian Booksellers stand virtually across from one another on Main Street. A few blocks up the hill (at 320 N. 4th St.) is Loome Theological Booksellers—the collection is housed in an old church—which has been referred to as the world's largest dealer in works of theology and philosophy.

Stillwater can become oppressively crowded during summer, on glorious fall weekends, and on holiday weekends. At such times it can still be appreciated from a distance. One option during the summer months would be to take a ride on one of the paddleboats that traverse the river almost daily at that time of year. Check for times and fees at the St. Croix Boat and Packet Company, 525 S Main St. (651-430-1234). An easier alternative would be simply to head up one of the steeply-sloping streets into the residential part of town. Stillwater has a large number of well-kept historic homes, with enormous porches and elaborate decoration. Because of the many ravines in town quite a few of the backstreets lead to dead-ends, but many of them offer commanding views over the streets of the city, where you can admire the numerous church spires and the glittering river moving by in the distance before you settle back to peruse that rare volume of essays by Jacques Maritain or Richard of St. Victor that you stumbled upon at a bookstore earlier in the day.

The north end of downtown Stillwater used to be less gentrified than the south end, but during the recent condo craze multi-story structures went up at an alarming rate, transforming the district into a canyon of up-scale residences. Yet you can still walk along in the shadows of the former Staples lumber mill—though it's now an antique mall. The co-op across the street is top-flight. For a fuller exposure to the town that once was, your best bet would be a visit the Warden's House Museum (602 N. Main St.) which has a number of displays relating to the early history of the area.

Stillwater sits at the upper end of Lake St. Croix, which extends downstream all the way to the confluence with the Mississippi. It was just north of Stillwater that the famous boom once stretched across the river to gather and sort the logs that had been cut and dragged to the river and to tributaries such as the Snake, the Namakogen, the Kettle, and other rivers farther to the north. As you leave Stillwater heading north on Highway 95, there are several pull-offs on the right side of the road at the Boom Site offering access to the river and commanding views of Lake St. Croix and the now-distant town of Stillwater huddled against its west bank.

Marine on the St. Croix

The drive north from Stillwater on Highway 95 takes you up through an impressive cut of sandstone—it's known to geologists world-wide as St. Croixian sandstone. Up top, the countryside is pleasantly rolling farmland and pasture, with no river in sight. (Thrill-seekers might be tempted to turn down Arcola Trail and then set out on foot across the Arcola Railroad Bridge, which spans the St. Croix at a dizzying height. Don't. The excursion is both dangerous and illegal.)

Ten miles upstream you will come to the hamlet of Marine. It was founded in 1839, and was the site of the first sawmill on the St. Croix.

Today Marine is a picture-book town, which has the further distinction of not having been unduly prettified. In fact, there isn't really much there. The General Store, which opened in 1870, remains well-stocked, because it still serves the daily needs of the residents. There is a bar, a restaurant, a miniscule public library, a gazebo in the park by the highway, and a log house by a millpond that was carted into the city by the local residents for their centennial celebration in 1937. This structure is thought to have been built by Swedish settlers during the 1830's. If so, then it has stood the test of time remarkably well. Yet perhaps we ought not to be surprised. Swedish settlers introduced the "log cabin" to the Delaware Bay region of colonial America as early as 1638—the Pilgrim Fathers had no knowledge of that form of construction—and it did not come into more widespread use by other ethnic groups until the eighteenth century.

MINGEI-SOTA

A movement took hold in Japan during the 1920s snd 1930s to preserve the crafts of the common people, whose handmade household articles were notable for their beauty and simplicity of design. These folk-arts, which the Japanese called *mingei*, and especially the art of wheel-thrown pottery, made their way to the West through the efforts of the Englishman Bernard Leach. It reached Minnesota in the person of Warren MacKenzie, who became a professor of pottery at the University of Minnesota following an apprenticeship with Leach in St. Ives, England. For many years MacKenzie's farm, studio, and showroom in the rolling hills between Stillwater and Mahtomedi were a mecca of sorts for young men and women interested in handmade pottery and the simpler, more natural lifestyle it evoked.

He and his students held sales occasionally, with Buffalo Springfield and Joni Mitchell tunes bursting from the boom-box.

In the course of time other potters have become rooted in the landscapes of the St. Croix, and for the last two decades some of them have held a sale every spring in mid-May. It's a wonderful opportunity to see the countryside, compare the differing styles of pottery, see the kilns, chat with the artists, and pick up a few teabowls or a serving platter along the way. The resident artists often invite friends to contribute, and the range of styles is considerable, though lingering echos of the *mingei* tradition can still be seen in the worls of Guillermo Cuellar, Jeff Oestreich, Robert Briscoe, Linda Christianson, and others.

For exact dates, maps, and more details about the artists involved, see **www.minnesotapotters.com.**

O'Brien State Park

The entrance to O'Brien State Park lies a few miles north of Marine on Highway 95. There are several pleasant walks down by the river, and you can also rent canoes to get out into the river's many backwaters, where you'll probably see plenty of herons and egrets, and perhaps a wild turkey, a cuckoo, a kingfisher, or some brilliant cardinal flowers.

The larger part of the park lies on the west side of the highway, however, and its twelve miles of trails will take you up through woods and fields and marshes that are set in near-idyllic proportion to one another. During the winter months the cross-country skiing is equally fine.

Scandia

Today the little community of Scandia lies at the heart of Minnesota's Swedish immigrant experience. This is because it was the first area the Swedes settled when they began arriving from Sweden in 1850. The eminent Swedish novelist Wilhelm Moberg wrote a series of novels about the area during the 1950s that were later made into films and also a musical. Some parts of the village haven't changed all that much. At any rate, you can visit its Gammelgården Museum, which consists of a number of old farm buildings and a parsonage set out across a small piece of land. Some of the buildings are furnished, others have museum displays.

The food at the Scandia Cafe is good and reasonably priced, though you're likely to see jambalaya and mini-corn dogs on the menu alongaide the Swedish meatballs.

Franconia

The bizarre and gigantic creations that lie scattered across the fields at the intersection of Highways 95 and 8 are hard to miss. That's the Franconia Outdoor Sculpture Park. Admission is free, and you can walk at your leisure among the unusual forms. You might even come upon one of the sculptors at work, which will give you an opportunity to inquire about inspiration, motivation, meaning, social relevance, natural resonance and other aspects of the creative process.

The grounds of the Gammelgården Museum in Scandia

A diferent aspect of Franconia reveals itself in the village, which can be found by taking the Franconia Trail down to the river bottom. The gravel road is the first left turn on Highway 95 south of Highway 8. In the woods at the foot of the long, steep hill you'll find impressive residential buildings that are similar to those at Frontenac, Upper Taylor's Falls, Upper Marine, and other river communities. At the end of the road you'll come to a small river landing.

Taylor's Falls

The intersection at the heart of Taylor's Falls is often hectic and congested, as travelers head eagerly to and from their cabins in Wisconsin along Highway 8, with semis often adding a further element of irritation to the mix. The main street of Taylor's Falls can sometimes seem equally congested. The best parts of the town are to be found on either side of the highway—up the hill to the Folsom House and the Angel District, with its prim white houses and estates, and down to the river and the attractions of Interstate Park.

The center of attention in the quiet residential streets above the town is the Folsom House. The man who built it, W. H. C. Folsom, had his finger in quite a few pies back when Taylor's Falls was the center of the lumber industry and its population was many times greater than today. The house he built is 1854 stayed in the family for five generations, and his descendants were in the habit of removing outdated furniture to the attic, so when the property was acquired by the State of Minnesota in 1968 they had a goldmine of antiquarian artifacts and information on their hands. The house is now open for tours between 1-4:30 daily (except Tuesday) and the guides do a good job of revivifying the era and highlighting the class distinctions between the Germans and Swedes who worked in the mills and lumber camps, and the New Englanders like Folsom who owned and ran such enterprises.

Once you've toured the Folsom House it might be worthwhile to stroll through the neighborhood up the hill, where many of the homes date from the same period. The similarities to a well-to-do New England village are striking. The area was known as Angel Hill, presumably because the families who lived there had already brought themselves quite close to heaven—at least in their own minds.

In those days most of the town of Taylor's Falls—the mills, the stores, the warehouses, the liveries, the saloons and boarding houses—was located on the flats down by the river. That part of Taylor's Falls is all gone now, and the area has become Interstate Park. For the passing tourist, a stop at the Glacial Park that runs along the river just below the highway bridge is highly recommended. You'll get some of your best views of the classic St. Croix Dalles from here by climbing out among the rocks behind the visitor center. And the asphalt path down to the river will take you past some intriguing geological phenomena—potholes. These large smooth holes in the basalt have obviously been cut by swirling water and grit over a long period of time. Yet they're many feet above the current level of the river. As usual, we have the glaciers to blame. Eons ago this valley was more than 200 feet below the water line, and the rushing waters of the glacial run-off from Lake Duluth scoured the bottom to make these strange and attractive features, which are, in fact, the largest and deepest of their kind in the world. There are several displays in the visitor center explaining in greater detail exactly what was going on in the area geologically way back then.

Geology aside, it's fun to wander down the winding path and scamper across the rocks amid the pines and maples. The path will eventually

take you to a riverboat landing, and on through the woods to the cliffs that are one of Minnesota's premier rock-climbing sites.

As you explore this small but beautiful area, you'll probably see more than a few canoes and kayaks moving past along the river between the cliffs, and you may even want to give it a try yourself. If so, you can rent these vessels at the other section of the park, which can be reached by car a mile or so further south along Highway 8. This very popular unit also has campgrounds and picnic grounds.

Wild River State Park

Upstream from Taylor's Falls the cliffs disappear and the landscape becomes less interesting. In fact, we are passing into a zone of Minnesota's terrain that has been largely ignored in this book. Yet Wild River State Park offers a textbook of local and regional features. It has a prairie restoration and both railroad and stagecoach tracks that can be located easily using GPS technology. And though the river itself has lost most of its drama and become merely a long stretch of water flowing through the woods, the ten-mile paddle from Sunrise to the park makes a very pleasant trip by canoe. (Call 651-583-2125 for more details.)

THE RED RIVER VALLEY

No one seems to know how the Red River Valley got its name—something about a sunset, no doubt. It's among the least "red" of Minnesota's rivers, and the region through which it flows is not a valley. The Red River meanders through the flat bottom of an enormous lake bed that dried up eons ago. The lake-bottom soil is rich, and the flatness of the land, combined with the effect of various ditching programs designed to eliminate lowland bogs and meandering tributaries, have made the valley one of the most productive agricultural regions in the world. Driving down the highway past expansive fields spreading off toward the horizon under a broad blue sky can be an exhilarating experience, and the long windbreaks of distant trees that run between the fields may remind us, as they catch the rays of the setting sun, of a luscious landscape by Claude Monet. The river itself plays very little role in the life of the region nowadays, except during times of flooding, but the handsome bridges that span it at infrequent intervals add one more element to an already pleasing landscape as they rise from the lush greenery of the river-bottom trees off to the west of Highway 75. A road-trip down the valley can also be enlivened occasionally by the appearance of a crop-dusting bi-plane coming in fast and low from the east and making an elegant turn just a few yards above the highway.

To fully enjoy a visit to the Red River Valley, however, it would be helpful to become familiar with the topsy-turvy history of the region, and the subtle topographic nuances you encounter as you move through it from west to east, crossing a succession of ancient beaches that mark the stop-and-go retreat of Glacial Lake Agassiz more than ten thousand years ago. At these points the tributaries to the Red River rush through canyons, and there are still a few undrained marshes (some of them now protected as parks and wildlife refuges) where birds either nest or congregate on their way to and from the Arctic.

A note in passing: it's widely presumed that the song "The Red River Valley" is from Texas, but Carl Sandburg thought it referred to the Red River of the North, and so did folklorist Edith Fowke, who selected and edited *The Penguin Book of Canadian Folksongs*.

The whitish line running up the center of the map marks the location of McCarthy Beach. The lake itself is long gone, of course.

HISTORY

The Red River Valley is Minnesota's back door. While much of the state's history is an east-to-west affair, the Red River comes at us north-to-south. And its modern history began in the north, where, in 1812, Lord Selkirk established a colony near Lake Winnipeg—it was known as the Red River Colony—for the purpose of giving a new lease on life to Scots who had been left landless by the spread of sheep farming in Scotland. Selkirk had read about the region west of Lake Winnipeg in Alexander MacKenzie's account of his explorations in the area, and being a gentleman of considerable means, he arranged to purchase 300,000 square kilometers of land in the area—more than enough to support the very small party of Scots who travelled west to the area in 1811. His arrangements were not well carried-out, however, and the fur traders already posted in the region were opposed to such activities, which threatened to undermine their sources of revenue. They burned down the settlers' fort twice, and during their second attack they also massacred 22 of the settlers.

Yet the settlement survived, and eventually it prospered, while the fur trade also continued to flourish once the two trading companies that were competing in the region merged in 1821. In time settlers who had moved south along the river to the region around modern-day Pembina, North Dakota, many of them half-French and half-Ojibwe, recognized the advantages of selling their furs in the new community of Saint Paul rather than in Winnipeg. Though this international trade route was technically illegal, the Americans paid more for furs. The journey was made practical by the wooden ox-carts that had been developed in the area to move furs and goods overland from place to place.

With the treaty of 1863, signed at a bend in the river near the modern-day hamlet of Huot, (see page 207) the Ojibwe Indians ceded almost 10 million acres of land in the region for white settlement, and immigrants began to trickle into the valley, Germans and Norwegians prevalent among them. In time the French-Canadian and Meti stock was gradually submerged in the tide, though parts of Polk and Red Lake Counties, especially along the Red Lake River, still betray some of the French influence of earlier times.

1 Fargo-Moorhead

The twin cities of Fargo and Moorhead sit on either bank of the Red River, though you hardly notice the river when you pass from one city to the other. Moorhead developed as a transportation hub back in the days when goods were hauled back and forth between Winnipeg and Saint Paul in long trains of large wooden carts, and it solidified its position when it was chosen as the Red River crossing site by the Northern Pacific Railroad. The trains still run right through the middle of Moorhead, and they blow their whistles the whole way through, so that even though the crossings are equipped with flashing lights and guard-arms, you may find yourself looking around a lot, a little unsure whether, at any moment, you're going to be obliterated by a speeding locomotive.

Though Moorhead's cultural life is enlivened by several local colleges, its two chief tourist sights are both replicas. Jerry Aps, a local shop-teacher, spent many years building a Viking sailing ship in an abandoned potato warehouse. The city of Moorhead later built the Heritage Hjemkomst Interpretive Center to house the vessel. A few

Guy Paulson's stave church sits on the bank of the Red River.

years later the museum accepted the offer of another resident, retiree Guy Paulson, to build a stave church on the riverbank outside the museum based on a church in the town of Vik, Norway.

Unfortunately, Aps died of leukemia before he had a chance to sail the ship across the Atlantic to Norway, but at the museum you can watch a video devoted to his son's efforts to complete the journey with the help of a few seasoned Norwegian seamen. As for the church, the design is unusual, to say the least, while both the richness of the wood and the delicacy of the carvings give it an appealingly medieval flavor.

A third exhibit, located in the basement of the museum follows the history of the Red River Valley from its formation during the last glacial period through the eras of oxcarts, steamboats, and railroads. To get an even more vivid sense of the role played by the Red River in the life on the region—or simply to unwind and enjoy the views—you can take an informative 45-minute excursion on the S.S. *Ruby*, which departs regularly on most weekends, and daily during the summer, from a dock located on the riverbank outside the museum.

A side-trip across the river to Fargo, North Dakota, will put a more urban edge to your exploration.

Along the central stretch of Broadway you'll pass coffee-shops, art galleries, an appealingly divey pizza restaurant, a shop selling antiques and religious statuary, and several upscale bars, including the HoDo Lounge of the Donaldson Hotel, on the corner of Broadway and First Street. The building dates from 1893, and it originally served as an Oddfellows Hall. It has recently been refurbished as a swanky hotel, with a dramatic sculpture in the foyer and a walk-up second-floor lobby. Each room has been carefully designed and decorated by a different artist, and many are equipped with large flat TV screens, Bose speakers, and other accoutrements. The artistic flourishes, which extend from the pictures on the walls to the shape of the bedstead, can be intriguing, though perhaps not entirely conducive to a good night's sleep. The hotel also schedules frequent poetry readings and musical performances, as if it were on a mission to put the lie to the image of Fargo presented by the Coen Brothers in their famous film, *Fargo*—none of which actually takes place there.

The Fargo Theatre, also on Broadway, is one of Fargo's treasures. Recently restored to Art Deco magnificence, it now shows classic and foreign films. Its antique Wurlitzer is often put to use during the intermissions.

The Radisson Hotel, standing a block to the east down First Street, is Fargo's only skyscraper. The rooms are nice and from the upper stories you can look off to see bridges and trees, church steeples and other buildings on both sides of the river. Those on a more modest budget will find plenty of motel options back in Moorhead at the junction of I-94 and U.S. 75.

Fargo's innovative Plains Art Museum (704 1st Ave N, 701-293-0903) is housed in a renovated warehouse. The permanent collection is strong in contemporary Native American and Plains artists you're unlikely to see elsewhere. The musuem frequently hosts regional and national exhibits, special events, and live performances, and it has both a café and a gift shop.

2 Buffalo River State Park

Though it sits at the intersection of Highways 9 and 10, Buffalo River State Park preserves a wonderful slice of the prairie expansiveness, with Moorhead State University's natural research area lying directly to the east and the Nature Conservancy's Bluestem Prairie Scientific and Natural Area off to the south. There is a campground, a picnic area, and a man-made swimming lake on the plain north of the river. Trails lead off through the woods along the river bottom, and also across the generally flat landscape of the prairie remnant. As the path begins to rise at the eastern end of the Wide Sky Trail, you'll be walking up the slope of Campbell Beach, which formed the edge of Glacial Lake Agassiz thousands of years ago. As you enjoy the open sky you're likely to hear the liquid song of a meadowlark or the astral chatter of a bobolink, both of which are common visitors to the park. More elusive prairie birds such as the upland sandpiper and the marbled godwit also show their heads occasionally, and in April, if you plan ahead, you can watch the prairie chickens do their courtship dance from a viewing blind. (Call the Nature Conservancy for details: 218-498-2679)

3 East Grand Forks

Grand Forks, or "les Grandes Fourches," as it was once known, developed where the Red Lake River meets the Red River. Already an important site for nomadic Native Americans during their seasonal buffalo hunts, it was often chosen as a rendezvous point by the French trappers who worked in the area during the eighteenth century. Oxcarts, steamboats, railroads, agriculture: The progression is a familiar one. Yet, as is often the case, Grand Forks also owes its existence to a single man and a single unusual event.

In those days Alexander Griggs, who had become a steamboat captain on the Mississippi in his youth, ran an operation transporting cargo up and down the Red River via flatboats. In 1870 he and his crew were stranded at the confluence of the Red Lake River and the Red River when the two rivers unexpectedly froze. They built a cabin and spent the winter there. During that long winter it occurred to Griggs that the area was well-suited for a town. The next spring he registered a land claim

and (with the aid of James J. Hill), he launched a steamboat to transport goods and settlers between Grand Forks and other points along the river. He encouraged others to settle in the area, and in 1875 he filed a land plat for the town of Grand Forks.

Grand Forks, North Dakota, and East Grand Forks, its neighbor across the river, were in the national spotlight in April of 1997, when the Red River overflowed its banks and flooded both cities. Within a day, sixty thousand people were forced to leave their homes and many buildings in downtown Grand Forks were on fire. Both cities have largely recovered, but the two neighborhoods most seriously damaged by the flooding, Lincoln Drive in Grand Forks and Sherlock Park in East Grand Forks, were never rebuilt. Instead, they've been turned into urban parks. The area along the river south of downtown Grand Forks is now a succession of pleasant picnic areas, playgrounds, and jogging trails. And the neighborhood just north of downtown East Grand Forks is now a Minnesota State Park Campground. You drive down city streets and turn up the driveway that leads to your campsite. The area could do with a little landscaping, but the sites are well-spaced, and the river is not far away. Across the street from the campground entrance is a row of bars and restaurants with expansive patios looking west toward the nearby river. And if you've forgotten an item of camping gear, never fear—there's a Cabella's right down the street!

4 Crookston

Although it stands out on the flat open plain of the Red River Valley, Crookston became a transportation hub during the decades when oxcarts passed through on their way to Saint Paul. In 1880 Crookston had ten hotels, and in 1895 Mark Twain paid the prosperous town a visit, the other stops on his itinerary being Duluth and Saint Paul.

When lumbering began to move west Crookston became a lumbering center, with millions of board feet of pine being floated down the Red Lake River from forests to the east. In fact, it was the Red River Lumber Company, based in Crookston, that popularized the mythic figure of Paul Bunyan in its advertising. Among the lumber barons active in Crookston was T. B. Walker, who later established an art museum in Minneapolis.

In more recent times Crookston has retained a degree of economic vitality through agricultural processing. Sugar beets have been a major crop in the Red River Valley since World War I, and in 1955 the American Crystal Sugar Company built a sugar beet processing plant in Crookston. A few years later the Dahlgren Company built a sunflower processing plant. It's a thrill to see fields of sunflowers ripening in the summer sun, and if you travel the area in the fall, you'll see sugar beets scattered along the roadside that have fallen off the heavily loaded trucks.

Crookston also received a boost in 1993 when its two-year technical college became a branch of the University of Minnesota. The college made a splash nationally when it became the first campus in the country to supply every full-time student with a laptop computer. Among projects that may return it to the public eye in the future are its researches into cellulosic biofuels.

Downtown Crookston has seen better days, but quite a few well-preserved buildings from the city's heyday remain standing. You can pick up a walking-tour brochure at the Chamber of Commerce office at 118 Fletcher Street. If you've only got time for a brief visit, then Widman's Candy Store would be the place to stop. It's located downtown at 116 & 118 South Broadway. The interior of the store dates back to its earliest years, the same family still runs the place...and much of the candy is still home made! Crookston's geography is complicated by the fact that the Red Lake River meanders this way and that through town, dividing it into a number of almost separate neighborhoods.

Old Crossing Treaty State Historical Wayside

An event of momentous import for both the Ojibwe and whites of Minnesota took place at a now-obscure park a few miles northeast of Crookston. To get there, take Highway 75 out of town going north, and turn right onto County Road 11 just past the University campus. Turn left on County Road 13 and watch for the brown signs that will direct you to Old Crossing Historic Wayside. Except for a statue of an Ojibwe warrior standing proudly next to a clump of bushes, holding a peace pipe, there is little to see here except the river and the trees and the fields. Yet it was on this site that a few Ojibwe chiefs signed a treaty in 1863 ceding almost 11 million acres of land to white settlement. Ter-

ritorial Governor Alexander Ramsey signed the document on behalf of the United States. The leaders of the Red Lake Band of Chippewa included Mons-o-Mo, May-dwa-gun-on-ind, Little Rock, Broken Arm, and Leading Feather. Red Bear of the Pembina Band and Little Chief of Turtle Mountain also participated.

Not so long ago, a cottonwood tree still stood in the park that was used as a post-office for ox-cart drivers passing through the region. Ox-cart tracks are still to be seen in the vicinity (though I've never been able

to locate them) and across the gravel road from the park you may spot a Catholic shrine of the Virgin Mary amid the trees. This shrine was built by Father Ernest Bossus, pastor of a nearby Catholic Church from 1926 to 1935, in thanks for a successful cataract operation.

5 Red Lake Falls

The quaint town of Red Lake Falls is situated on the crest of an ancient beach at the confluence of the Red Lake and Clearwater Rivers. As early as 1798 Jean Baptiste Cadotte established a fur-trading post at the confluence of the two rivers. At the time the Hudson's Bay Company was working to extend its trade network to the south. It was also interested in securing reliable supplies of buffalo meat from the prairies immediately to the west, which was the essential ingredient in the pemmican that sustained the voyageurs on their long and arduous journeys through the northern forests.

In the spring of 1798 the geographer and surveyor David Thompson visited Cadotte at Red Lake Falls, and he described the man as follows:

Mr. Baptiste Cadotte was about thirty-five years of age. He was the son of a French gentleman by a native woman, and married to a very handsome native woman, also the daughter of a Frenchman: He had been well educated in Lower Canada, and spoke fluently his native Language, with Latin, French and English. I had long wished to meet a well educated native, from whom I could derive sound information for I was well aware that neither myself, nor any other Person I had met with, who was not a Native, were sufficiently masters of the Indian Languages. As the season was advancing to break up the Rivers, and thaw the snow from off the ground, I inquired if he would advise me to proceed any farther with Dogs and Sleds: he said the season was too far advanced, and my further advance must be in Canoes.

More than a half-century later, in 1863, the United States government purchased much of the real estate in the area (11 million acres) from the resident Ojibwe near the present-day hamlet of Huot. A decade later Pierre Bottineau, a native of the Red River Settlement near Lake Winnipeg, brought a large number of French-Canadian settlers from the Twin Cities to settle in the area.

A survey of the area's early residents would expose surnames on the order of Gervais, Bazile, Labissonniere, Benoit, Cloutier, Pepin, and

Desmarais, all of which testify to the early influence of French-Canadian stock. But with the passage of time and the influx of new immigrant groups, many parts of the valley became heavily Norwegian in flavor.

Today the river itself may be the most appealing thing in Red Lake Falls. Tubing is a popular activity; in fact, much of the river's 190-mile length from Red Lake to the Red River is navigable by canoe. The river passes through marshes, farmland, deep canyons, and heavily-wooded sections. A week-long festival is held each year in early June to celebrate this unusual watercourse, with activities taking place at the various communities stretched out along the route.

Glacial Ridge National Wildlife Refuge

In 2004 the federal government established the Glacial Ridge National Wildlife Area on 2,000 acres of land donated by the Nature Conservancy. The refuge will eventually encompass 35,000 acres, making it the largest tallgrass prairie and wetland restoration project in U.S. history. As the area included in the refuge expands, it will provide habitat for grassland birds, greater prairie chickens, and sandhill cranes, and it also supports a wide array of prairie wildflowers. Migrating waterfowl will make use of its fields and wetlands. The funds for land purchase and maintenance will come from sales of the federal Duck Stamp. The restoration of this vast acreage to its natural wetland condition will not only provide valuable wildlife habitat, but also help control flooding on the Red Lake River and preserve the wells of the Crookston water supply which are located nearby.

Though the region is one of great promise for hunters, birders, and other wildlife-lovers, a visitor to the refuge today will hardly know that she's passing through it. Aside from a sign and a project description on Highway 2 south of Marcoux, the landscape encompassed by the refuge is largely indistinguishable from the surrounding terrain.

6 Thief River Falls

Thief River Falls lies at the confluence of the Thief and the Red Lake Rivers. It was originally a lumbering town, and later a wheat distribution center. It had the distinction of being at the cross-roads of the Great Northern and Soo Line railroads, which may explain why the train station is so impressive. Thief River Falls is now the largest city in the region, and it's still growing. There are several attractive city parks along the riverbanks, and plenty of local restaurants, banks, and motels. Many of the town's residents are employed at the Arctic Cat factory where snowmobiles and ATVs are manufactured. You can tour the plant at 1 PM on most days during the production season, and by all accounts the tour is a good one. (Call 218-681-8558 for more information.)

Yet for all of this, an aura of remoteness hangs over the city. Thief River Falls lies in the region far beyond the range of the most prosperous Red River Valley farms. The production value per acre of Pennington County is half that of Polk County, immediately to the west, and the countryside is more likely to be given over to pasturage, woods, marshes, and bogs.

7 Agassiz National Wildlife Refuge

Thief River Falls makes a good jumping-off point for Agassiz National Wildlife Refuge, Minnesota's largest wildlife refuge and perhaps its best. The Agassiz refuge offers a spectacular display of wild-

Agassiz National Wildlife Refuge: there is something irrationally hopeful about the sight of seemingly endless expanses of wetlands teeming with bird life.

life that varies by the season. Seventeen species of ducks commonly nest there each year, and as many as 100,000 migrating ducks pass through every fall. Franklin gulls nest by the thousands, and herons, grebes, and cormorants are also common. The refuge sustains two packs of gray wolves, a healthy population of moose, and plenty of deer. Migrating warblers, shorebirds, and sandhill cranes can also be easily spotted during spring and fall. And even newcomers to the birding world may be surprised to find how many beautiful ducks and shorebirds can be seen here from the comfort of a moving car.

Because the refuge is managed with the interests of the animals at heart, access to its 61,000 acres is limited, but there are several short hiking trails at the visitor's center, a four-mile driving loop, and a hundred-foot observation tower overlooking the teeming wetlands.

As you gaze out across the countryside here, it may be worth reflecting on the fact that before the Red River Valley was heavily ditched and drained, a much larger part of it looked like this.

The Aspen Parkland

The higher elevations on the eastern edge of the Red River Valley, from Red Lake Falls all the way to the outskirts of Winnipeg, form a domain known as the tallgrass aspen parkland. (In Canada the region goes by the name Boreal Plains.) It's a cold, dry, windy place, which keeps trees to a minimum and makes the region susceptible to spring fires. There are probably more deer stands than houses in the region, though ranches do dot the countryside amid the fields and forests. The vast, gently hilly fields dotted with copses of aspen give the parkland region a charm all its own.

The vegetation made an impression on early visitors, as can be attested by such place names as Eckvoll and Espelie ("oak vale" and "poplar slope" in Norwegian). A number of railroad properties in the area were never given over to farming, and many of them were purchased by the state during the 1960s. Following another flurry of land acquisitions during the 1990s, a number of large blocks of parkland became wildlife management areas.

Backpacking campsites line the South Fork Two River as it heads toward Lake Bronson.

8 Lake Bronson State Park

Lake Bronson is named after the Bronson family, whose farmstead lies at the bottom of it. The lake was created as a hedge against drought during the 1930s by damming the South Fork Two River. Lake Bronson is one of the few lakes in the area, and it offers water-based recreation to visitors from Manitoba and North Dakota as well as northwestern Minnesota.

Those who visit from other parts of the state may be less interested in the lake, however, which is pleasant but far from extraordinary, than in the wildlife and surrounding landscape. The park lies in the midst of aspen uplands, and there are several miles of beautiful open hiking trails across its eastern reaches. Western grebes are often sighted on the lake (a true sign that we're approaching the West), moose are sighted in the park with some frequency, and hikers also encounter bears from time to time. There is a grassy, almost suburban campground along the lakeshore, and quite a few rings of more wooded and secluded sites a mile or so down the road beyond the swimming beach. The park also has four backpacking sites along the river and several canoe-in sites on the far side of the lake. (218-754-2200)

9 Skull Lake Wildlife Management Area

If a visit to Lake Bronson State Park has whetted your appetite for a larger dose of Aspen Parkland, there are areas to the north that offer more of the same. Most accessible, perhaps, is Skull Lake Wildlife Area. Take County Road 15 due north out of Lake Bronson. (It later becomes County Road 4.) Where the road finally turns right, you can turn left onto a narrow gravel road that will take you into the area. A half mile in there's a parking lot and a place to camp. From here a two-rut foot trail leads off to the northwest.

The area is remote, and before heading in you might want to notify the DNR office in Karlstad (218-436-2427) to let them know you'll be up there. They can also advise you as to recent sightings of the local population of elk. An even less likely event—but no less thrilling to some folks—would be to catch sight of the rare and elusive yellow rail, which nests here in relative abundance.

Four miles to the east on County Road 4 you'll come to another two-rut road heading north toward the Canadian border. It will take you into the Caribou Wildlife Management Area. A mile up the road there's another designated camping spot. The landscape is flatter and the terrain is boggier but there's no telling what you might see up there.

Open fields stretch off toward the Canadian border at Skull Lake WMA.

THE BOGS

The word *bogeyman* comes from the bogs, and it suggests how mysterious and threatening the boglands remain to most of us. Minnesota has more than 7.5 million acres of bogland—far more than any other state except Alaska. It would be difficult to reach any destination north of Duluth without driving across miles and miles of it, though it usually passes unnoticed. The peat that forms the floor of these bogs is highly-prized by gardeners, but very little of it is actually harvested, and most of Minnesota's bogland remains inaccessible and all but unexplored. Hardly a summer goes by that a local newspaper in Cook, Big Fork, or Roseau doesn't carry the story of an elderly couple who goes blueberry picking on the edge of the local bog, only to re-emerge, tattered and torn, days later, with a harrowing story to tell of disorientation and desperation. That may explain why this section of the book is largely devoted to towns and landscapes lying on the fringes of the area.

Bogs serve important ecological functions, acting as water filters, overflow basins, and habitat for a small but interesting number of plant and animal species. They have increasingly become a winter playground for snowmobiles and ATVs—a practice that, without regulation or restraint, may lead to damage that will take many lifetimes to repair.

But what is a bog? A bog is a floating mat of sedges upon which sphagnum moss begins to grow. This moss, also called peat, develops because the oxygen present is insufficient to allow for normal decomposition of the plant matter. Over time the mat eventually becomes so thick and stable that evergreen shrubs, and eventually tamarack and black spruce trees, begin to grow on it. Though such regions may sometimes dry up completely and become forest-lands, the bogs that we're familiar with remain wet and largely inaccessible to foot traffic. Because the soil and water are acidic, they support little wildlife, and the small rodents that do enjoy the bog environment—bog lemmings, shrews, and voles—are not easy to catch sight of. A number of interesting plants thrive there—bottle gentians, rosemary, bog-laurel, sundews, pitcher-plants, moccasin flowers, and bog-orchids. Perhaps the most colorful sightings you're likely to make in the bog are of warblers: the Connecticut warbler, yellow-rumped warbler, Nashville warbler, and palm warbler often nest there.

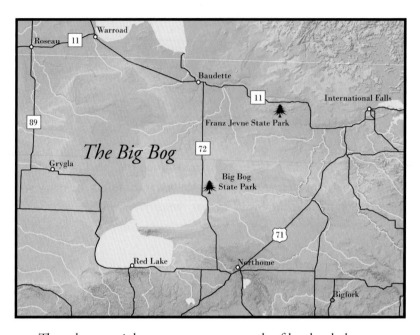

Though you might come across a stretch of bogland almost any-where in northern Minnesota, there are two large swathes of it. One stretches from Aitkin in a northeasterly direction toward the Iron Range and beyond (not included on map above). If you drive High-way 53 between Cloquet and International Falls you'll see plenty of it on both sides of the road—tightly packed black spruce and tama-rack groves above a velvety carpet of bumpy green moss. An even denser chunk of bog lies between the Red Lake Indian Reservation and the Canadian border. This giant bogland began to form more than 7,000 years ago in the flat lake basin formed by the retreat of Glacial Lake Agassiz, and in some places the layer of peat can extend up to fifteen feet below the surface. Moraines and shallow deposits of sand scattered throughout the area also support jack pine and spruce forests.

Big Bog State Park

Bogs are probably not a place anyone would chose to spend a long vaca-tion. Yet they have their own appeal, and a visit has recently been made more inviting by the creation of Big Bog State Park, on the northeastern tip of Upper Red Lake.

The lower section of the park will appeal mostly to fisherman who want to try their luck with the famous walleyes of Upper Red Lake, which are staging a comeback after suffering a debilitating decline during the 1990s due to overfishing. (In 1989, the Red Lake Band of Ojibwe harvested 950,000 pounds of walleye. In 1996, their nets brought in only 15,000 pounds.) This section offers a landing and a few campsites in the woods along the Tamarac River just before it flows into the lake, and a few interpretive hiking trails along the shore of the lake itself. It's a pleasant site, and archeological excavations confirm that it once served as a camp and burial site for the native peoples of the area. In more recent times a British fur trade post was located nearby, though the experts disagree on precisely where it was located.

The lake itself is Minnesota's largest, if you consider only those that are entirely within the boundaries of the state. It's also among the most unusual. Much of Red Lake's shoreline remains undeveloped, and a zone of reeds, marshes, and bogs rings large stretches of it.

Ten miles north on Highway 72 you'll come to the northern section of the park. It's been developed on an island of sand that cuts into the largest undisturbed patch of bog in the lower 48 states. A one-mile metal boardwalk extends out into the bog, which is actually twenty

A number of interesting plants thrive in the bog: bottle gentians, rosemary, bog-laurel, sundews, pitcher-plants, moccasin flowers, and bog-orchids.

miles wide and fifty miles long. A walk along even this short stretch will give you a feel for how immense the bog actually is. As you stroll across the level boardwalk through the tamarack and spruce, you'll pass open sphagnum bogs, black spruce bogs, peat bogs, and white cedar swamps. Other features that have been sculpted by the water as it flows at a snail's-pace through the vegetation include circular islands, oviod islands, raised bogs, and ribbed fens, most of which are most easily seen from the window of an airplane. Trails that were created by the last remaining caribou herd in Minnesota, which petered out during the 1930s, are also still clearly visible—bogs do not change in a hurry.

Interpretive displays along the way offer more scientific commentary than most of us can digest at one go, and they also detail a fascinating sidelight in the bog's history: In the early twentieth century the area was opened to homesteading. Massive drainage projects were undertaken—the canals are still plainly visible, of course—and farmers moved into the area. The scheme was ill-devised from the beginning, the farmers were unable to support themselves or pay the taxes on the land that had been reclaimed, and the counties that had drained the land, unable to pay off the loans they'd taken out to finance twenty years of drainage operations, faced bankruptcy. The state of Minnesota agreed to assume the loan payments in return for the land. Programs were put in place to resettle the farmers, and the water seeped back into the bogs. The entire episode only goes to show that even the most obscure of Minnesota's regions often harbor a secret and fascinating history.

International Falls

The transition from the rocky terrain of the Canadian Shield to the flat landscapes of the boglands can be seen in the contrast between the rugged outline of Rainy Lake and the straight, quiet course the Rainy River takes once it leaves the lake on its way to Lake of the Woods. International Falls sits where the Rainy River leaves the lake, right on the fringe of the bog region.

The city's great claim to fame is as the nation's "icebox." It frequently records the lowest minimum temperature in the United States. But the city retains some of the flavor of earlier times, perhaps because it's an

The Boise-Cascade paper plant in Fort Frances, Ontario, looms across the Rainy River.

active rail center, and you're likely to see long rows of aspen trunks and huge mounds of fresh woodchips sitting by the roadside as you tour the city. Also difficult to miss is the enormous Boise paper mill that stands in the middle of downtown, which is reputed to be the world's second-fastest. Beyond the wood products industry, the economy of International Falls also receives a boost from the proximity of Rainy Lake and Voyageurs National Park. (see the Arrowhead section for details.)

The best way to familiarize yourself with the region would be to stop in at the Koochiching Museum at 214 6th Avenue, in the shadow of the paper mill (218-283-4316). The back half of the museum is devoted to a fine selection of artifacts from the early history of the area, with stone tools from the Archaic period, Ojibwe crafts, trade items from voyageur days, and a collection of miniature steamboats modeled after the ones that plied Rainy Lake and the Rainy River before the railroads arrived. The front half of the museum is devoted to the career of International Falls' most famous resident, Bronko Nagurski. There are few alive today who actually saw Nagurski play, but in his day he was a sort of Babe Ruth of professional football. Leaving aside the three world championships he earned as a professional wrestler, Nagurski is the only athlete to be named NFL All-Pro at three different non-kicking positions. Today the NCAA annually awards a Bronko Nagurski Trophy to the nation's best college defensive player. Watch the video, read the newspaper clippings, examine the memorabilia, and then decide for yourself if Nagurski was the greatest football player of all time. He was certainly among the most versatile.

International Falls is well endowed with mom-and-pop motels, as well as several upscale chains. A trip across the border to Canada can also add to the fun, presuming you've remembered your passport. Though the cultural differences are small, everything seems a little *different* on the other side, and following Highway 11 out across Rainy Lake can be a pleasant trip.

Franz Jevne State Park

The journey from International Falls to Baudette takes you down the south side of the Rainy River along Highway 11, and it can be a lonely trip. Perhaps the best place to enjoy the beauty of the river is Franz Jevne State Park. It's a small, hilly piece of land with a number of primitive campsites and a nice picnic area. You can walk down to the river through the trees and stroll the bank or watch the pelicans fishing in the rapids. The river itself is broad and smooth, but it's moving with considerable force. (After all, much of the water that leaves the Boundary Water Canoe Area reaches Hudson's Bay via this route.)

The entire scene is one of quiet beauty, the riverbank on the Canadian side is largely pastoral, and as you gaze across the river you may spot a few of the many Indian mounds that line the bluffs in the area.

The largest of them all stands on the south side of the river a few miles to the east, where the Big Fork River flows into the Rainy River. Three stories tall and more than a hundred feet long, it may be as much as two-thousand years old. For many years it was open to the public as a state historic site. The Laurel Indians, perhaps a distant ancestor of the Dakota, gathered here every year, centuries ago, to fish the Rainy River for sturgeon (which can run to more than ten feet in length) and they interred hundreds of their dead in the mounds nearby. The Minnesota Historical Society finally closed the site, which it deemed inappropriate for a tourist attraction, not to mention the remote location and the

dwindling number of visitors. But standing on the riverbank at Franz Jevne State Park, one can easily imagine the days when travel was by water and the livelihood of a community depended on its success at spearing the passing fish. The Laurel people, too, probably camped in the woods and watched the pelicans in the rapids, and it isn't difficult to understand why they chose to bury their dead along the banks of this lovely and bountiful river.

Baudette, Warroad, and Lake of the Woods

Lake of the Woods is a world unto itself. It covers almost fifteen hundred square miles and has more than fourteen thousand islands, though the part of it that lies in Minnesota consists largely of a massive sheet of open water. Baudette lies on the Rainy River a few miles upstream from the lake, and both the town and the resorts that dot the riverbanks nearby cater to fishermen heading out onto the big lake. It's an active little town with a border crossing and a decent number of restaurants and motels.

The best place for the passing tourist to see the lake is at Zippel Bay State Park, a few miles north of town (218-783-6252). It has several campgrounds, a marina, and a three-mile long beach where you can stroll as you look out across the seemingly endless expanse of water to the north. The rare piping plover can occasionally be seen on the beach, though you're far more likely to see terns, gulls, spotted sandpipers, and other common species. During the off-season, when there are few people around and the waves are rolling in, Zippel Bay Beach can seem like the last place on earth.

The town of Warroad is the only port on the American side of Lake of the Woods. The west end of town is dominated by an immense Marvin Windows factory. If you head out to the marina you'll pass the Seven Clans Casino along the way. It's fun to watch both the birds and the boats from the observation tower at the marina.

At the end of the parking lot a historical marker recounts the history of Fort St. Charles, which was built by the French in 1732 and abandoned thirty years later when the British won control of the entire continent during the Seven Years War. A reproduction of the fort stands on the original site—but that's at the tip of the Northwest Angle, sixty miles away by car, with two border crossings and the last twenty miles on gravel. If you're looking for *remote*, that would be a good place to start. Call Angle Island Resort for details 800-223-8101.

Roseau

Roseau is far and away the largest city within the boglands. Much of the economic vitality of the town is rooted in the Polaris snowmobile factory on its outskirts. Polaris began its life as a manufacturer of farm machinery, but during the mid-1950s it became the first company in the world to market recreational snow-machines. Though Japanese manufacturers later entered the market, Polaris still ranks among the top four snowmobile manufacturers world-wide. You can tour the enormous plant on most days at 4 p.m. Inquire at the museum or gift shop for details (205 5th Ave SW; 218-463-4999).

Alongside the gift shop there is a snowmobile museum that tells the story of the company's rise and exhibits its bulky early machines, its brilliant design successes, its racing machines, and its occasional misfires. The adjoining restaurant may be the best place in town to eat.

Roseau lies on the western fringe of the Bog region. It's surrounded to the east, north, and south by wetlands, but to the southwest the drier

Red River Valley zone begins almost immediately outside of town. The problems that the town experiences with flooding is the direct result of the fact that the countryside is already saturated with water.

The Roseau Bog, just north of town on Highway 310, is a favorite with wild-life enthusiasts looking for wolves, northern hawk owls, boreal owls, and other unusual species amid the black spruce, tamarack, and cedar thickets.

Nearby Hayes Lake State Park contains a section of the Roseau River, an artificial lake, and lots of bog trails where you can hunt for orchids, gentians, and other unusual species—or just enjoy the solitude.

When is a bog not a bog?

Words such as "bog," "swamp," and "marsh" are often used interchangeably. They aren't the same thing.

Bog (or Peat bog): Characterized by vegetation which is not decaying rapidly, and thus accumulates as peat. Sphagnum moss is a common inhabitant of bogs.

Fen: Similar to a bog, but the nutrient levels are higher because it is fed and drained with streamwater. Sphagnum moss may be present, but is absent in rich fens.

Marsh: Wetland with plants like cattails that grow in the mud underwater but stick out above the water level.

Muskeg: A spruce bog covered with tussocks of Ericaceous shrubs (plants related to blueberries).

Swamp: A flooded forest. Cypress and tupelo typically grow in swamps. Forests that have been inundated by beaver action aren't swamps, because the trees will eventually die due to the elevated water table.

THE IRON RANGE

There had been speculation about the mineral riches of north-eastern Minnesota even during the period of French exploration in the eighteenth century. After all, the native tribes had been extracting copper from rich veins in the Keewinaw Peninsula (now a part of Michigan), just across Lake Superior, for over 5,000 years. In 1850 a U.S. Geological Survey team reported iron ore near Gunflint Lake, which further heightened interest in the area. In 1865 the state of Minnesota hired its own geologist to scope out the area near Lake Vermilion. He didn't find iron, but something far more valuable—gold. This started the state's only real gold rush, and a road had soon been constructed from Duluth to the southern shore of the then-remote lake. In classic gold-rush fashion, a town soon sprang up, with saloons, dry goods stores, and boarding houses. Unfortunately, nobody found any gold. Nor could the place where the state geologist had originally made his find be relocated. The entire episode ended as quickly as it had begun.

One man who visited the area during the rush, however, George R. Stuntz, remained convinced that there was money to be made mining in the region. And Stuntz felt that iron, rather than gold, would prove to be the money-maker. Mining iron ore would be a large scale operation requiring a massive infrastructure, however, which Stuntz lacked the capital to put into place. He elicited the interest of East Coast businessmen, including Charlemagne Tower (after whom the town of Tower was later named) and conducted several tours of the area to convince his would-be investors of its potential. Finally, more than fifteen years after his original visit, Stuntz and his East Coast partners formed the Minnesota Iron Company. And in a pattern that would recur again and again in the industry's history, one of the first things the company did was petition the Minnesota State Legislature to give it a tax break. The legislature readily agreed to such a deal—that someone was prepared to spend millions developing the forests and bogs of northern Minnesota was music to their ears.

In 1884 the firm opened the Soudan Mine, setting the stage for Minnesota's long run as one of the world's major iron ore producers.

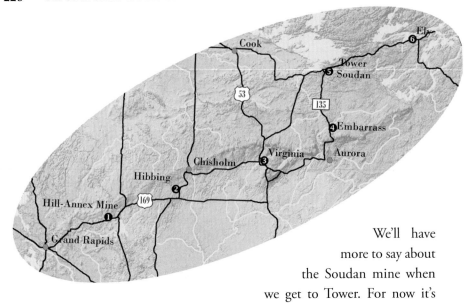

We'll have more to say about the Soudan mine when we get to Tower. For now it's enough to mention that the ore extracted from the mine was so rich in iron that the region was soon crawling once again with prospectors. And this time not all of them came away empty-handed. A new vein of ore was discovered north of Lake Vermilion and the town of Ely soon developed nearby.

It took somewhat longer to unearth the deposits that were eventually to outstrip all others, because the iron took the form, not of hard ore-bearing rocks, but of soft crumbly iron ore lying close to the surface. These deposits lay in the region to the west of the Soudan mine. Stuntz had taken his associates over the country several times without noticing anything unusual. In was not until November of 1890 that an agent working for a Duluth family named Merritt uncovered samples of the soft red ore about ten miles east of where the city of Virginia later developed. The Merritts named their find the Mesabi Range making use of the Ojibwe word for "giant."

Although the Merritts had little experience in big business, they succeeded in acquiring a number of land parcels at very reasonable prices, and were soon deeply involved in the project to build a railroad from the Mesabi Range to Lake Superior. Meanwhile, more experienced miners and financiers from the East also became interested in the region, along with lumber families who already had leases in the area and were looking ahead to the time when the forests would be gone. The history of the Iron Range is enlivened by ambitious local figures like Merritt and Stuntz, but by the time mining operations had gotten into high gear, many of them were in the hands of men with names like Rockefeller, Carnegie, Morgan, and Frick.

The men who flooded the area in droves in search of work were more likely to have names like Smabi, Gustavson, or O'Brien. More than forty languages were commonly spoken on the Range during its early years. At first the miners were predominantly Cornish, Scandinavian, French-Canadian, and other northern European extractions, many of them originally drawn to the area by the lumber trade. With the passage of time, workers from the Slavic countries of southeastern Europe became increasingly prominent in the mix. In 1900 half the residents of the Mesabi Range were foreign-born. All of this lent a degree of color to the social life of the towns, and its legacy lingers in the voice-patterns and local customs of the Range's citizens to this day.

The significance of the region to America's economy can hardly be over-estimated. From 1900 to 1980, the Mesabi Range contributed about 60 percent of the nation's iron ore output. The advanced shipping infrastructure that developed along the Great Lakes and the St. Lawrence Seaway was put in place largely to handle the ore moving east from Minnesota to the steel mills of Indiana and Pennsylvania. Production began to decline slowly during the 1950s, and the high-grade ore was eventually depleted entirely. But by 1960 a staggering 2.5 trillion tons of ore had been mined and transported from the Iron Range to the loading docks in Duluth, Two Harbors, Silver Bay, and other port cities on Lake Superior.

In recent decades mining activity on the Range has centered around a low-grade ore called taconite, which we'll explore when we reach Mountain Iron. The latest technological innovation has been a new "nugget" iron-making process pioneered by Kobe Steel, Ltd., which has granted a license for the construction of a $235 million manufacturing facility in Hoyt Lakes. Annual iron-nugget production capacity is expected to be 500,000 metric tons. The iron output from the nugget plant, unlike taconite, will be of the quality required by the new generation of mini-mills that are coming to dominate the industry. All of which is very good news for the residents of the Iron Range.

Hill Annex Mine State Park

The area we call the Range actually consists of three distinct deposits. We crossed the Cuyuna Range on our journey from Aitkin to Grand Rapids. In its day this range produced more than a hundred million tons of ore, which is nothing to sneeze at. Yet the figure pales in comparison with that of its neighbor to the northeast, the Mesabi Range. The output of the Mesabi, which runs from Grand Rapids in a northeasterly direction past Hibbing and Virginia to Babbitt, was truly staggering during the first half of the twentieth century. Mesabi, quite fittingly, is the Ojibwe word for "giant." But more about that later.

Though Grand Rapids is better known for logs than ore, the nearby town of Calumet is the home of the Hill Annex Mine, which offers a perfect introduction to the region. The Hill Annex Mine is the world's largest open pit mine that is open for tours. Mining began here in 1913 and continued until 1978. In that span of time it produced 63 million tons of iron ore, making it the state's sixth largest producer. Eventually the high-grade ore gave out, and the mine was sold to a state agency, the Iron Range Resources and Rehabilitation Board for a dollar. In 1988 the mine became a state park. It is now a national historic site.

The Hill Annex Mine is one mile long, three-quarters of a mile wide, and up to 500 feet deep. You probably won't get a chance to see the bottom, however, unless you bring your scuba tanks. Once the mines were shut down, the pumps were turned off and the pit gradually refilled with water. Pines took root on the banks, and the entire site began to develop an odd and eerie beauty all its own.

To get a more complete picture of the operations during its productive period, you can take a 90-minute tour, often conducted by someone who used to work in the mines. You may even get a pontoon ride out into the middle of the lake. Some of the tours feature fossil hunting, but the guides usually restrict themselves to the mine's history and changing production methods. You can visit the old mine clubhouse and view some exhibits pertinent to the site. Even without the tour, a view down into the blue-green waters of the red, steep-sided mine is stunning. (For more information call 218-247-7215)

Hibbing

Hibbing is often considered the hub of the Iron Range. It is far and away the largest town in the area and it lies in the heart of the Mesabi Range, surrounded by vast open pits.

The town was founded by an immigrant from Germany named Frans Hibbing, who arrived in northern Wisconsin all but penniless and found work, first as a farmhand, and later as a timber cruiser. By the age of thirty Hibbing had established a real estate business in Duluth, and by that time he had also learned a few things about mineral exploration. In 1892 he headed up into the Range with a crew of thirty men looking for ore deposits. He found what he was looking for. The next summer the townsite of Hibbing was platted, and named in his honor. Hibbing returned the favor by taking a personal interest in the town's development, financing the construction of a water plant, an electric plant, roads, a bank, a sawmill, and a hotel with private funds.

Such relationships were common on the Range in those days, and they were deemed either generous or paternalistic, depending on one's point of view. They were put to the test in an unusual way in Hibbing, where the ore deposits proved to be so widespread that the mining companies, having surrounded the town on three sides with gaping mines, deemed it necessary to move the town itself in order to get at the valuable deposits below. By 1919, when the move took place, Hibbing had more than 20,000 residents. They agreed to move to a new site two miles to the south, only after the mining companies agreed to provide generous financing for the businesses that were to be established at the new site. Many of Hibbing's original homes and businesses were also painstakingly lifted from their foundations and moved to new locations.

In all, about 200 structures were moved to the new city. These included a store and even a couple of large hotels. A new high school was built at the new site, to the tune of almost $4 million dollars, and it remains noteworthy today for its marble floors, brass railings, statues, murals, crystal chandeliers, lavish auditorium, and fancy detailing throughout.

In fact, many towns on the Iron Range were endowed with parks, schools, and community buildings that were far more substantial than the norm, due to the property taxes the communities received from the mining companies.

There is no way to fully comprehend the amount of ore that was mined on the Mesabi Range, or the number of cars, airplanes, tanks, appliances, computers, cables, bridges, and other items that were manufactured using the steel it helped to produce. But a visit to the Hull Rust Mine on the outskirts of Hibbing might give us a clue. This enormous hole in the ground is more than three miles long, up to two miles wide, and 600 feet deep, and it's often billed as the world's biggest open pit mine. It was the first mine to be opened on the Mesabi Range, and since ore shipping began back in 1895, more than 1.4 billion tons of earth have been removed from it. At its peak the various operations taking place within its expanse produced a quarter of all the ore mined in the United States.

Although most sections are no longer in operation, eight million tons are still extracted yearly from the pit by the Hibbing Taconite Company. And we ought not to forget that although it has seen better times, the Mesabi Range still produces 75% of the iron ore mined in the United States.

To experience something of Iron Range life first-hand, stop in at the Sunrise Bakery, 1813 3rd Avenue E, to sample miner's delicacies like pasties (a Cornish meat pie), potica (a traditional Slovenian nut bread), or porketta (an Iron Range specialty of rolled pork roast, seasoned with fennel, garlic and other spices). The bakery has been going strong since 1913, and if you fall in love with one of their old-world treats, you can order up some more from their easy-to-use website.

For a more complete immersion in the mining traditions of the Range, make it a point to visit Ironworld Discovery Center in nearby Chisholm. Here you'll be able to examine museum displays running from the dim recesses of geological time to the latest advances in taconite processing, and visit recreated dwellings from various life-ways and cultures of the past, including a logger's cabin, an Ojibwe camp, and a Finish Sami sod-roofed home. The oral histories alone are worth an extended visit. The center is especially lively on those summer weekends when festivals take place dedicated to the music, costumes, food, crafts, and other traditions of Polish, Swedish, German, and other ethnic groups. (For further information call 800-372-6437).

Bob Dylan

In the minds of many visitors who take little interest in the dusty red ore that built the region, Hibbing is best-known as the boyhood home of Bob Dylan. Dylan was born in Duluth in 1941. The family moved to Hibbing when Bob was seven. His name in those days was Robert Allen Zimmerman, and there are plenty of stories afoot about various musical performances he gave at high school talent shows or in the local bars. Among the bands he played with were The Golden Chords, The Shadow Blasters, Elston Gunn, The Rock Boppers and The Satin Tones. You can drive by Dylan's boyhood home, on the corner of 25th Street and 7th Avenue E, and attend the Friday night fish fry at the Moose Lodge, if you want to see the venue where

Bob Dylan's childhood home

Dylan's bands often played when he was a teen. Zimmys, a restaurant on Howard Street, features Dylan memorabilia and also serves some of the best food in town. The Hibbing Public Library has a Bob Dylan exhibit in the basement, with yearbook photos and posters that you might not see elsewhere. But the best way to evoke the talented songwriter's memory might be to slip one of his CDs into the car stereo as you cruise the streets of this proud and yet slightly depressed mining town, and remind yourself, as you listen to some of his plaintive or angry ballads, that Bob himself never really felt at home here.

Dylan graduated from Hibbing High School in 1959 and moved to Minneapolis briefly to attend the University of Minnesota before moving on to New York City. Two years later he released his first album.

Whether Dylan left town on a Greyhound Bus no one seems to know. If he did, it would have been fitting, not only because buses have traditionally been the favored means of transportation for the drifters, outcasts, and blue-collar workers that appear more than occasionally in Dylan's poetic lyrics, but also because Hibbing is the home of the American bus industry. Two local entrepreneurs, Carl Wickman and Andrew "Bus Andy" Anderson, started a bus line in 1914 to ferry iron miners to and fro between Hibbing and the nearby town of Alice. Their single "bus" was a Huppmobile that carried only a few passengers. The service was popular, new routes were added, the two businessmen expanded their range of operations little by little. The result was Greyhound Bus Line.

In 1989 a Greyhound Bus Museum was finally established in Hibbing to celebrate this fascinating chapter in the nation's transportation history (218-263-5814). There are several buses parked in the parking lot outside, including the original Huppmobile that started it all. Inside you'll find plenty of miniature models, goofy exhibits, and a video that you watch from the seats of a bus.

Just outside Hibbing you may see a plaque identifying a spot of unusual geographic interest. It marks the spot where three watersheds meet. If you dropped a glass of water on the spot, some of it would end up in Hudson's Bay, some in the Gulf of Mexico, by way of the Mississippi River, and some would eventually make its way to the North Atlantic by way of the Great Lakes and the St. Lawrence Seaway. You may see roadside signs marking the Laurentian Divide at various places on your journey across the northern reaches of the state, but this is the only spot in Minnesota, and one of only two in the country, where not two, but three drainage systems meet.(The other one is in Montana's Glacier National Park.)

The towns we'll be passing between Chisholm and Virginia all played a part in lumbering and mining during the first half of the century. Buhl has re-entered the limelight in recent years by bottling water from an aquifer 700 to 1000 feet underground and selling it in

New York City, among other places. It has been tapping the aquifer for local use since 1901, and selling the water aggressively for close to twenty years.

Mountain Iron

The Mesabi Range got its start in Mountain Iron, where ore was first discovered in 1890. And the future of mining on the Range may also be seen here at the Minntac Mine, which is North America's largest taconite mining operation.

The extraordinary bounty of the Mesabi Range was due not only to the relative ease with which ore could be extracted from the open pit mines, but also to its unusually high iron content. Well, nothing lasts forever. As the high grade ore began to peter out on the range scientists turned their attention to a low-grade ore called taconite. These deposits had been discovered as early as 1870, and they were plentiful, but the ore had only a 30-50% concentration of iron, and the methods of extracting it were deemed to be too costly.

During the 1940s, however, as the richer ore deposits were depleted, scientists at the University of Minnesota led by Dr. E.W. Davis developed a cheaper way to extract the iron from taconite. In the later 1950s the Reserve Mining Company built a taconite processing plant at Silver Bay, Minnesota, and before long they were producing 6-10 million tons of pellets a year.

The taconite industry could not fully compensate for the decline in iron mining, but it continued to provide jobs during a period of widespread unemployment on the Range. The Minntac plant employs more than 700 people and turns out 18 million tons of ore annually.

For more information on this fascinating chapter in the industry's history, you can stop by and take a tour of the plant, and you might even get a chance to watch as the miners set off a blast in the pit below.

Virginia

Local pride has always been strong on the Iron Range. Hibbing has always been the largest and most important among its cities, but Virginia has traditionally prided itself on having a touch of class not

Like many Range cities, Virginia sits on the edge of an open-pit mine

found on the streets of its neighbor to the west. The main business district burned to the ground twice during Virginia's early years, but she picked herself up each time, and when lumber baron Frederick Weyerhauser established the Virginia and Rainy Lake Lumber Company there in 1908, its mill was the largest and most modern in the world. In its prime the mill yards covered a square mile of real estate. The company employed 3,000 lumberjacks and 1,800 workers at the mill itself. When the plant closed its doors in 1929, it signaled the end of a golden era in white pine logging. In less than 100 years, almost 68 billion board feet of pine had been cut from northern forests—enough to fill boxcars to the moon, and halfway back!

Virginia was also a mining city, with as many as twenty mines in operation simultaneously. The Messabe Mountain Mine, run by the Merritt brothers who had originally discovered the ore, was, in its day, the largest in the world. As a result of the wealth generated by these two outsized enterprises, citizens of Virginia started referring to their city as "The Queen City of the North" and she retains that label today.

As you'll notice as you approach Virginia, there are plenty of open pits dotting the landscape as reminders of that vigorous era. Though most of them have long-since been shut down, you can drive up to the Mineview in the Sky observation platform as you leave town on Highway 53, if you haven't yet had your fill of very large holes in the ground. The overlook has an information center, and there are several enormous earth-moving machines parked in the parking lot.

The real draw for visitors to Virginia, however, is the architecture on Chestnut Street downtown, which is lined with store fronts and marques from a vanished age.

You might well begin your tour of the six-block district at the train station at the west end of Chestnut Street. This three-story orange sandstone building, which now houses a bank, was built in 1913. At one time, a large pine stood in the turn-around at the front of the depot and we can easily imagine how festive it might have looked, all lit up on winter nights before Christmas. In those days Virginia was a rail center, with four railroads running twenty trains a day in and out of the bustling city. In the early days a "Lumberjack" express also ran roundtrip daily from Virginia to Cusson, hauling forest workers to their appointed rounds. The final passenger train left the Virginia passenger station in 1961.

The track overlooks Silver Lake, where the log pond, the log unloading docks, and sawmills No. 2 and No. 3 of the Virginia Rainy Lake Lumber Company were once located, and also the generating plant of the Virginia Municipal Heat & Light Company. The lake is now the home to what is billed locally as the World's Largest Floating Loon.

For a whiff of former days, why not stop in at the Italian Bakery (205 1st Street S). They've been open since 1905, and they're still turning out potica and other Range specialties at very reasonable prices.

Embarrass

A few miles north of Virginia on Highway 169, you'll see a turnoff to the right down County Road 21 toward the hamlet of Embarrass. This tiny village is sometimes in the news, because its weather station occasionally records the lowest daily temperature in the United States. If you can spare the time for a detour, it might be worth paying Embarrass a visit, though perhaps not for the weather. For much of its history, Embarrass has been a center for a community of Finnish farmers, and many of the old wooden farm buildings these newcomers from the Old World built are still standing, as a reminder both of the very heavy Finnish settlement in northern Minnesota, and also of the fact that alongside the lumbering and mining activities for which Northern Minnesota is well-known, there was also a stalwart contingent of independent-minded farmers who came to the area just to work the land. In 1941 the *WPA Guide to Minnesota* reported that of the town's 652 residents, only two were non-Finns.

A nice piece of Finnish handiwork

It might be a mistake to suggest that the Finns came here just to farm, however. In fact U.S. Steel, which controlled much of the mining activity in the area, engaged in an aggressive campaign to exclude Finns from their work force, especially after the labor strikes of 1915. Nor was it the giants of industry alone who exhibited such racist behavior. The Finns were widely looked down upon by other ethnic groups, and it was not an uncommon sight in those days to see a sign at a public beach—NO INDIANS OR FINNS.

As you approach Embarrass from the west you'll see the tiny visitor's center as you cross Highway 135 (218-984-2084). From here, if the center is open, you can take a heritage tour which visits several of the nearby homesteads. Tour guides will point out the Finnish construction techniques and share stories of those early days of pioneer farming. If you're on your own, follow the signs to the campground that lies east of town. Proceed past the campground and you'll arrive at a group of farm buildings that were built more than a hundred years ago in classic Finnish style.

After you've taken a look around, stop in at Sisu Tori, the local gift shop in the village, to read the announcements on the bulletin board or pick up some traditional Finnish baked goods. Then make your way north on Highway 135 to Tower.

Tower

If Virginia is a gateway to the north end of Lake Vermilion, Tower is right on the lakeshore at its larger southern end. Yet Tower's greatest claim to fame is undoubtedly the nearby Soudan mine. Unlike the open pit mines of the Mesabi Range, the Soudan mine is a shaft mine. It was opened in 1884, and was the first successful mine on the Iron Range. It later became a National Historic Landmark, and has been left pretty much just the way it was the day they shut it down in 1967. A tour of the mine would certainly be worth your while. But be prepared for a claustrophobic experience. A cable car will take you down a shaft to a point more than 2,000 feet below ground. Then you'll be carried by train more than a mile to the deepest area of the mine.

Because it required a good deal of tunneling, it was relatively expensive to extract ore from the Soudan mile. Yet the ore itself was famous for its high oxygen content, a valuable feature in producing steel, and a small amount of Soudan ore was often mixed with ore from other mines to improve the smelting process. When techniques to inject the oxygen artificially were perfected, however, demand for the expensive ore from the Soudan Mine withered.

During its many years of operation, the Soudan mine had an enviable safety record, and it was often referred to as the "Cadillac of iron mines." Now that the ore has been played out, the subterranean chambers of the Soudan mine have been refitted as a scientific laboratory by the University of Minnesota High Energy Physics Lab.

Physicists have long been on a quest to measure a tiny particle called a neutrino, which seems to make up a large part of the stuff of the universe, although it has almost no mass and travels with ease through all sorts of matter. The best place to study these tiny midges is deep underground, where most other sub-atomic particles have been filtered out by the surrounding bedrock. Little did the crusty men who dug the

Soudan mine a hundred years ago imagine, that the caverns, tunnels, and shafts they were creating would one day be used to explore the behavior of the tiny flecks of "dark matter" that are rocketing this way and that throughout our universe. Yet today the Soudan Underground Laboratory is the foremost underground science and engineering laboratory in the United States. Scientists from around the world come here in hopes of isolating the fundamental forces that rule the universe. If you're even vaguely interested in Weakly Interacting Massive Particles or Dark Matter, you ought to stop down to see the Main Injector Neutrino Oscillation Search detector and other fancy machinery. (For more information on either the mine or the lab call 218-753-2245)

Ely

Outdoorsmen and wilderness enthusiasts approach Ely with gleeful emotion. The town lies at the end of the road, in the heart of the woods, and on the edge of the Boundary Water Canoe Area Wilderness. It is the home to the famous International Wolf Center, and it has long been associated with such modern heroes of outdoor adventure as polar explorer Will Steger, wolf guru L. David Mech, black bear expert Lynn Rogers, wildlife photographer Jim Brandenburg, and nature–writer Sigurd Olson.

Yet like its neighbors on the Range, Ely got its start as a mining center. You'll see an overgrown pit where some of the excavations took place as you come into town: it's now filled with water and called Miner's Lake. There were five mines in all in the vicinity of Ely, and taken together they produced more that 80 million tons of iron before the final one shut down in 1967.

Author, adventurer, and former *Minneapolis Tribune* columnist Jim Klobuchar grew up in Ely, and in his essays he has captured the flavor and meaning of the era when immigrants from all over the world worked the mines perhaps as well as anyone:

> *The memory of Europe brought them few glints of rekindled joy— the old country with its thin pantries and the boots of the emperor's army and dead ends. But it was, after all, their homeland and the*

cradle of their family, and it taught them the songs. So they sang the songs and spoke the language, but the Iron Range was the new frontier of their lives....The men went into the mines. The women hung the family clothes on the line when the temperature was 15 degrees below zero....It wasn't the Austrian government that ruled their lives now, or the czar in Russia. Now the mining companies disbursed the money and made most of the rules.

But in the mining towns of Minnesota there was one abiding difference from the times and places that had squashed them down before they came to America. Fear had gone out of their lives. So had futility. True, the dirt of the mining towns might have been a little deeper than the dirt of the old country. They were embarrassed by their ignorance of the language and having to sequester themselves in their self-protective colonies where people spoke a language they could understand and nobody laughed at their crudities. But there were schools in this town. Their children would grow up speaking English. If they did their lessons, they would escape their shantytowns and the dark red pits where the immigrant men worked.

By the time its mines were played out Ely had long-since established itself as an outdoor recreation center. The lakes surrounding Ely are studded with lodges and resorts built early in the twentieth century, and it continues to sustain a healthy business outfitting canoe trips, motor-boat trips, and fly-in fishing trips deep into the untamed wilds to the north.

Yet the very richness of its untapped resources have made the hinterland beyond Ely a battleground between conflicting interests, both commercial and recreational, almost from the beginning. (For more on Ely's role in outdoor recreation and environmental learning, see pages 268-270.)

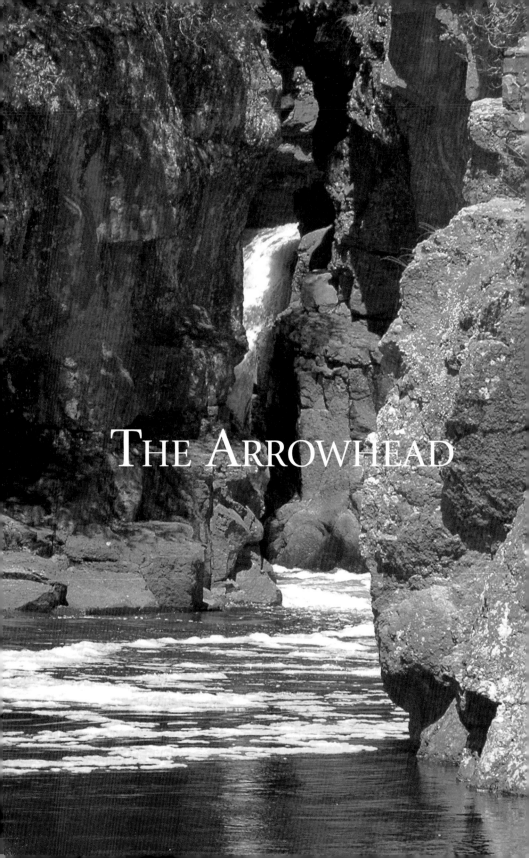

THE ARROWHEAD

Minnesota's Arrowhead region is the wildest and arguably the most beautiful part of the state. Much of it consists of evergreen forests that have never been set to the plow. Nearly all of it was logged at one time or another, and logging operations continue to provide livelihoods for local residents, but today the region's glistening lakes are once again surrounded by evergreen forests. The western edge of the Arrowhead is vaguely defined by the bogs north of Aitkin and the southwestern shores of Lake Vermilion. The eastern edge is far more clear-cut. A long succession of rolling hills and towering cliffs meet the expanse of Lake Superior to create the tourist mecca we know as the North Shore.

Roads were late in coming to the region, and many early settlers were miners, lumberjacks, and fishermen who traveled by boat up and down the coast. Copper-mining has long been associated with the region, though the production has never amounted to much, and is dwarfed by that of Michigan's Upper Peninsula. Yet if it weren't for *rumors* of copper, the Arrowhead would probably be in Canada today. Ben Franklin worked hard, during the negotiations that led to the Treaty of Paris in 1783, to insure that the North Shore was included as part of the American rather than the British domain precisely because of its alleged copper deposits. Though both gold and copper were mined in the area sporadically during the later half of the nineteenth century, it was only with the discovery of iron ore deposits that the interior of the region took on a degree of economic vitality.

The area's first roads and rail routes stretched inland from the lake to the mines in Tower and other locations in the interior, but during the early decades of the twentieth century a highway was laboriously constructed between Duluth and the Canadian border, and before long resorts began to spring up along the shore. By that time adventurous souls had also begun to explore the lakes and rivers that crisscross the roadless tracts of forested land. Following decades of bureaucratic wrangling and spirited public debate, much of the area along the Canadian border was set aside as the Boundary Waters Canoe Area.

In recent times the highway up the shore has been improved, passing lanes have been added, tunnels have been cut through the cliffs at several places to eliminate hairpin cliff-side curves, and now the motor trip from Duluth to Grand Portage is as safe and easy as it is gorgeous. On summer weekends the state parks and highway pull-outs are thronged with tourists who have come north to escape the heat of the Twin Cities and to admire the many waterfalls that thunder through the woods on their way to Lake Superior.

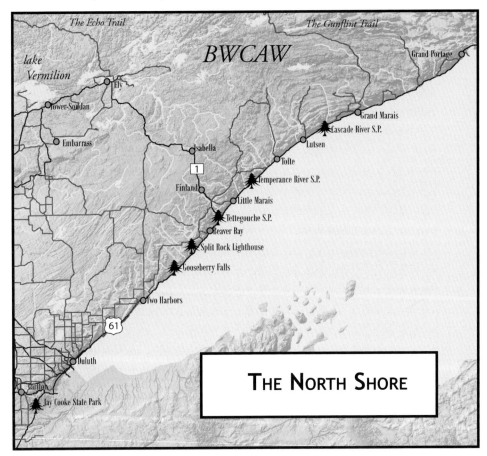

The Echo Trail   The Gunflint Trail

BWCAW

lake Vermilion   Grand Portage

Ely

Tower-Soudan

Embarrass   Grand Marais

Cascade River S.P.

Isabella   Lutsen

1   Tofte

Finland   Temperance River S.P.

Little Marais

Tettegouche S.P.

Beaver Bay

Split Rock Lighthouse

Gooseberry Falls

Two Harbors

61

Duluth

Carlton

Jay Cooke State Park

THE NORTH SHORE

I. THE NORTH SHORE

Carlton and the Saint Louis River

On July 2, 1864, President Lincoln signed a bill authorizing a grant of 47 million acres of land across the undeveloped northern tier of the United States to the newly-formed Northern Pacific Railroad. In return, the NP agreed to build a railroad to service those remote regions. Completing such an enterprise required not only land, but also capital, however, and the company struggled for years to convince investors that building a railroad across thousands of miles of largely-uninhabited terrain would eventually become profitable. It was only when New York financier Jay Cooke, (who is sometimes described as the man who financed the Civil War), lent his prestige to the project, that sufficient funds were obtained to start laying track. You can visit the spot today where groundbreaking took place on February 15, 1870, at Thompson Junction, a few miles east of Carleton, and a few miles west of the area we now know as Jay Cooke State Park.

Several Minnesota cities, including Brainerd and Moorhead, owe their prominence within the state to the railroad. The Northern Pacific also absorbed the smaller Lake Superior and Mississippi Railroad, which ran 155 miles from St. Paul to Duluth. By 1873 the line had reached Bismarck, Dakota Territory, and tracks had also been laid from Kalama to Tacoma in Washington Territory. But troubles with financing continued, and in that year Jay Cooke himself, who had not only promoted the company but invested heavily in it, was forced to close his Philadelphia banking house. This closure undercut confidence in the banking system and was a contributing factor in the Panic of 1873, during which nearly a quarter of the railroad lines in the country went bankrupt and the nation entered a severe economic depression that lasted until 1877.

The Northern Pacific was only one of many ventures that Cooke was involved in during his long career—he later recouped his fortune investing in Utah silver mines. Yet there is no denying that Cooke was fond of Duluth, which he envisioned as a second Chicago. Yet a glance at the map would suggest that while Duluth has access to eastern and European ports via the Great Lakes, it lacks Chicago's many connections to the nation's heartland. By 1900 Chicago's population had exceeded a million. Duluth's was hovering around 30,000.

Jay Cooke State Park

The countryside between Carleton and Duluth is rocky—in fact, there are a number of impressive outcroppings within the city of Carleton itself. And the Saint Louis River tumbles down across several layers of convoluted slate and graywacke as it passes through Jay Cooke State Park on its way to Lake Superior, making the park one of the loveliest in the region. During the Depression CCC workers built a number of handsome buildings in the park, as well as a long suspension bridge across the roiling river. Whitewater kayaking is popular along several stretches, and in times of low water, some sections of the river can easily be crossed by jumping from rock to rock.

The park has picnic areas, a wooded campground, and fifty miles of hiking trails. The Munger State Biking Trail skirts the northern edge of the park on its way to Duluth, passing through several striking areas. And the hilly country on the south side of the river, where many of the trails are, is quite wild.

As you spend some time hiking or kayaking in the park, you can ponder the fact that in 1665, when Louis XIV had only recently become king of France and London was being beset by fire and plague, two ambitious Frenchmen, Radisson and Groseilliers, were trading in this vicinity. They returned to Quebec from their first venture in the Northwest with furs valued at $40,000—a harvest which may well have saved the floundering colony.

Kayakers descending the St. Louis River

However, Louis XIV's minister, Colbert, had forbidden men to trade in the country west of Montreal, fearful that his colony's personnel would vanish into the brush, and the brothers-in-law were not only fined, their furs were confiscated, and they were prohibited from returning to the region. Undaunted by this rebuff, the two enterpreneurs turned to England for support, and as a result of their efforts the Hudson's Bay Company was formed a few years later, thus setting off a struggle in which the French were eventually vanquished from the continent. The St. Louis River itself remained a vital conduit into the interior for many decades, as it brought the voyageurs close to the watershed of the Mississippi, and also to the northern lakes via the Pike River and Lake Vermilion. (For more park info call 218-384-4610)

Duluth

One of the most dramatic vistas to be found in Minnesota greets the visitor traveling north on Interstate 35 on the way to Duluth. After passing through miles of inhospitable bogland, the terrain gets rockier, the land rises, and hints of a deep valley can be seen to the south. As you come over the rise of Thompson Hill, the mouth of the St. Louis River, Duluth harbor, and Lake Superior suddenly spread themselves before you in the distance, and you feel that you've entered another world. You have.

Duluth is the most dramatic, extravagant, and romantic of Minnesota's cities, largely because of its position on Lake Superior. At one time it was home to more millionaires per capita than any other city in the world, and the sources of its wealth—mining and shipping—are still plainly to be seen along the waterfront. For many years Duluth was the busiest port in the United States, and occasionally in the world (when measured in tonnage), with huge masses of iron ore rolling down from the Mesabi Range, and grain and coal arriving by rail from as far west as Montana and Wyoming. The local economy was also bolstered by a U.S. Steel plant and other industrial enterprises. The decline of both mining and lumbering in the region has long-since taken it toll on the city's economic vitality, giving it a somewhat weathered appearance, though this has also had the effect of preserving many of Duluth's architectural treasures.

Yet ever since its inception Duluth has also come in for its fair share of abuse. As far back as 1871, when it was a struggling city of three-thousand souls, a congressmen from Kentucky made use of hyperbole to ridicule a proposed federal land grant to build a railroad from Hudson, Wisconsin, to Duluth harbor. In one brief passage the congressman takes up the issue of Duluth's climate:

Then, sir, there is the climate of Duluth, unquestionably the most salubrious and delightful to be found anywhere on the Lord's earth. Now, I have always been under the impression, as I presume other gentlemen have, that in the region around Lake Superior it was cold enough for at least nine months in the year to freeze the smoke-stack off a locomotive. But I see it represented on this map that Duluth is situated exactly halfway between the latitudes of Paris and Venice, so that gentlemen who have inhaled the exhilarating airs of the one or basked in the golden sunlight of the other may see at a glance that Duluth must be a place of untold delights, a terrestrial paradise, fanned by the balmy zephyrs of an eternal spring, clothed in the gorgeous sheen of ever-blooming flowers, and vocal with the silvery melody of nature's choicest songsters. ...

According to one contemporary report, the congressman's speech brought the House to uproarious laughter no less than sixty-two times—though the grant was awarded nevertheless. Unbeknownst to the congressman, Lake Superior *does* provide a moderating influence on the climate of the region, fanning the shore with cool off-shore breezes in the summer and warming it ever-so-slightly during the winter with its residual heat. Ever-blooming flowers? No. But Duluth is one of the United States premier bird-watching cities. During the spring countless warblers pass through its many parks on their way to nesting grounds in the North Woods, and during the fall hawks from all over central Canada pass down the North Shore and funnel by the hundreds of thousands past the birders who congregate on the slopes of Hawk Ridge on Skyline Drive above the city. During the winter months snowy owls are often seen lurking amid the grain elevators and bridges of Duluth Harbor. (I once met a birder on the beach in LaJolla, California, who had just returned from a birding trip to Duluth…and this was in February!)

Perhaps the quickest way to tap into Duluth's history would be to take a boat tour of the harbor. You'll pass the enormous grain elevators and learn about the role played by Duluth in supplying the Great Lakes steel industry with iron ore. A tour of Glensheen, a mansion that sits on the lake at the east end of town, would give you some insight into the lifestyles of the men who orchestrated, and profited from, these large-

The Venerable Duluth Pack

In these days of synthetic fabrics, the phrase "Duluth Pack" may have lost some of its allure, but a generation ago these canvas packs were as strongly associated with wilderness travel as Fisher Maps and Old Town Canoes.

The pack has its humble roots in the small shoe-store of a French-Canadian immigrant named Camille Poirer. He arrived in Duluth in 1870 and prospered in the boom-town environment fueled by Jay Cooke's railroad and other local endeavors. In 1882 Poirer filed for a patent on a new type of canvas pack-sack that closed with buckles and had shoulder straps to comple-

ment the traditional tumpline across the forehead. (The pack also had an umbrella holder!) Known then as the Poirer Pack, this sturdy, utilitarian product soon took on a more generic name— the Duluth Pack.

In 1911, Poirer sold off his pack business to the newly-estab-

A crusty camper and his Duluth Pack

lished Duluth Tent and Awning Company, which had opened a shop on 1610 West Superior Street. In addition to the packs, the company made tents, awnings for businesses, hay wagon covers, and heavy canvas aprons. Though the product line has changed with the times, the Duluth Tent and Awning Company still makes a classic "Duluth Pack." You can pick one up at its upscale showroom near the end of Canal Street. And if you happen to have an aging pack (mine is now thirty-five years old), you can get the straps repaired at the original workshop which is still located on Superior Street in West Duluth.

scale endeavors. It was built in 1905 for Chester Adgate Congdon, a Duluth attorney, and is is now maintained by the Duluth campus of the University of Minnesota. The buildings and grounds, with their idyllic lakeshore setting, are a perfect place to wile away an afternoon—or to ponder the dreadful murders that took place here in 1977.

Yet for many visitors Duluth's appeal is rooted less in its history *per se* than in its position as the gateway to the North Woods. A detour off of I-35 at Canal Park offers both a refreshing break from freeway travel and a fine introduction to the delights of the North Shore. Park at the first slot you see once you pass the Dairy Queen on Canal Street and continue east on foot down the south side of the street. You'll pass Northern Lights Bookstore, where you can pick up a blank journal or some vacation reading material; the Sivertson Gallery, which carries a fine collection of prints, photographs, pottery, jewelry, and gift cards; and the Duluth Pack Store, which carries everything from canoes to candy-bars, though it specializes in the famous Duluth Packs that it manufactures locally (see previous page for details).

If you continue on to the east you'll come to the Duluth Maritime Museum (218-727-2497), which is chock full of exhibits about the shipping industry and other aspects of life on the big lake. Be sure to check the monitor that lists the ships that will be arriving and departing from the harbor. While the port of Duluth is no longer as prominent as it once was, it still ships more grain and ore annually than any other port on the Great Lakes, and vessels flying flags from all over the world dock there regularly. These huge ships pass through the channel just outside the building, and it can be a special thrill to watch them approach from the distance, then glide between the concrete walls of the channel with only a few feet to spare on either side. The horns will blare, and you'll see the vertical lift bridge that connects the city with the long sandbar on the opposite side rise to let the freighter pass.

To get a fuller dose of the maritime atmosphere, you can take the lakefront boardwalk for a mile or two along the waterfront. It passes several shopping complexes, including one housed in the old Fitger's brewery, and proceeds on to Leif Erikson Park.

Another option would be to drive out Lake Avenue—it runs parallel to Canal Park Drive—across the lift bridge to Park Point. As you

A foggy day on Park Point

continue east along the long sandbar through quiet neighborhoods, the harbor will be to your right, and you'll occasionally catch sight of the big lake to your left between the houses and the dunes. You'll eventually come to a parking area at 45th Street. (There are other informal parking areas along the way, but please don't trespass.) Hike out beyond the grassy dunes and you'll find yourself on a six-mile strip of beach. Yes, the waters of Lake Superior are cold, but along this stretch of shoreline, which is shallow and sandy, the sun warms the water, and you'll often see adventurous folks cavorting in the waves. Refreshing. Brisk. Perhaps a little shocking.

The North Shore Scenic Drive

Just outside Duluth the highway splits, and depending on how much of a hurry you're in, you can take the expressway to Two Harbors or the scenic drive along the lakeshore. The scenic drive is somewhat slower, needless to say, but you'll pass the first North Shore resorts, and two nice restaurants—the Scenic Café and the somewhat more elegant Nokomis Restaurant a little further north—both of which are well above average. You'll also pass two villages—French River and Knife River—that were involved in copper mining endeavors during the late nineteenth century, before dwindling into obscurity. About fifteen miles east of Duluth you can take a side-trip out Stony Point Road, which has a certain quiet charm. And in Knife River there are several no-frills shops that sell smoked fish.

Two Harbors

Two Harbors provides beauty, historical interest, and services to satisfy any traveler's needs. It has restaurants and fast food outlets, a Pamida department store, and it's also a good place to pick up some pasties—the meat pies that the Cornish miners introduced to the area long ago—for a picnic lunch at one of the many wayside rests further up the shore, or even in Two Harbors itself. Though many travelers barrel right on through the little town, a detour down the streets of Two Harbors to the waterfront is well worthwhile. You may see an ore boat being loaded at the huge, specially-designed loading docks, and there are also several interesting museums along the waterfront, including one operated by the Lake County Historical Society that's housed in the old train depot.

The first shipment of ore left Two Harbors in 1884, and by 1890 more than a thousand ships were passing through the mouth of Agate

An ore boat leaving the docks at Two Harbors

Bay every year, carrying not only ore, but also timber, coal, and passengers. A lighthouse was constructed in 1891, and most of the original
buildings are still standing. The complex is now managed as a B&B, so
if you're feeling flush you can stay overnight! (1-888-832-5606)

Once we leave Two Harbors the landscape becomes more varied,
the resorts less often resemble motels, and the shore becomes a
rugged cliff-lined coast. The far shore gradually disappears from view,
and Lake Superior itself takes on the look of a mighty sea. It's along this
stretch, too, that we pass a succession of parks and wayside rests whose
spectacular cliffs, forests, and waterfalls fully expose the unusual geology
of the region.

The cliffs are the result of volcanic activity that took place one to
two billion years ago—too long ago to be comprehended—and formed
a ridge running from the North Shore all the way down to Kansas.
Geologists have identified more than a hundred such cataclysmic events
along the North Shore, and it must be very gratifying to be able to tell
them one from another. But when we look at these handsome forms,
all we need to know is that very hot molten rock surfaced, cooled, and
solidified a very long time ago. We can still see these sheets of rock today
because during recent times the glaciers scoured the area and removed
the sediments that had accumulated on top of them. The soils that have
developed since that time are poor. They're capable of sustaining the
boreal forests that visitors love so much—the pine, spruce, lichens, bogs,
and birch—but little else.

Lake Superior itself provides the final element in the ensemble. It
consists of melt-water left by those massive sheets of ice which settled
into the depression created by the glacier's enormous weight. The many
rivers and streams that cascade down from the interior of the region find
their way through the numerous faults and cracks between the volcanic
extrusions to the level created by the lake. As we look at the plunging
torrents of water and the cavities that have been cut into the rock by its
swirling force, it may be difficult for us to accept the fact that although
the rocks themselves are very old, the rivers are mere infants.

Expansive lake, rugged cliff, tumbling torrent, and (seemingly) primordial forest—as a recreational ensemble the North Shore is hard to

beat. And it's our good fortune that much of this terrain has been incorporated into parks, trails, and wayside rests.

Gooseberry Falls State Park

Gooseberry Falls State Park is the most popular park on the North Shore. This is probably because it's the first one the visitor comes to when arriving from the south. Many travelers feel no need to proceed further, and considered on its own merits the park certainly has a great deal to offer.

In the first place, it's the most expansive of the North Shore parks. There is no better place, perhaps, to envision the lava flows that surfaced in the area a billion years ago than along the shoreline just south of the Gooseberry River's mouth, where massive shelves of rock slope gently toward the incoming waves. On a windy day, (or a quiet one,) these lichen-covered rock shelves, with pools of water and tufts of yellow grass scattered here and there, are the perfect setting for a meditative stroll.

Paths lead along the riverbank and up through the woods above this stretch of waterfront to the visitor's center, a large and attractive building that houses a gift shop and several interpretive displays. Continuing on foot further upstream toward the highway bridge, you'll come to the park's chief glory—a series of three waterfalls that drop more than 100 feet. Wandering across the rock shelves beneath the falls will give you a sense of involvement that most waterfalls can't provide.

At this point, however, you've just begun to enter the park. There are several more falls on the far side of the highway bridge, and miles of hiking trails on both sides of the river. The trails on the east side make for excellent cross-country skiing in winter, and bivouac shelters are located at several spots with commanding vistas of the forests and rocky hills below. (Call 218-834-3855 for park details.)

Split Rock Lighthouse State Park

Navigation had always been tricky along this stretch of coast, with compasses being thrown out of whack by the ore deposits, and during a disastrous storm in November of 1905 seven ships went down and 215 people drowned. The owners of the vessels lobbied hard in

Congress to establish a lighthouse in the vicinity, and within a few years Split Rock lighthouse was perched on the clifftop in the then-roadless region to guide freighters on their way to and from Two Harbors and Duluth. For many years it had the distinction of being the highest lighthouse in the Coast Guard's system. (Highest above sea-level, that is. Lake Superior itself is at a higher elevation than any other body of water accessible to ocean navigation.)

The lighthouse was finally shut down in 1969, though it still serves as a landmark for small boats. And since that time it has lost little of the aesthetic appeal that made it not only the highest, but also one of the most often-visited lighthouses in the system. The federal government deeded the property to the state of Minnesota in 1971, and it has been operated as a historic site by the Minnesota Historical Society since that time, while the attractive countryside surrounding it has become Split Rock Lighthouse State Park (218-226-6377).

The park itself offers a marvelous picnic area along the rocky beach below the lighthouse, and to many visitors this view is enough. An added thrill, during times of low water, is to hike across the isthmus to the rocky island just off shore. (Open only after August 1 due to bird nesting). The countryside beyond the picnic area is also attractive—wooded and rocky—though its been given over to a number of walk-in campsites, and during the summer months there's little to see from the path. In winter, on the other hand, this area makes for some splendid, if occasionally treacherous, cross-country skiing, as the trails rise and fall along the lakeshore and up across the jumbled and rocky terrain.

The historical lighthouse is also well worth a visit, especially if you're interested in the early history of the region (218-226-6373). At the interpretive center you can watch a better-than-average documentary on the lighthouse, its keeper, the arrival of tourists, and shipping on the lake. Exhibits in the building provide more information along the same line. Tours of the nearby lighthouse and the lightkeeper's house leave from the center regularly, but after watching the film and wandering through the museum, you may feel you already know the place inside and out. You can also wander the grounds on your own, and the guides scattered here and there are eager to share their expertise about the buildings and the era, as well as about current shipping practices out on the big lake. From the lighthouse you can sometimes see the Apostle Islands off on the eastern horizon, and looking to the northeast up the shore you'll probably see Palisade Head, Shovel Point, the distant crest of the Sawtooth Mountains, and other landmarks forty or fifty miles up the coast.

As if all of that weren't enough, one of the finest inland day-hikes in the region follows the Split Rock River upstream for several miles before crossing it on a sturdy bridge and descending again along the opposite bank. The trailhead—Split Rock River Wayside—can be found a few miles south of the park entrance, near milepost 43.5.

Beaver Bay and Silver Bay

Beaver Bay is the oldest continuously inhabited settlement on the North Shore. It was founded in 1856 and sustained itself by means of a sawmill that provided lumber for the communities springing up, and often disappearing again, at other places along the lake. On the other hand, Silver Bay, just a few miles up the highway, is the *youngest* town on the North Shore. It was built in 1954 by Reserve Mining Company to house the workers at its taconite plant, which looms imposingly on both sides of the road as you pass by. Not surprisingly, Silver Bay resembles a post-war suburb, with long rows of ramblers, a mini-mall, a Dairy Queen, and other amenities. Though it has never been in danger of disappearing, Silver Bay's fortunes have fluctuated wildly along with those of the American steel industry, and the town took a serious hit when Reserve Mining shut down its local operations in 1986. (Three years later the plant was reopened on a smaller scale by the Cypress Minerals Company.)

For the passing visitor Silver Bay's chief draw might be the fine cross-country ski trails that the city maintains in the hills on the far end of town. These trails will take you past some of the most harsh and remarkable terrain in Minnesota.

Tettegouche State Park

This park contains of a cornucopia of natural wonders within its more than 9000 acres. Some are easy to enjoy, others will require some effort.

First on the list would be Palisade Head, which can be reached by a steep narrow road off of Highway 61 about two miles south of the main park entrance. It consists of an imposing mass of igneous rock the peak of which stands 350 feet above the lake. There is a parking lot at the top of the bluff, though otherwise the area remains undeveloped

Shovel Point, as seen from Palisade Head

except for an ugly communications tower. The views from the top are superb in all directions, and the cliffs that rise more than 200 feet directly out of the lake have been a popular rock-climbing spot for many years.

The main park is located at the mouth of the Baptism River. It can be a pleasant place to wander. Park at the wayside rest and follow the path along the bluff to a stairway leading down to the attractive cove where the river meets the lake. From the same parking lot you can also proceed northeast through the woods along the bluff to Shovel Point. In fact, this may be the most pleasant short hike on the North Shore. After a brief, stiff climb up the backside of the point, you descend through a forest of stunted pines growing amid the rock. Eventually the woods give way and you find yourself facing an austere and beautiful slab of rhyolite with the lake looming on either side. A boardwalk has been erected out to the point to preserve the delicate plant-life on the rocky windswept shelf.

Shovel Point does not have the sheer height of Palisade Head, but it's a more evocative piece of rock.

If you drive on past the wayside rest into Tettegouche Park, you'll find a number of hiking trails through the woods, one of which leads to the highest waterfall in Minnesota. The terrain is unusually hilly, and many of the trails have a steep and closed-in quality that won't appeal to everyone. But it's a special thrill to come upon a gem of a lake nestled amid the wooded semi-mountainous countryside, and on the west shore of Mic Mac Lake you'll find a small but remarkably well-preserved logging camp.

The camp was built by the Alger-Smith Lumber Company in 1898 to house the loggers who were harvesting the Norway and white pine in the area. Once the marketable trees were gone a group of Duluth businessmen bought the camp to use during their fishing trips. It was later sold outright to one of the members, Clement Quinn, who owned it for fifty years. Throughout all this time the pristine character of the camp was preserved, and with time the land itself returned to the beautiful condition in which we see it today.

The State of Minnesota took over the camp and in 1979 it was included in the newly-formed Tettegouche State Park. Today several of the cabins are available for rental throughout the year. (For more park information call 218-226-6365.)

Highway 1

In a area of few roads, Highway 1 is a landmark. Known locally as the Ely-Finland Trail, it connects the North Shore with Ely and the Range. It might be worthwhile to head inland here, for much of the countryside between Illgen City, where Highway 1 meets the lake, and Finland, a hamlet located seven miles inland, is attractive, with distant hills and cliffs framed by expansive pastures and woodlands. The Baptism River runs through the valley created on the backside of the Sawtooth Mountains, and the region seems like a land apart.

You can return to Highway 1 via County Road 6, or continue up County Road 7 to Crosby-Manitou State Park. This unusual park has been specially designed with backpackers in mind. The twenty-two campsites are widely spaced along the banks of the Manitou River, and are accessible only on foot. The country is remote, the woods seem primordial, and the silence is broken only by the rushing river, the chatter of birds, and the occasional buzz of a mosquito. If you're not in the mood for an overnight stay, a hike to the cascades followed by a picnic at Benson Lake can also be nice.Enjoy!

Father Baraga

The lakeshore between Little Marais and Tofte is less heavily developed than some other stretches of the North Shore, though the curious traveler will find plenty of byways to explore. For example, at the mouth of the Cross River you'll come upon a very large granite cross. This is an oversized replica of a wooden cross pounded to a tree by Father Frederic Baraga in 1846. Baraga was a Catholic missionary from Austria who had come to the New World to do God's work. He was a man of prodigious energy, and he made a distinct impression on the inhabitants of Lake Superior. One contemporary remarked: "There is hardly a locality on the lake which is not connected with the history of his life, either because he built a chapel there, or wrote a pious book, or founded an Indian parish, or else underwent danger and adventures there, in which he felt that Heaven was protecting him."

In the most famous of these tales, news reaches Father Baraga in the Apsotle Islands of an epidemic that has broken out at one of his North Shore missions. Without delay he sets off across the open waters of Superior in a birchbark canoe, against the advice of his voyageur guide Dubois, who has never heard of anyone completing such a daring crossing. Yet Father Baragas will not be deterred. The weather turns ugly, but the wind is at their back, and after paddling through the night the two finally approached their destination. In his book *Kitchi-Gami*, the German ethnologist Johann Georg Kohl described the scene as it was related to him by Dubois's cousin:

> *Long rows of dark rocks on either side, and at their base a white stripe, the dashing surf of the terribly excited waves. There was no opening in them, no haven, no salvation.*
>
> *'Paddle on, dear Dubois— straight on. We must get through, and a way will offer itself'.*
>
> *[Dubois] shrugged his shoulders, made his last prayers, and paddled straight on, he hardly knew how.*

By sheer luck (or divine intervention) they landed in the tranquil mouth of the river we now know as the Cross River, and Father Baraga cut down a few trees and erected a cross in thanksgiving.

Baraga later composed the first grammar book of the Ojibwe language. In fact, his dedication to his flock was so unflagging and sincere that legends began to develop around him, and his zeal inspired twenty other missionaries from Europe to the wilderness. In 1930, on the centenary of his arrival in the New World, a movement was set in motion to canonize him.

The wooden cross erected by Baraga at the mouth of the Cross River was replaced long ago by a more imposing one made of white granite. But it would be a good thing if this granite cross were removed and replaced by a wooden one more in keeping with the spirit of the man and the flavor of his times. The Ojibwe call the Cross River "Tchibaiatigo-zibi" which means "wood of the soul river," presumably in reference to Father Baraga's wooden cross.

Temperance River State Park

If Gooseberry is the most expansive of the North Shore parks, the Temperance is the most closed-in. The water plummets and swirls between walls of lava that are often no more than a few feet apart. A hike up to the bridge and back doesn't take more than a few minutes, though the trail continues on to several other waterfalls further upstream. It's fun to scramble up the cliffs and then walk out onto the exposed shelves of rock. Peering over the edge of the rock into the seething gorge can give you a moment of true *frisson*. (Be sure to keep young children well in hand.) It's also fun to wander through the woods to the mouth of the river, which received its name because it's the only North Shore river that doesn't have a bar at its mouth. (Call 218-663-7476 for park details.)

Tofte

The town of Tofte has been considerably built up in recent years, with gas stations, resorts, condominiums, and restaurants. But the two best things in Tofte, from the traveler's point of view, are the general store and the fishing museum. The store is located on the corner just beyond the turn-off for the Sawbill Trail, one of the major entry-points to the BWCAW. It has everything you're likely to have forgotten—batteries, playing cards, potato chips, a corkscrew—for either a foray into the wilderness or a weekend at a lakeside cabin.

The fishing museum, on the other hand, has the lore of the region. It's small—but aren't most museums a little too large? It has fishing boats and displays and video interviews with people named Tofte and Fenstad. It preserves what the town of Tofte is beginning to lose—its connections with the past.

The waterfront in Tofte is relatively flat, but if you drive a mile or two up the Sawbill Trail you'll see the trailhead to Carleton Peak, the highest point on the North Shore at 1529 feet. The fairly easy hike to the summit is three-and-a-half miles round trip.

Lutsen

It's difficult to approach Lutsen without thinking of the death of the Swedish king Gustavus Adolphus in the battle of Lützen in 1632. There is a bit of disparity between the two Lutsens, of course. The population of Lutsen township even today is only 350-odd souls. The Swedish king, on the day when he lost his life at Lützen, led 25,000 men into battle. No doubt the early Swedish immigrants who named the town wanted to pay homage, in their own modest way, to the principles of Swedish sovereignty and religious freedom. More simply put, Gustavus Adolphus was their *hero*.

Today Lutsen is best known for its eponymous ski resort. Lutsen Resort has plenty to offer during the summertime too, of course—from kayaking to golf. And the passing tourist ought not to miss the short hike around Oberg Mountain, which is one of the best on the North Shore. The two-mile trail follows a series of switch-backs up through the woods, then circles the rounded peak, with a series of nine spectacular overlooks along the way. To reach the trailhead, turn up the hill on the Onion River Road (Forest Road 336) about five miles north of Tofte. The trailhead is two miles in on the right-hand side.

Cascade River State Park

Every North Shore river has its own unique character, and strange as it may seem, as you ascend the banks of the Cascade River you find yourself reciting a favorite poem by Li Po or Wang Wei. It may be the cedars that crowd in on either side of the torrent; it may be

the classically balanced twists and turns of the river's path as it drops from level to level; it may be the rough-hewn wooden bridges and overlooks that provide a succession of splendid views; or it may be the mist that hovers in the air above the pools at the base of each segment of whitewater. No doubt all of these qualities contribute to the beauty of the river's descent. It's a short hike up the west (and prettier) side of the river and down the other side again. Longer trails take you further upstream, and on this, as on many of the other North Shore rivers, it comes as a surprise to see how flat the countryside becomes once you finally reach the crest of the hill. (Call 218-387-3053 for park details.)

Grand Marais

Grand Marais sits on a picturesque harbor and conveys the atmosphere of a seaside resort town rather than a wilderness outpost. In recent times many local businesses have given way to galleries, brew pubs, and gift shops, yet the village remains a pleasant place to visit, and is considered a "destination" for folks staying at cabins and resorts an hour or more down the shore. You can rent a kayak, eat a pizza, outfit a canoe trip, charter a sailboat, ski the cross-country trails on the hills above the town, or throw stones along the beach. One thing you won't want to miss, however, is a trip out beyond the Coast Guard station to the rocky peninsula called Artist's Point that extends out into the lake beyond the concrete breakwater. Both children and adults will enjoy wandering among the crevices and across the lichen-covered sheets of

Slabs of volcanic rock slope off into Lake Superior at Artist's Point in Grand Marais. The Sawtooth Mountains can be seen in the distance.

rock on the way out to the point, or simply watching the waves roll in. And there are times in winter when ice-sheets of a remarkable pale blue pile up here in huge heaps along the shore.

Among North Shore communities Grand Marais has a good deal to offer in the way of dining, from old fashioned cafes like the Blue Water Cafe and My Sister's Place, to pleasant seafood joints like the Angry Trout, to modern establishments like the Crooked Spoon and the Lake Superior Brewing Company. And the Ben Franklin Store on Wisconsin Street downtown may be setting some sort of record for inventory items per square foot. Sewing supplies, games, clothing, work gloves, tools, shoes, postcards, jigsaw puzzles—it's all here, now all you've got to do is find it.

B eyond Grand Marais the countryside levels out, the vegetation gets scrubbier, the resorts are fewer and often less substantial, and the landscape takes on an almost forlorn sub-arctic look. The many beaches are usually deserted, and they can make a pleasant stop.

It might be worthwhile stopping in at Naniboujou Lodge, which was established as an exclusive hunting retreat during the 1920s. (Babe Ruth, Ring Lardner, and Jack Dempsey were among its charter members.) The Ojibwe-inspired decoration on the walls and ceiling of the dining room are definitely unusual, and the spacious grounds evoke an atmosphere of an entirely different era of leisure. (218-387-2688)

Grand Portage National Monument

T he Ojibwe considered the hills above Grand Portage as a prime area for tapping maple trees long before the first white explorers arrived in the area. They also fished in the bay and passed through the nearby woods regularly on their way past the cataracts of the Pigeon River when traveling from Lake Superior to the waterways of the interior. The fur traders, in their turn, came to recognize its value as an *entrepot* for storing trade goods and furs, and as a rendezvous site where Voyageurs arriving from Montreal and those who had wintered in the interior could meet and exchange their cargoes. A fort stood on the spot from 1730 to 1805, and between 1778 and 1802 it was the headquarters and western supply depot for the North West Company. In time the traders and their Indian clients all but eliminated the beaver from the region, trade dwindled, and the fort was abandoned.

The site of the original stockade was rediscovered in 1922, and several archeological excavations have taken place since, resulting in a partial reconstruction of the site. The large palisade is impressive, but the buildings inside are even finer. They've been constructed in a French style that allows the coarsely-planed timbers to slide up and down along tracks in the vertical support beams, which prevents the structures from

becoming unstuck during the expansion and contraction of the changing seasons. Within the interior of the fort you'll find a great hall, kitchen, warehouse, and a lookout tower. A second handsome hall stands just south of the fort, along with replicas of the elaborate birch bark structures that the Ojibwe natives of those times would have lived in.

A visit at any time in the summer can be a treat, and the park personnel can tell you anything you want to know about voyageur or Ojibwe life during that bygone era. But things truly come alive during the annual Rendezvous Days (often the second weekend in August) when a powwow is held and historic re-enactment takes place on an elaborate scale, with music and dancing, food and crafts, gambling, pipe-smoking, and all the rest.

At other times of the year the area can get rather quiet, though the view from the top of the hill behind the fort our across Wauswaugoning Bay is sublime in any season. Looking out beyond the islands, it's easy to drift back to the times when travel was exclusively by birch-bark canoe, "civilization" was a long ways away, and white and native peoples worked together in the grand commercial enterprise of supplying European dandies with top-hats. (Call 218-475-2202 for more information.)

The Grand Portage Reservation encompasses much of the area around Grand Portage, and a modern lodge and casino just over the hill from the monument offers lodging, gaming, a swimming pool and sauna, a restaurant, and a pleasant view of the bay. A few miles further north, on the Canadian border, you can visit Grand Portage State Park, which offers a one-mile hike to the 120-foot Hill Falls of the Pigeon River. More ambitious souls can set out from the palisade up the 8.5 mile Grand Portage trail itself, which is still widely-used by recreational canoeists.

SECTION II: THE HINTERLANDS

The BWCAW

Though it doesn't have quite the cachet of the Grand Canyon or Yosemite, the Boundary Waters Canoe Area Wilderness, located on Minnesota's border with Ontario, is the most popular *wilderness* area in the United States. This may be because it's easier to reach a truly remote place via canoe than by hiking or mountain-climbing. Boy Scouts, Girl Scouts, church groups, serious fishermen, and weekend paddlers alike fall in love with the sparkling lakes, rocky hillsides, and towering pines of the region, and return again and again.

The forests of the region were logged along with everything else at the turn of the twentieth century. But Congressional leaders were soon alerted to the unusual character of the area, and in 1909 the federal government established a 1.2 million acre Superior Refuge, which later that year became Superior National Forest. Between 1922 and 1926 the U.S. Forest Service built several roads into the previously remote areas of the forest, including the upper end of the Gunflint Trail, the Echo Trail north of Lake Vermilion, and the Fernberg Road, which heads east from

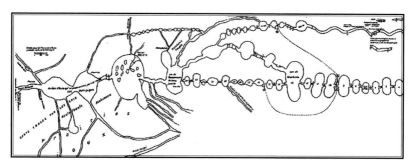

An early map of the boundary waters

Ely toward what we now know as the Boundary Waters Canoe Area. In the same era, under pressure from conservationists who decried the despoliation of the area, a 640,000 acre wilderness area was established by the Department of Agriculture. The proclamation did allow logging, but prohibited road building or recreational development of any kind. A proposal in 1925 to build a dam in the heart of the area was defeated only after a bitter five-year struggle in which, following a pattern that would be repeated time and again, most locals favored development, while dedicated "outsiders" worked hard, under the leadership of the Isaac Walton League and other organizations, to preserve the area's pristine character.

During the Depression the federal government pursued a policy of purchasing lands that had fallen delinquent and building portages and trails in the wilderness area. Finally, after several further battles to stop power-plant construction on various rivers, in 1938 the Forest Service established the Superior Roadless Primitive Area, which included most of the present BWCAW.

Yet development on the fringes of the area continued throughout the 1940s, and fly-ins became increasingly popular. In 1949 President Truman issued an executive order prohibiting such flights, but resort-owners continued to make them while challenging the president in court. The litany of move and counter-move continued for decades, with the federal government gradually authorizing more funds for land purchase while attempting to restrain, though not eliminate, both logging and motorized recreational use. In 1964 Congress passed the Wilderness Act, though disputes and rulings involving snowmobiles, the mining of copper near the area, and other issues, have continued to keep activists, legislators, and forest service personnel busy to this day.

Today the Boundary Waters Canoe Area Wilderness includes more than a million acres, and extends for 150 miles along the Minnesota-Ontario border. What makes the region so special? No doubt it's the presence of pristine wilderness crisscrossed by sparkling lakes that are easily navigable by canoe, where bald eagles, loons, beavers, and moose are common, and the sound of an internal combustion engine is never heard. The rocky shoreline, towering white pines, intimate bays, and commanding vistas make for a very winning package. Though more than 200,000 people visit the area each year, there are more than two thousand campsites strung out along 1200 miles of paddling routes within the park, with even more opportunities to explore on the north side of the border in Quetico Provincial Park. Visits are strictly regulated by point of entry to insure that overcrowding doesn't spoil the effect—or the great fishing!

Anyone planning a visit ought to keep in mind that the area is genuine wilderness. There are no signs, and no "services" other than the campsites scattered here and there. To make a foray into the area requires a degree of preparation. Fortunately, there are plenty of outfitters in Ely, Tofte, Grand Marais, and along the Gunflint Trail that can provide you with equipment, supplies, and valuable advice.

While it isn't difficult to travel in the BWCAW, certain rudimentary skills are essential. You've got to know how to paddle and steer a canoe, read a map, and set up a campsite. It would be wise to familiarize yourself with first aid techniques, anticipate traveling in the face of high winds, and bring clothing that will remain comfortable and warm when soaking wet. Canoes *can* capsize, and hypothermia is not a joke.

On the other hand, anyone who has done some camping and paddled a canoe is likely to have a wonderful time in the region. Several guidebooks are available describing many routes in admirable detail. Yet it can be a challenge for a beginner to chose a route of appropriate difficulty and interest. Most visitors naturally want to find an easy route with spectacular scenery and ample wildlife that also offers complete solitude. That is not going to happen. Yet the park is well-managed, and the quota systems are surprisingly effective in insuring that even the most appealing places in the park seem remote at least *some of the time*. What follows are some general remarks about the region that may be helpful in planning a trip.

The landscape of the BWCAW differs a good deal from one area to another. In the eastern section, from McFarland Lake west to Gunflint Lake, the lakes tend to be long and thin, though the towering hills and cliffs in the area give it a remarkable beauty that makes the often nasty wind worthwhile. The area north of Brule Lake is made up of long skinny lakes set in flat terrain without quite the same stature. Many of the classic island-dotted lakes of the region will be found south and west of Saganaga and Sea Gull Lakes, extending west to the vicinity of Ely. However, in recent years much of this area has been devastated by forest fires, leaving it charred, treeless, and rife with schrubbery and wildflowers. Fortunately many of the campsites were spared, due to soil compaction, and the countryside further to the south, from Ogishkimunchi east to Little Saganaga and Tuscarora, remains pristine. These same lakes can also be approached from the south via Sawbill Lake.

The region from Snowbank Lake west to Basswood Lake includes many large lakes and bays that are open to motorized travel. It's also the area closest to the town of Ely, which adds to the sense of crowding. This area may lack the remoteness of some other regions, but it also provides access to some very fine country to the east, and to outstanding routes through the Quetico country north of the border.

North of the Echo Trail are several rather brushy zones, though they offer intriguing options to the connoisseur, especially when high water levels make river travel along the Nina-Moose and Little Indian Sioux rivers feasible.

Here are a few tips for making a canoe trip more pleasant.

• All campsites in the BWCAW have a fire grate and a privy in the woods. They are marked with dots on all commercial maps of the region. In planning the stages of a trip, it's important to consider the distances between campsites. If the one you're planning to use is occupied when you get there, it's nice to have an alternative in mind.

- Plan to set up camp early in the afternoon.
- Bring a cook stove. Fires are nice but stoves are quicker, and fire bans are sometimes put into effect which could ruin your trip.
- Consider eating a simple breakfast—granola, instant milk, dried fruit, beef jerky, coffee—and breaking camp early. Pancakes may be tasty but it's also nice to traverse the lakes before the wind rises, when the mist is still hovering in the coves and the portage trails are empty. This also makes it easier to cover ground and still make camp early enough to get the site you want.
- Loop trips are nice. On the other hand, things never look the same coming and going, and foregoing the "loop" experience opens many new travel opportunities, especially on short trips.

Permits are required for entry into the BWCAW. They're easy to arrange for on-line at www.BWCAW.org. Each entry point has a limited number of permits daily, however, so it's wise to make arrangements at least a month or two in advance of your trip. The many outfitters in Ely, Tofte, Grand Marais, and along the Gunflint Trail will be able to help. That having been said, it is often possible to secure a permit on short notice, especially if your travel-dates remain flexible.

Ely

Many visitors to Ely are on their way to the BWCAW, but Ely also makes a marvelous travel destination in its own right. It has quite a few lodges and motels, and a number of coffee-shops and restaurants catering to tourists, canoe-camp and outfitting staff, and the lucky souls who have set up housekeeping on the shores of nearby lakes. And there is quite a bit to do right in town.

First on the list for many is the International Wolf Center, located east of town on Highway 169 (218-365-4695). Minnesota has long been home to the most robust wolf population in the lower forty-eight states. In 1985 the Science Museum of Minnesota mounted an exhibit, "Wolves and Humans," to examine the facts and fables of wolf behavior and lore, and to display various artifacts related to this creature. The exhibit was so popular that efforts were made to find a permanent home

Ely, the town at the edge of the woods

for it. Where else but in Ely, where the earliest modern wolf research was conducted by Sigurd Olson and Milt Stenlund, and significantly extended more recently by L. David Mech, the foremost international expert in the field? If you visit the center today you can see material from the original exhibits and also watch the resident wolf pack at play. The center offers an array of programs that include video presentations, howling trips, radio tracking, snowshoe treks, family activities, dogsledding, and flights over wolf country.

The North American Bear Center opened in 2007 on the west end of town. It's the culmination of years of work by famed bear researcher Lynn Rogers, who has studied bears in the vicinity of Ely for decades.

Rogers, too, was involved with an exhibit at the Science Museum of Minnesota. That exhibit never made it to Ely. (Then again, much of it was about grizzly bears.) The new center is in its infancy, and lacks the pizazz of the Wolf Center across town. But it's worth visiting nevertheless, to see footage of bear behavior that Rogers and others have gathered out in the field. And to see Ted, the 800-pound live bear on display at the center. (218-365-7879)

For a brief look at the surrounding countryside—which is why most people come here in the first place—take the Echo Trail north from the east end of town up past Shagawa and Burntside Lakes. There are some nice campsites at Fenske Lake, though further on the trail the lakes are few and far between and the countryside gets a little scrubby.

Lake Vermilion

Lake Vermilion is sometimes referred to as the prettiest lake in the state. (The National Geographic Society once ranked it among the top ten lakes nationwide!) It's situated at the edge of the same geological formation that arcs down from the north to give the rugged beauty to the BWCAW. But unlike that somewhat remote region, Lake Vermilion is easily accessible by car. For those who lack the time or the where-withal to venture out into the northern wilderness by canoe, Vermilion offers plenty of pines, cliffs, and sparkling waters—but without quite so much effort.

Of course, this combination of qualities also makes Vermilion a very popular lake, which somewhat undermines the sense of peace and solitude to be found on the lakes further to the north and east. On the other hand, the lake is 40 miles long and it has more than 1200 miles of shoreline. The northern half is still largely inaccessible except by boat. To travel from one end to the other by boat through a labyrinth of bays and channels can take half a day or more, and there are still plenty of isolated coves, pristine rock shelves, and undiscovered fishing spots along the way to satisfy any visitor. In fact, mail is still delivered to many places on the lake by boat six days a week. The mail run is 80 miles long, it takes three and a half hours to complete—and you can ride along! The mailboat leaves Arenson's Marina 9 a.m. every day but Sunday from June 1 to Labor Day. Call 218-753-4190 for more information and reservations.

The "upper" end of the lake around Wake-Um-Up and Norwegian bays (actually downstream from the "lower" end), is somewhat less bustling than the area around Tower, where Fortune Bay Casino also contributes to the commotion. A trip by car north around the west end of the lake on County 24 to Vermilion Dam, where the Vermilion

River leaves the lake, will take you through some interesting scrubby landscapes where the exposed bedrock of the border country meets the shallow soils of the glacial lake plain to the west. From here you can continue north to Crane Lake or to a turn-off where the Echo Trail runs east through the woods to Ely.

Voyageurs National Park

If you continue north on Highway 53 past the quaint towns of Cook and Orr, you will eventually reach the entrance to Minnesota's only national park. Voyageurs National Park, like Lake Vermilion, lies on an exposed edge of the Canadian Shield, which includes some of the world's oldest rock formations. The park consists of four large lakes and several smaller ones set in a landscape of forests, bogs, and beaver ponds. In the time since the last glacier departed some twelve thousand years ago, a thin layer of soil has built up on the basalt and granite bedrock to support the classic boreal forest ecosystem we know as the North Woods.

The large lakes included in the park once formed part of the main thoroughfare used by the Voyageurs on their way to winter trading posts deep in the interior. A trading post was established on nearby Rainy Lake as early as 1688. Nowadays canoeists still ply the waters, though the area is dominated by fishermen and families making use of houseboats available for rent at resorts near the park. With only ten miles of roads, Voyageurs is definitely a water-based park. The first-time visitor might even wonder if it might better have been named Voyageur's National Parking Lot. The four entry points—Crane Lake, Ash River, Kabetogama, and Rainy Lake—are nowhere near one another, and the visitor arriving without a watercraft will find precious little to do at any of them other than wander around the visitor center or take a short hike through the woods. But even such fleeting glimpses of the park make it obvious why there are so many boat trailers lined up in the parking lots. The countryside is spectacular, even when viewed from the end of the dock.

If the itch to see what's out there gets to you, there are scores of resorts north of the Kabetogama Visitors' Center (218-875-2111) that can provide you with anything from a kayak to a family houseboat, not

A view from Blind Ash Bay Trail out across Kabetogama Lake

to mention on-shore accommodations. And there are state forest camp-grounds near both the Ash River Visitors Center (218-374-3221) and the Kabetogama entry points.

The Kettle Falls Hotel lies on a spit of land from which you can look *south* across the bay to Canada! It offers visitors a genuine step back in time. The hotel was built in 1910, and is accessible only by means of a ten-mile boat trip through the islands. (218-240-1724)

Local residents have traditionally been luke-warm, if not actually hostile, to Voyageurs Park. After all, the lakes have always been there, and the arrival of the park meant removing locals from their cabins and placing added restrictions on how the lakes and islands could be used. The arrival of a new park superintendant in 2007 and the influx of twenty million dollars to build a new headquarters and visitors' center in International Falls may have inspired a rapprochement. (For more information on International Falls see pages 218-219.)

Though permits are required for overnight stays in the park, there are no quotas. To experience what the park has to offer fully will require some advance planning, but even the passing visitor will enjoy the hikes and views along the shore.

FOR FURTHER READING

The best source for information about lodging, seasonal events, contact information, and general background, is the Moon Guide by Tim Bewer called simply *Minnesota*. The *Minnesota Travel Companion*, by Richard Olsenius, has good maps, many brief entries about small towns, and a number of interesting vintage photographs. The *Compass Guide to Minnesota* by Greg Brenning offers a useful overview of the state accompanied by good color photographs. The *Great Minnesota Touring Book* by Thomas Huhti provides a large number of short itineraries which often contain details not available elsewhere.

The state's geology is made intelligible to travelers in Constance Jefferson Sansome's *Minnesota Underfoot*. If you're interested in birds, you'll want to obtain a copy of Kim Eckert's *A Birder's Guide to Minnesota*, which will lead you down some interesting county roads, regardless of whether you're lucky enough to meet up with a wimbrel or a black-backed woodpecker. Anyone interested in the early history of the state would enjoy William Warren's nineteenth-century classic *History of the Ojibwe People*. And if your interest lies in immigration history, you could hardly do better than the anthology put out by the Minnesota Historical Society, *They Chose Minnesota*. The *Streams and Rivers of Minnesota* by Thomas F. Waters remains a classic overview of the state's many watersheds. More detailed studies in the Rivers of America series by Evan Jones (on the Minnesota River) and James Taylor Dunn (on the St. Croix) are also worth seeking out. *Where the Sky Began* by John Madson is a thoughtful look at many aspects of prairie life. Robert Beymer's two-volume guide, *Boundary Waters Canoe Area*, makes planning a trip to that area a lot easier. And *Books and Islands in Ojibwe Country* by Louise Erdrich, brings us close to the spirit of the border country around Lake of the Woods.

A (very) short list of literary works depicting Minnesota life would include *Songs of the North* by Sigurd Olson, *Main Street* by Sinclair Lewis, *On the Banks of Plum Creek* by Laura Engalls Wilder, *Lake Wobegon Days* by Garrison Keillor, and *The New Land* by Wilhelm Moberg. *The North Country Reader*, edited by Jean Ervin, contains essays and stories by contributors as diverse as Henry Schoolcraft and Gordon Parks.

About the Author

John Toren was born in Minneapolis and raised in the hamlet of Mahtomedi, on the east shore of White Bear Lake. As a youth he spent many weekends at the family cabin on Lake Vermilion and worked for three summers as a guide in the Boundary Waters Canoe Area. In 1975 he and a friend canoed from Lake Superior to Lake Winnipeg in nineteen days. He eventually received degrees in both history and anthropology from the University of Minnesota and did several years of graduate work in European history.

In recent decades Toren and his wife Hilary have traveled to many far-flung places in Europe and the United States. A few of these adventures are described in his first book, *Mountain Upside Down* (Nodin Press: 2003). For the past twenty years Toren has also published a quarterly magazine, *Macaroni*, which has been nominated twice for the Utne Independent Press Award for General Excellence.

Over the years Toren has lectured on subjects as diverse as flamenco culture, bird-watching, and French painting of the nineteenth century. He often gives travel presentations about Spain, Greece, the French provinces, and the American Southwest. His articles and reviews have appeared in the *History Channel Magazine*, *Minnesota Monthly*, *Twin Cities Magazine*, the *Minneapolis Observer*, *Rain Taxi*, the *Star-Tribune* and other publications. Toren currently spends much of his time, when he isn't out exploring new territory, as a free-lance editor and book designer.